The Human Side of Selling

The Human Side of Selling

by ROBERT E. MOORE

AUTHOR OF "MAN ALIVE"

Illustrated by I. K. Anderson

Harper & Brothers, Publishers, New York

THE HUMAN SIDE OF SELLING

Copyright, 1951, *by* Harper & Brothers
Printed in the United States of America

All rights in this book are reserved.
No part of the book may be used or reproduced in any manner whatsoever without written permission except in the case of brief quotations embodied in critical articles and reviews. For information address Harper & Brothers, 49 East 33rd Street, New York 16, N. Y.

FIRST EDITION

E-A

This book is dedicated to the men and women everywhere who believe in the brotherhood of all mankind.

Contents

Preface   xiii

INTRODUCTION

1. How to Earn More Money—and Get More Fun Out of Life   1

    WHETHER YOU ARE AN "AMATEUR" OR A "PROFESSIONAL" SALESMAN, YOU CAN GET MORE OF THE GOOD THINGS YOU WANT IN LIFE WHEN YOU KNOW THE SELLING FORMULA OF THE STARS.

PART I
The "Material" Side and the "Human" Side of Selling

2. Why Some Salesmen Fail—While Others Earn A Fortune   8

    AN AMAZING CONTRAST OF FAILURES AND SUCCESSES IN SELLING—AND THE REASON WHY!

3. The Star Salesmen—the Champs—Know the Human Side of Selling . . .   16

    CUSTOMERS ARE HUMAN BEINGS.
    SALESMEN ARE HUMAN, TOO.
    EVEN THE BOSS IS HUMAN!

PART II
Customers Are Human Beings

4. What Do You Know About "The Man Behind the Dollar"?   23

    IS THE CUSTOMER "ALWAYS RIGHT"? THE NEW CUSTOMER IN BUSINESS AND AT HOME—HUMAN—HIS PROBLEMS, FRUSTRATIONS, RESENTMENTS, INTERESTS, AMBITIONS, PLEASURES, WANTS ARE SIMILAR TO YOUR OWN.

CONTENTS

5. *How To Grow Wealthy Selling Retail Customers* — 30

   DO YOU SELL IN A GROCERY, HARDWARE, FURNITURE, OR DEPARTMENT STORE? DO YOU SELL BUILDING SUPPLIES, AUTOMOBILES, FARM EQUIPMENT? DO YOU WORK FOR A BANK, A RAILROAD, AIRLINE, A HOTEL, OR A RESTAURANT? YOU WILL LEARN HOW MANY MEN AND WOMEN IN JOBS JUST LIKE YOURS ARE "EXTREMELY SUCCESSFUL."

6. *How To Develop the Most Profitable, and the Happiest, Relationship with Your Dealer Customers* — 59

   WHAT DO YOUR DEALERS REALLY THINK OF YOU? HOW CAN YOU GET ALL THE BUSINESS YOU WANT FROM RETAILERS—AND MAKE THEM FRIENDS AND BOOSTERS?

7. *What Every Salesman Should Know About the Wholesaler Customer—and How To Sell Him* — 72

   HIS PLACE IN THE ECONOMY. HOW HE CAN HELP YOU MOVE A LARGE, PROFITABLE VOLUME OF YOUR PRODUCTS WHEN YOU KNOW HOW HE WANTS TO BE SOLD.

8. *How One Word Can Help You Sell More Insurance—and Move Up Rapidly into the Million-Dollars-A-Year Class* — 81

   HOW A STAR SALESMAN, A FARMER, AND A YOUNG NAVY VETERAN DID IT.

9. *How the Customer in the Medical and Dental Professions Wants To Be Sold* — 88

   ARE YOU LOSING BUSINESS YOU COULD GET EVERY DAY, IF YOU REMEMBERED WHAT THE DOCTORS THEMSELVES SAY IN THIS CHAPTER?

10. *Who Are the Institutional Customers—and How Do They Want To Be Sold?* — 96

    HOTELS—RESTAURANTS—CLUBS—HOSPITALS—SCHOOLS. ARE YOU SEEING THE RIGHT PEOPLE, AT THE RIGHT TIME AND IN THE RIGHT WAY?

CONTENTS

11. *When the Industrial Customer Will Buy—and How To Sell Him*   108

    IT IS EASY TO SELL TOP INDUSTRIAL EXECUTIVES AND DEPARTMENT HEADS WHEN YOU USE THE METHODS OF SUCCESSFUL INDUSTRIAL SALESMEN.

12. *How To Make "Cold" Purchasing Agents Good Customers and Warm Friends*   117

    WHO SAID THEY'RE "COLD"? WHEN YOU REALLY UNDERSTAND THEM, YOU WILL KNOW THEY NEED YOU AND WANT TO BUY FROM YOU.

13. *Why the Buyer of Advertising Is Never Tough When You Sell His Way*   125

    SOME SPACE, TIME, AND DISPLAY SALESMEN SHOULD KNOW HIM BETTER. HE WILL BUY IF YOU "TALK HIS LANGUAGE."

14. *How To Impress and Sell the Management Customer*   133

    TOP EXECUTIVES, BOARDS OF DIRECTORS—THEY BUY BIG WHEN YOU THINK BIG IN YOUR CONTACTS WITH THEM.

15. *How To Find Prospective Customers*   142

    THE BEST SALESMEN USUALLY HAVE THE BEST, AND THE MOST, PROSPECTS. HERE'S HOW THEY GET THEM.

16. *Never Let A Customer Forget You!*   150

    AND NEVER FORGET A CUSTOMER—HE CAN BE YOUR "GOLD MINE" AS LONG AS YOU KEEP HIM "IN GOOD CONDITION."

17. *Your Customers Need You*   158

    YOU CAN BE ONE OF THE MOST WELCOME PEOPLE TO COME INTO THEIR HOMES OR PLACES OF BUSINESS.

PART III

Salesmen Are Human, Too—What To Do About It

18. *How A Salesman Is "Born"*   167

    ARE YOU A BORN SALESMAN? NOW YOU WILL KNOW!

CONTENTS

19. *He Knows His Stuff—Let's Call Him In*   172
    INVARIABLY THE MARK OF THE STAR SALESMAN—IT ALWAYS PAYS BIG REWARDS.

20. *An Honest Joe—He Gets Our Business*   178
    CUSTOMERS PREFER TO BUY FROM THIS TYPE OF SALESMAN.

21. *He's So Darn Enthusiastic, It Must Be Good!*   185
    TOP PERFORMANCE EVERY TIME—AND ALWAYS CLOSE TO THE TOP IN SALES.

22. *He Wears Red Neckties and Gets the Green Light*   192
    THE IRON FIREMAN RED-NECKTIE STORY, AND HOW EVEN THE STARS KEEP IMPROVING THEIR "PERSONALITIES."

23. *He's A Showman—Corny, but Completely Convincing*   202
    COLOSSAL, STUPENDOUS, OR SIMPLE BUT EFFECTIVE SHOWMANSHIP, AND HOW IT CAN BOOST YOUR SALES.

24. *He Rides 'em Hard—These Four Vicious Nags and One Mean Little Jackass*   210
    FEAR—RESENTMENT—REGRET—DOUBT—DELAY.

25. *He Is Proud To Be A Salesman—A Professional Salesman!*   219
    "WHAT ARE YOU DOING THESE DAYS?"

PART IV
Even the Boss Is Human!

26. *Who Is This Character—The Boss?*   227
    HAS A JOB TO DO, TOO. MUST SHOW A PROFIT. YOUR SUCCESS CAN DETERMINE HIS SUCCESS.

27. *He's Working For You*   235
    KNOWING THIS FACT IS A POWERFUL FACTOR IN THE SUCCESS OF TOP SALESMEN.

CONTENTS

28. *If You Were the Boss* — 241

   IS THIS A GRIPE—OR AN OPPORTUNITY? IT CAN BE EITHER.

29. *How to Sell Yourself into the Job You Want* — 249

   IF IT IS WORTH HAVING—BUT HOW DO YOU KNOW? AND WHAT ARE YOU WILLING TO DO TO GET IT?

30. *Loyalty Is the Badge of A Noble Man!* — 258

   IT HAS A DEFINITE DOLLAR-AND-CENTS VALUE TO THE SALESMEN BIG ENOUGH TO KNOW IT.

CONCLUSION

31. *America Needs A Great Army of Salesmen* — 266

   THIS IS "YOUR SHINING HOUR OF OPPORTUNITY!"

32. *You Can Make Your Community Proud of You* — 275

   TAKE PART IN LOCAL GOVERNMENT, IN EDUCATIONAL WORK, WELFARE WORK. BE A STAR IN YOUR HOME TOWN.

33. *Follow the Way of Champions to Success* — 282

   IT WORKED FOR THE GREATEST MICHIGAN CHAMPIONSHIP FOOTBALL TEAMS—FOR STAR SALESMEN EVERYWHERE—IT WILL FOR YOU!

34. *The Radar of Human Relations* — 290

   WHEN YOU TUNE IN THE HUMAN SIDE OF SELLING, YOU COME WINGING IN SMOOTHLY ON THE BEAM—TO GREATER SUCCESS, INCREASED EARNING POWER, MORE HAPPINESS IN "THE GREATEST PROFESSION IN THE WORLD."

Index — 295

"Nothing Ever Happens Until a Sale Is Made"

Preface

IF IT has been your good fortune to hear one of the dynamic speeches of Arthur Motley, President of *Parade* Magazine, you will no doubt remember how he emphasizes this significant fact: *Nothing ever happens until a sale is made!*

You are constantly making, or losing, sales every day of your life. Whether you are an "amateur" salesman or a "professional," your success and happiness depend to a large extent on your ability to sell other people.

In this book you will meet many of the country's greatest salesmen and learn the reasons for their success. The time you spend with them can pay you a substantial profit by adding much practical know-how to your selling education.

Joseph P. Hardie, Vice President in Charge of Sales of Bristol-Myers Company, gave me this definition of education: "Education is the accumulation of knowledge which eventually enables a person to understand the other fellow's point of view."

Mr. Hardie also said, "I am one hundred per cent in accord with the belief that The *Human* Side of Selling is being gravely overlooked by too many sales people today. Being human, and thinking of the other fellow, to my mind is the key to good salesmanship."

To the star salesmen and women, the friendly human executives, the understanding educators and patient editors who have been my critics and counselors, my sincerest gratitude.

R. E. M.

The Human Side of Selling

INTRODUCTION

CHAPTER 1

*How to Earn More Money—
and Get More Fun Out of Life*

IF you live all alone on some far-off tropical island you do not need this book. Put it aside and go on out of your hut, climb a few trees, and gather yourself an armful of coconuts. Your life is a simple one. You have no one to sell. You don't want to earn more money (you can't eat money anyway), and how could you possibly get more fun out of life?

However, if even one other person is on that island with you, by all means read on. You might want to "sell" your friend on the advantages of climbing those tall trees and shaking down the coconuts for you each morning as a desirable form of exercise.

In the broadest sense of the word, we certainly are all "salesmen." Unless we live alone and never come in contact with anyone else we all are in one of two classifications of salesmen:

(1) *Amateur* Salesmen, or
(2) *Professional* Salesmen.

As amateur salesmen we are engaged in some form of selling all day long. From early morning when we sit down to breakfast and say "Good Morning!" to the family and someone asks "What's good about it?" all through the day, in our association with friends, fellow workers, the boss, and everyone we meet, we are selling our opinions, our ideas, ourselves.

This book is primarily for professional salesmen—the men and women who earn a living by selling. Nevertheless, it may help amateur salesmen to look for and try to understand the other fellow's

point of view, and help them sell their way through life more successfully.

Charles M. Schwab said, "Many of us think of salesmen as people traveling around with sample kits. Instead, we are all salesmen every day of our lives. We are selling our ideas, our plans, our energy, our enthusiasm to those with whom we come in contact." Think that over and you will understand how important selling is to your happiness as well as to your success in business.

As Maxwell Schultz, executive vice-president of Willmark Research Corporation, expressed it, "Everyone, whether he is an amateur or a professional salesman, used the A.I.D.A. selling formula to sell his ideas to others."

Mr. Schultz said:

The lawyer selling his case to a jury, the doctor selling hope for recovery to a very sick patient, even a child, when he wants to sell his dad on the idea of increasing his allowance, must go through those four A.I.D.A. steps: He must get *Attention*. He must arouse *Interest*. He must create *Desire*. And, finally, he must get *Action*.

Every successful salesperson follows that formula. The salesman behind the counter, or on the street, must first get the prospective buyer's Attention, then arouse his Interest, create Desire, and get Action. If he misses any of those steps, he will not sell.

Of course, a knowledge of the "mechanics" of selling is not enough for amateur or professional salesmen. The presentation to the prospective customer must be permeated with the *Human* Side of Selling. The successful salesman today is the one who is genuinely interested in his customer and helps his customer buy intelligently.

Mr. Schultz is a noted lecturer on scientific selling. He knows what makes top salesmen successful. Through his nation-wide organization he works with more than a thousand companies which employ hundreds of thousands of salespeople. Invariably, he has found that the most successful are those who understand the *Human* Side of Selling.

If you are working as a salesman now, in any form of selling, you can't help earning more money and getting more fun out of life after you read this book. Why is it possible to make such a positive statement? Because the following pages are chuck full of examples of horribly wrong ways of selling, and the one happy, easy, successful way—and if you're interested enough in your selling career to have this book in your hand right now you surely will use the selling methods described which have made fortunes, and so many warm friends, for top salesmen everywhere.

Looking over the chapter headings you may wonder how you will profit by reading about some form of selling in which you are not engaged. If you sell insurance or automobiles or building materials, for instance, you may say, "Why should I read about selling farm equipment?" In the discussion of successful farm-equipment selling are several ideas which salesmen in many other industries could use profitably. I'll bet some alert salesmen will use their cameras to increase their sales and keep customers happy after they read about a certain successful tractor salesman in Chapter 5.

It has been said that there is nothing new under the sun and genius consists in finding new uses or new applications for proved methods or ideas. If that is true, you may find many challenges to your genius in chapters which have nothing to do with your immediate selling but may contain ideas or successful methods of other salespeople which you might apply successfully to your own work.

You will visit with outstandingly successful salespeople and business leaders such as Mr. J. C. Penney, who said, "Millions of people trade at our stores because of our values, quality, style, and friendly service. But the greatest of these is friendly service." And emphasizing the importance of the *Human* Side of Selling, Mr. Penney added, "Many men, with otherwise mediocre talents, have still won marked success through their honest friendliness."

That statement by the man who started selling behind a counter and built one of the largest retail store systems in the world, more than 1,600 stores, may suggest to you the great power of the *Human* Side of Selling. Mr. Penney knows it. You will know it intimately after you read this book. It can help you become as successful as you care to be.

During the peaceful years between wars, every free country needs a great army of salespeople. During a wartime period, when so many experienced salesmen are called into service, there is always

HOW TO EARN MORE MONEY

a shortage of salespeople, particularly of salespeople who understand the *Human* Side of Selling. War or peace, prosperity or depression, salesmen and saleswomen are always needed.

Look in the Want-Ad Section of your newspaper any day and you will see more opportunities for salesmen and saleswomen than for any other job classification.

If you can sell, you need never worry about earning enough to support yourself and your family. During the bitter depression of the early nineteen-thirties the president of a small bank in the South decided to commit suicide. His bank had failed. He had lost every cent he had. There were so many people unemployed that he couldn't see how he possibly could support his family. He was through. Perhaps his life insurance money would keep his family going for a few years at least. He walked up the stairs to his study, sat down at his desk, opened the drawer, and pulled out a revolver. He pointed it at his head. As he was about to pull the trigger he saw a copy of *Specialty Salesman Magazine* which his wife had placed on his desk. Something made him hesitate. He put down the revolver and opened the magazine.

A few days later, Mr. H. W. Minchin, general manager of *Specialty Salesman Magazine,* received an air-mail letter from that banker. The brokenhearted man told Mr. Minchin how he was about to shoot himself, but the last-minute ray of hope—that he might support his family by selling—made him wait and write what might be his last letter. He told Minchin he would not kill himself until he received a reply to his letter asking whether the publishers of *Specialty Salesman* could suggest some way he could sell enough to make a living for himself and his family. If he did not receive a reply in a few days he would go ahead with his decision to commit suicide.

In a three-page reply Mr. Minchin suggested a number of ways that ex-bank president could sell. He pointed out that the man must be interested in serving the people in his town and could continue to serve them as a salesman. He suggested several lines he might sell. He urged him to try selling before he threw in the sponge and killed himself.

Two months went by and Minchin wondered what had happened to the bank president whose outlook on life had been so gloomy. One day he received a friendly, enthusiastic letter in which the would-be suicide told him that he had followed his suggestions and was now a successful salesman. He no longer had any thoughts of taking his own life, in fact was making more money than he ever had as a banker, had more friends, and was happier than he had ever been in his life.

That is a true story. You may say it is exceptional. I hope it is. Nevertheless, the experience of that former banker as a salesman does emphasize the great security and peace of mind that can come to you—and all other men and women who sell—especially when you know the *Human* Side of Selling.

You can profit by the experience of some of the most successful salesmen and sales executives in America, which we will discuss in the following pages. Invariably you will find that they earn more money and get more fun out of life because they know the *Human* Side of Selling.

This book can show you how to make more money and have much more fun as a professional salesman. Read it with a pencil. Mark the paragraphs you want to review. Bend back the corners of the pages that will help you most. Tear the book apart if you wish. But don't be like the Brown County, Indiana, mule.

According to Dickman Stone, food editor of the Indianapolis *Star-News* and noted restaurant merchandiser, the people of Brown County, Indiana, manage to live without working. Recently one of the old residents passed on and left his 50-acre hillside farm to an ambitious young nephew who had never lived in Brown County. When the nephew took over the farm he found the fifty acres were all covered with scrub oak. He decided to clear the farm and plant it, and he went into town to buy a mule to pull the old plow.

He bought a mule at an auction and led him out to the farm. Two days later he was back in town with the mule. He told the auctioneer he had sold him a blind mule.

The auctioneer said, "Why, son, I've sold that mule nineteen or twenty times and no one ever told me it was blind. What makes you think that mule is blind?"

The young man said, "That mule sure is blind. I took him out to work in the field and he ran right into trees and fell over stumps. He's as blind as he can be!"

The auctioneer laughed. "Heck!" he said, "that mule ain't blind, son. He just don't give a damn!"

Perhaps you will read this book and think it rather interesting; you may enjoy it thoroughly. Yet, if you merely put it down and do not use the additional knowledge you have acquired about the *Human* Side of Selling you will be very much like that Brown County mule.

If you really want to earn more money and get more fun out of life, this book will help you in two ways: (1) by showing you the mistakes that are holding so many other salespeople back from success and (2) the easy, confident, sure way to profit by the *Human* Side of Selling.

PART I

The "Material" Side and the "Human" Side of Selling

CHAPTER 2

Why Some Salesmen Fail— while Others Earn a Fortune

IT is estimated that 90 per cent of those who fail to succeed as salesmen fail because they do not understand the *Human* Side of Selling.

Whether you are a department store salesclerk or an automobile salesman, whether you sell in a drugstore or sell air-conditioning systems to factories, whether you sell groceries or hardware, insurance or radios, whether you sell stocks and bonds on Wall Street or sell hosiery house-to-house in Missouri, there is one factor in your selling that you share with every other salesman. *You sell people—Human Beings.*

One salesman said, "Wouldn't selling be a pleasure if we didn't have to bother with customers!" He was not a happy nor a successful salesman. I'd call him a "sales scarecrow." A scarecrow, you know,

Sales Scarecrow

usually looks like a man, but his head is full of straw and his stretched-out arms, flapping in the breeze, frighten crows away. Aren't some salespeople like that? Don't they actually drive customers away?

Harry Hansen, noted literary editor of the New York *World-Telegram and Sun,* was driven away by sales scarecrows when he walked into four stores and tried to buy a topcoat. You can't scarecrow Mr. Hansen—or any other customer—and get away with it. The *Human* Side of Selling will slap you right in the eye. Listen to Mr. Hansen:

> You may think me rude, but nobody is going to sell me a new topcoat. No, sir, but nobody. I am going to sell myself one. I've been walking through the aisles where the brand-new topcoats are displayed—in herringbone, worsted, gabardine, covert cloth; in brown, tan, gray, and smoky fog; in form-fitting, loose-fitting, reversible, lined and unlined models, and one of these days I am going to take one down and say: "Wrap it up." But no one is going to sell me one.
>
> I'll tell you why. I have been in four stores and have been jostled by a half dozen salesmen. They take for granted that all they have to do is slap a coat on my back, rub their hands across my shoulders, and make a sale.
>
> When I say it's too loose, they pinch up both shoulders and say: "See that? A good fit."
>
> When I hesitate, they begin looking around for the next customer and say, "Be right with you, sir."
>
> That's not selling. That's giving me the bum's rush. Selling is an art.

Harry Hansen expressed it so well! Selling is an art. And you will read, in one of the following chapters, about an artistic clothing salesman. He doesn't give his customers the bum's rush. His customers do not walk out. In fact, they keep coming back so regularly that he earns more than fifteen thousand dollars a year selling men's clothes. He knows the *Human* Side of Selling.

Walkouts are costly experiences for any store. Mr. Hansen walked out of four stores. He wanted to buy a topcoat. He did not buy. The stores lost the profit on the sales. Scarecrow salesmen lost—actually turned away—the sale. Most of us have had similar experiences—too frequently. Millions of dollars of sales are being turned away every day by salespeople who do not know the *Human* Side of Selling.

When I drove my two-year-old Buick into a Buick dealer's service shop the other day and left it for an oil change and lubrication I walked out through the display room. That is, I started to walk out, but I saw a beautiful new super-convertible and stopped in my tracks. I walked around that car. I opened the door, looked inside, sat behind the wheel. None of the three salesmen in the room came near me, although anyone could see I was politely drooling.

After a while I asked one of the salesmen the cost of the car. He told me, and went back to his conversation with the other men. I walked out of that display room, hailed a cab, and daydreamed about that robin's-egg blue convertible all the way to the office. Not one of those salesmen even bothered to ask my name. They evidently were so interested in their own affairs that they cared nothing at all about Robert E. Customer Moore.

I may have been a red-hot prospect then. I am cold as ice now. Being human, I have no desire to buy a car from that dealer under any circumstances. Those salesmen lost the best type of customer—a satisfied user.

At a recent automobile show I became interested in a rather handsome Packard. A salesman who approached me asked bluntly, "What are you driving now?" I told him I was driving a Buick Roadmaster and asked whether the Packard was a better car.

Lo and behold! his reply was one that certainly would inspire confidence in a prospect and excite him into prompt action! He said, "Well, I think it is a better car. Of course, you have 152 horsepower and this is only 150, but I personally think this car rides better."

"Why does it ride better?" I asked.

"Well, I think it does," he said. "It may be just a personal opinion, but I really think it does."

A sales scarecrow futilely waving his personal opinion in the air. Here was an interested prospect whose curiosity had been aroused by Packard advertising. The salesman had only to parrot that advertising, even if he had no interest in me as a *human* being, no curiosity about why I might want to own and drive a Packard. He sold me on *not* buying that car more effectively than he could if he had been a competitor's salesman.

In our chapter on the *Human* Side of Selling automobiles we will contrast those sales scarecrows with an automobile salesman who built the *Human* Side of Selling cars into a 10-million-dollar business.

Fred Sutherland, vice-president and general manager of the George Spies Industries, Chicago, called an electrical contractor and asked for an estimate on a plant wiring job. The price seemed reasonable and he gave the contractor-salesman the order. After the wiring had been installed, the contractor said, "The job is finished, but you had better not let a fire marshal see it. It violates the fire law."

Mr. Sutherland is a forthright gentleman. He blew up—in spades. He asked the contractor why in x-x-x-x he had specified and quoted on inadequate wiring. The man replied, "I thought you wanted a low-cost job." He obviously was thinking of dollar signs and wiring—and not at all of the customer and his needs.

Fred Sutherland made that electrical contractor tear out the illegal wiring before he left the plant and install the heavier conduit specified by law. In Chapter 11 you will meet a decided contrast to that man—an electrical contractor in a little Florida town who is selling some of the largest power, lighting, and air-conditioning installations in the state—at prices as much as two and a half times higher than competition. He is in demand—he knows the *Human* Side of Selling.

The Superior Sleeprite Company, a large manufacturer of furniture and bedding, had one territory which had never been productive. Salesman after salesman failed to sell the dealers in that area enough to pay traveling expenses. According to Harold Baum, promotion manager, "It was a no man's land where salesmen starved to death—until we turned it over to Nate Schaeffer." In the chapter of the *Human* Side of Selling to dealers you will read how futile are the calls made on dealers by sales scarecrows. And you will read how Nate Schaeffer irrigated an arid sales area with the *Human*

Side of Selling and harvested twenty thousand dollars a year in commissions.

During a period between World War II and the Korean War, when unemployment was high and sales volume was dropping in almost every industry, the editors of *Fortune* magazine asked themselves, "What's the matter with American selling?" and made a widespread study to find out. Their findings were summarized in three words: *"Salesmen aren't selling."*

A staff member of *Fortune* was sent on a two-week shopping tour. He reported:

I called on every type of drugstore, chains, neighborhood pharmacies, large independents, the kind that are called "chemists," and the cut-rates; and I called on them in all types of localities in the Northeast, from rural villages to large cities. My technique was this: I would amble up to the counter—plainly in no hurry—and say I wanted some razor blades. If, after a reasonable pause, the clerk had not seized this opening and suggested a brand, I would ask for a 10-cent package of Gillette Thin Blades. Then, still in no hurry, I would wait for a query as to how was I fixed for shaving cream and after-shave lotion.

I waited a long time. Before I was through I had given clerks in some ninety-five stores a fair crack at me. Yet, incredibly, in only five did they suggest a companion item, and in only nineteen did they suggest a brand of blades. In only three did they do both. When it came to the matter of the "large economy size," only six tried to upgrade me from the 10-cent package, and of them only three mentioned the fact that I could save money that way. With most clerks the nearest approach to a suggestion was a closing "Will there be anything else?"—delivered in such a thank-you-call-again tone of voice as to be useless.

Only six of ninety-five salesclerks bothered to think it was not logical for a man to buy just one 10-cent razor blade. And of the six only three—three out of ninety-five salesclerks—thought enough of the customer to tell him he could save money by buying a larger package of blades! How scarecrowish can our selling be? But the *Fortune* editor found scarecrow salesmen wherever he went. His report continued:

During my drugstore tour I was testing another type of outlet once famed for its use of suggestion, for I was stopping for gas. And in most cases that is just what I got: gas. I stopped at fifteen stations—big ones, the kind with lubritoriums and irradiated rest rooms—but at only five did the attendant ask to check the oil and water. In none did I hear the old prewar refrain, "Fill 'er up?"

It is incredible that there are so many scarecrow salespeople in every type of business. On all sides you see them indifferent to opportunities to make sales or actually driving sales away. Their lack of understanding of the *Human* Side of Selling leaves them inept failures as salesmen, or at best frustrated, bungling mediocrities. But let us read some more of the *Fortune* editor's report of his experience in the land of the Lilliputian salespeople:

Next I would shop for an item expensive enough so it might properly be expected to call forth some rather intensive sales effort. Tires I badly needed, and since the hundred-odd dollars in cash I would hand over for them constituted a pretty fair carrot to dangle before salesmen, I set off to tempt them.

My first call was at a B. F. Goodrich agency. There was no one in the showroom, but by searching a bit I found the owner out in back working away at a recapping machine. The tires on my convertible, I explained, were in bad shape and I was interested in getting a new set, preferably the low-pressure type.

The owner shot me a confidential sort of glance. "Want to know something," he said, "just between you and me?"

Yes?

"These low-pressure jobs . . . they're not worth the difference."

No? I wondered.

"No." He pulled a memo book from his hip pocket and ran his finger under a line of figures. "The size you'd have to take would cost you about $28 apiece."

"Good bit of money for a tire."

"That's no lie, brother. It isn't all either. You'd have to get a set of tubes too. Set you back another three, four dollars apiece."

We looked at each other inconclusively for a few moments. At length he folded up the memo book and put it back in his hip pocket. "Those babies," he said, nodding to the convertible out front, "sure would run a man into money." I agreed, and thanked him for his trouble. "Nothing at all," he said, inching back toward his recapping machine, "and if you're interested in regular Goodriches, I got plenty of those on hand." He laughed, "Too damn many!"

At my next call, a Lee tire store, I was similarly dissuaded. In the calls that followed, the story was much the same. Not a word of Goodrich's "rhythm-flexing cords," of Dayton's "1296 road-gripping toes," of Firestone's "road-gripping skid-resistors." Nor of the obvious fact that the more expensive tires have more rubber, and hence a good deal more life, in them. Instead, answers were more generally along the lines of that of the salesman who explained with a wink to show he was nobody's fool, that the principal difference was "the extra twenty bucks on the price tag."

Out of fourteen calls the results were as follows: in three stores I was virtually talked out of buying; in two no one would wait on me; and in another the manager was busy listening to Gabriel Heatter at the time, and was too transfixed to give the matter his full attention. In five the salesmen did little more than answer the questions I asked of them, and none of them could think of any particular reason, plausible or otherwise, why their tires were any better than the competition's. Similarly, none suggested that I get five rather than four tires, though that had been my intention.

In the chapter on the *Human* Side of Retail Selling you will read some welcome contrasts to the experience of the *Fortune* editor with the sales scarecrows who are so incredible, and seem to be so numerous.

Hundreds of scarecrow salesmen have failed to sell insurance. Many sell only enough to earn a fair living. But some sell more than a million dollars a year—they know the *Human* Side of Selling. And that makes the big difference between failure and success in any kind of selling.

You may be a slap-happy scarecrow salesman if you ignore it, or don't know it. You can earn as much as you care to, and enjoy life more than ever before, when you know and are guided in your selling by the *Human* Side of Selling.

CHAPTER 3

*The Star Salesmen—The Champs —
Know the* Human *Side of Selling*

WHILE 750 sales executives attending an Edison Electric Institute convention listened intently, Jack Lacy, head of the Lacy Sales Institute, told them: "There are two basic reasons why people buy from a salesman: (1) they think he can give them more for their money than anyone else; (2) they like him. And the second reason is far more important than the first."

Mr. Lacy said: "Many companies today have sales training programs. Most of them are good. Too many, however, are mainly product education programs. They train the salesman to know the company's products or services thoroughly, but they do not train him to understand selling psychology.

"According to the dictionary, you know, psychology is the science of the mind. It explains *why* people act and think and feel the way they do. Training in selling psychology would show the salesman how and why people decide to buy *from him*.

"Training in selling psychology would show the salesman the vital importance of the second of the two basic reasons why people buy. He would know that if prospective customers dislike him they automatically dislike his product, but if they like him well enough they will look for ways to do business with him."

Jack Lacy knows probably as well as any man in the world how vital to a salesman's success is the *Human* Side of Selling. He has been a star salesman of food products, books, advertising, transportation, insurance. When he sold insurance, he soon topped a million dollars a year and became the leader of his company. He has been

One for All and All for One—Me!

a brilliant sales manager and has trained more than a hundred thousand salesmen.

In Jack Lacy Sales Clinics, sponsored by Sales Executive Clubs all over the country, he has helped an army of men and women become successful salesmen by showing them that "the head of the prospect is the thing that pays off. The difference in salesmen is the effect they produce *in the mind* of the prospective customer!"

The unsuccessful "weak-sister" salesman doesn't think of the mind of his prospective customer. You might say he doesn't think of the customer at all. Usually he just goes through the motions of presenting his product without considering what the customer needs, wants, or should have.

The drugstore salesmen discussed in the preceding chapter, who permitted a customer to buy one razor blade and didn't even try to sell him more, certainly were not thinking about the customer. The customer might as well have placed a coin in a slot machine and served himself.

Those salesmen are the "scarecrow" type largely responsible for the growth of the self-service store, which is eliminating retail store salepeople who do not sell.

In the selling profession you either sell or eventually you go. And you sell most successfully when you know the *Human* Side of Selling, when you think in terms of the *people* you sell instead of the *things* you sell.

The day a salesman becomes aware of the *Human* Side of Selling can mark a turning point in his life. *Parade,* the Sunday picture magazine, reported such a turning point in the life of John Fox, who launched a vigorous new industry.

According to *Parade:*

It was a sultry afternoon in Hingham, Massachusetts. All that week John Fox had trudged from one house to the next, begging housewives to try samples of frozen, concentrated orange juice.

It was disheartening work. World War II had been over only a few months. Housewives were tired of substitutes. Hadn't their husbands and sons been grumbling about the Army's powdered eggs and dehydrated potatoes?

THE STAR SALESMEN

"And now 'frozen concentrated orange juice'! No, thanks. I'll squeeze my own." The answer was always the same.

Wearily, Fox rapped on the kitchen door of another home.

An angry housewife peered out: "My maid is sick. I'm waiting for the grocer. I am having fourteen women for tea. And you! There should be a law . . ."

The door slammed.

Perhaps on any other day John Fox would have walked away. But not today. He opened the door and walked in. He could hear the hostess greeting a guest.

Putting on an apron, he tackled a pile of half-finished sandwiches. Suddenly, the housewife reappeared. Her look of surprise froze into a glare of anger. There was a chilly pause, and then they both laughed.

Fox made orange juice. Several women gave him orders. One, a volunteer worker, introduced the frozen juice at a nearby hospital.

Soon the boom was on. And it's still on. You see, the reception these Hingham women gave Fox's product marked the birth of an industry that sells nearly a half million cans of frozen orange juice a year! And salesman Fox? Today he is president of one of this industry's leading companies.

Parade called that experience of John Fox "The Turning Point." What made it a turning point in his life? At that moment he forgot that he wanted to sell a product (frozen orange juice) and thought about the *customer* and what he could do to help her.

What did she want? Well, she was in a jam. No help. Fourteen women coming in for tea. What would you want? A helping hand. When John Fox helped her finish those tea sandwiches he didn't have to *"sell"* her his frozen orange juice—she *"bought"* it, and helped him sell her friends.

As Jack Lacy told that meeting of sales executives, the most important reason why people buy from a salesman is that *they like him*. What makes customers like a salesman? Is it "personality"— some personal magnetism which a few salesmen have and many lack? Well, the "personality"—the personal magnetism—of John Fox was the same all week long. Yet he didn't sell a single can of orange juice . . . until something happened. What?

Why, *he became interested in the customer*—in helping her—and consequently the customer LIKED HIM and wanted to do business with him!

There you have the *HUMAN Side of Selling.*

When a salesman realizes he isn't selling a "thing," that he is selling "PEOPLE"—when he becomes interested in the PEOPLE he sells, genuinely interested in helping them—he has found the Aladdin's Lamp that brings selling success.

When you have that "Aladdin's Lamp," selling is easy. When you do not, it is hard, discouraging work. I know. I'm one of the bright young men who worked their way through school selling magazine subscriptions from house to house, from town to town.

Ringing doorbells my first day was a series of discouraging experiences. "I'm too busy. Haven't time to talk to you!" housewife after housewife said as she firmly closed the door.

My early eagerness rapidly drained away. I didn't make a single sale all day. No one could be more of a sales "scarecrow" than I was all that day.

That first evening I asked our crew manager why I failed so miserably when I had tried so hard. He said, "Trying hard is not enough. Making a lot of calls is not enough. What you say and do when you are face to face with the prospective buyer makes or loses the sale. Come with me tomorrow and I'll show you what I mean."

The next day I saw a magnificent demonstration of the *Human Side of Selling.* When a woman came to the door and said she was too busy, she was mopping her kitchen floor, he said, "Let me help you." And he said it sincerely. He meant it, and they knew somehow that he did. The doors opened. We washed dishes, mopped floors, hung wash on the line, and the busy housewives *bought* our magazine subscriptions. They even phoned friends and relatives and urged them to subscribe to the magazines sold "by those nice young men."

You might ask what making tea sandwiches, mopping floors, and hanging up wash have to do with selling frozen orange juice or magazines. They have nothing to do with selling the *products,* but everything to do with selling the *people.*

With all my young enthusiasm, earnestness, knowledge of my

product, willingness to work and work hard, I had not sold even one magazine subscription. However, when I was shown that I was selling *people,* not magazines, I took orders for more magazine subscriptions than I had ever hoped to sell.

You might say, that's all right for house-to-house selling, but how does it apply in other types of selling? You can't wash dishes for a customer who comes into a store, or drives into a service station for five gallons of gasoline. You don't have to wash dishes, or help a prospective customer with her housework even when you do sell from house to house. *The* Human *Side of Selling requires only that you have a genuine interest in the customer, you want to help the customer do the things the customer wants to do, and you treat the customer with the respect, the courtesy, and the friendliness you would appreciate if your positions were reversed.*

When you are selling in a store or in a service station, very often the *Human* Side of your selling is the only reason why people continue to trade with you—or never come back. Other stores, other service stations, may be just as convenient, may have the same quality of products, in fact the same products. The way you treat the customer, therefore, will determine whether the customer comes back. We will discuss that in Chapter 5.

In any type of selling, the unsuccessful, bungling salesman—the sales scarecrow particularly—thinks in terms of the *things* he sells, and the *things* that interest him.

Ask a salesman who is just getting by in his selling what interests him most about his job and he probably will say, "the salary," or "the commission"—and how little he has to do to earn it.

His next interest will be the clock—and how soon each day he can get away from his selling job.

Next, the sales he makes, the orders he gets.

Finally, the product or service he sells, and the organization he represents.

The star salesman, on the other hand, thinks of the *people* he sells, how he can help them, how the product or service he sells can benefit them.

The customer is the most important factor in every sale. Remem-

ber that. *There are two other influences, however, which have a deep effect on the* Human *Side of Selling: they are* (1) *the salesman himself and* (2) *his boss.*

Yes, we salesmen are human and, strange as it sometimes may seem, each of us knows that the boss is human too.

The top salesman constantly studies himself, continually seeks to improve and strengthen the human qualities that make him a more successful salesman. He also learns all he can about his employer and his objectives, so he can help the boss in every way he possibly can.

The customer, the salesman, and his boss should be like the famous Three Musketeers—one for all and all for one. When they are, the salesman is guided almost completely by the *Human* Side of Selling and is certain to be a top-flight successful salesman, respected by his associates and customers, with solid financial security, with countless friends. He will be confident, relaxed, and happy—a star in "the greatest profession in the world."

PART II

Customers are Human Beings

CHAPTER 4

What Do You Know about the "Man behind the Dollar"?

THERE probably isn't a salesman alive who at some time hasn't questioned the Marshall Field slogan: "The customer is always right!" How can the customer be "right" when she is impatient, grouchy, doesn't know what she wants in the first place, takes up a lot of our time and then may walk away without buying anything? How can the prospective customer be "right" when he is discourteous, abrupt, often cruelly blunt in his refusal to buy?

Of course, the customer isn't always right. Customers are *human* beings, and therefore they can be just as inconsiderate, as petty, as ornery as we salesmen are at times.

And because customers are *human,* they can be as sweet as angels at other times.

We know that even the best customers are not always right. Why, then, did Marshall Field adopt the slogan: "The customer is always

Welcome Friends—We Sure Love to See that Beautiful Dollar of Yours Coming Our Way!

right!"? Marshall Field was not naïve. He knew what he was doing. Why?

When Marshall Field opened his little store in Chicago back in 1852, he soon learned what every successful merchant learns, what every star salesman knows—*the customer is the man behind the dollar*.

It is not your store nor your company, not the merchandise you sell, nor the work you do that puts the dollars in the cash register or the salary in your pay envelope. It is the customer—the man behind the dollar—and he can give those dollars to you or to someone else, as he chooses.

Marshall Field wanted the *man behind the dollar* to bring those dollars into his store. What could attract them to Field's when other stores had the same, or similar, merchandise? He found that the attitude of the salespeople—the way the salespeople treated customers—was far more important than the merchandise they sold. So he adopted his famous slogan and made it the policy of the store. It attracted so many customers that Marshall Field's store became one of the largest and most successful retail establishments in the world.

Because the customer is the *man behind the dollar,* the customer is indeed the most important factor in every selling transaction. To sell the *man behind the dollar,* we ought to know him better. Who is he? What does he want of us? What can we salesmen do to induce him to give more of those dollars to us?

Who is he? He is a *human* being. One day he may be on top of the world. The next day he may be the victim of frustrations, defeat, insecurity or suffering. When you meet him he may be cheerful and optimistic, or grouchy and unhappy.

He has seen man's inhumanity to man explode into world-wide war, revolution and counterrevolution. He has seen, or has read about global depressions, class conflicts, conspiracies, civil war, dictatorships, sabotage, executions, the brutality of the strong inflicted on the weak or unwary.

The apparent triumph of brutality, dishonesty and ruthless power gives him a sense of insecurity, makes him inclined to be suspicious of strangers until he is sure their motives are friendly.

Usually he is a reasonably well-balanced person. But he may be mentally ill. According to *Today's Health* magazine (published by the A.M.A.), there are six million Americans who are sufficiently maladjusted and unhappy to require psychiatric treatment. *Look* magazine, in an article about the serious need for more psychiatrists, reported: "One American out of ten becomes mentally ill. It still comes as news to many people to learn that mental illness is pre-eminently our No. 1 health problem."

When a customer appears to be short tempered and disagreeable, remember that he may be unhappy, under pressure, suffering from nervous tension, even mentally ill. Be kind to him!

Your customer has much the same problems that you have, at home, in business, in relation to the world at large. Sometimes he can cope with them easily. At other times they overwhelm him. Unfortunately salesmen who do not understand him, or are indifferent to him, add to his confusion and feeling of unimportance.

During wartime shortages, he stood in line. He paid premiums for the car or other things he needed. He ate humble pie and remembers how he was shoved around by those salespeople and merchants who forgot to be human. He had to accept all sorts of substitutes. He had to take what he could get. And he actually was laughed at when he had money in his pocket and wanted to buy.

Yes, the customer—the *man behind the dollar*—was made to feel unimportant, in fact, quite little.

And your customer (whether that customer is a housewife at the counter in a grocery store or a vice-president at his desk in the office of a huge corporation) *is* little. We all are little people. And we know it.

Deep down inside we have a subsconscious perspective which keeps us in our place in relation to the teeming millions on this spinning globe of ours. And occasionally, when we look up at the stars on a clear night, we realize what infinitesimally small bits of life we are in the vast universe.

We all are little people. But in each of us is a fiercely burning fire of individuality. We are capable of tremendous bigness. Nothing is beyond our reach. And we bestow our favor on the comparatively few who recognize and respect the bigness in us and do not accentuate our unimportance. We love the few who appreciate and encourage our bigness.

What does that mean to a salesman? It means that customers will resent and refuse to buy from you if you treat them as though they are not important, if you make them feel little. And it is easy to do just that by lack of attention, indifferent service, by your appearance, your manner, by the tone of your voice, by being late for appointments or not preparing for them.

An advertising manager has told me he is constantly amazed by the fact that so many salesmen seem to make no preparation for their appointments with him. They don't even know what products his company manufactures. They talk about the *things they want to sell* and have not taken the trouble to find out how those things might be of service to his company.

That advertising manager did not tell me that those salesmen make him feel little. But it is certain that they do not make him feel important. They seldom get an order.

There is one salesman who gets all the orders he wants from that advertising manager. He has studied the company's products and its markets and has learned the management's sales objectives. He goes out of his way to help the company improve its distribution, increase its sales. He doesn't have to sell that ad manager. The ad manager buys.

A. M. Sweeney, general sales manager of the General Electric Company, Bridgeport, said, "We have recently decided to abandon, as far as possible, the use of the word 'Salesmanship' or 'Selling.' We are now stressing the idea that no one *likes to be sold,* but they *love to buy.* So, we are going to talk to our salesman about Buymanship for want of a better name. *Helping* the customer *buy* will be our approach."

What makes a customer *want* to buy from us salesmen?

We will discuss specific customers, and what makes them want to buy, in the following chapters. All customers, however, are HUMAN, and they prefer to buy from the salespeople who give them

Recognition—and Prompt Attention
Respect—and Courtesy
Genuine Interest
Help in Doing the Things the Customer Wants
    to Do, in Achieving His Ambitions
Appreciation.

Remember that your customers are little people. In relation to the world at large, no one is very important. You might say we are just so many social security numbers! Each individual, however, is the most important person in the whole world to himself. And quite important to his family and friends. If you show that you *recognize his importance,* he will like you and will be more inclined to buy from you.

How do you show that you recognize the customer's importance? By giving him immediate attention when he comes into your place of business. By calling him by name. By keeping appointments promptly. In so many ways!

Do you remember the corner grocer who gave each child who came into his store a piece of candy? He would say, with a big friendly smile, "Here, Mary, I have something for you!" It wasn't the fact that she got something for nothing that made Mary happy; it was the recognition! She knew that grocer was glad to see her—*she liked him,* and as she grew up preferred to buy at his store.

Customers appreciate respect. Marshall Field showed it when he told the world that in his store "The customer is always right!" Never argue with a customer. If you see that he is mistaken in his judgment of your products or service, or is unfriendly and disagreeable, be courteous and patient with him. John A. Quigley, vice president and general sales manager of Bayuk Cigars, Inc. agrees with that advice. But he says, "Where the customer obviously is misinformed or uninformed about a product or idea, agreeing with him would deny him the benefits of the right slant and the profits that could accrue to him. Opposition to his thoughts may result in momentary unpleasantness, but if you handle it diplomatically, and events prove the course you recommend is right, you will have gained his confidence and respect. I recently had an experience of this nature where an unfriendly large account became convinced that we had his best interests at heart and is now one of my company's top customers."

When you take a genuine interest in the customer you come closer to his heart, and to his buying impulse. It is natural for a person to like someone who really is interested in him. Make this experiment—notice a customer's new hat and tell her you like it. Nine times out of ten, she will reward you with a warm, friendly smile and tell you how glad she is that you like it. Don't be insincere. Customers can feel it. But let them know you are interested in them personally, and they will want to buy from you.

To hit the jackpot in sales, help the customer do what he wants to do most at the time you call on him, or when he comes into your place of business. Show him how you, and the products or service you sell, can help him achieve his immediate ambitions, and he will buy from you.

Remember to thank him for the order. And show your appreciation in every way you can. M. K. Moore, who sells orders that amount to thousands of dollars to businesswomen, sends them a bouquet or a small box of candy with a short note of thanks after she receives their orders. Instead of making sales, she makes customers who prefer to buy where they are appreciated.

One insurance agent calls me several times before the day I have to renew my policy, but never after he receives my check. Another phones after he gets my check, thanks me, and asks me how he can be of service to me in any way. Which one gets my additional business? You're right. The one who shows by his appreciation that he is interested in me as much as he is in my dollars.

A successful gasoline service station sends a card to customers each month thanking them for their business and the opportunities they gave the station to serve them. Other stations write: "Our records show you haven't been in for a long time . . ." Which one gets the business? The one which shows its appreciation.

Some students of customer relations say that today's customer is more sophisticated, more cynical than prewar customers. They say the customer today knows he can get along without a new car every year, or new electrical appliances, or a new home, new furniture, the latest clothes. And consequently he is harder to sell. That may be true. But the customer of today is just as much a *human* being as the prewar customer was.

Yes, the customer, regardless of his frustrations, insecurity, sophistication, is *human*. He needs and wants many things. Above all, he needs and wants people near him who recognize his importance, his inherent capacity for greatness.

He is the *man behind the dollar* who pays your salary, or commissions. He can make you a great success as a salesman, if you will treat him as though he indeed is one of the most important persons in the world to you. If you do, you will know the tremendous power and personal satisfaction of the *Human* Side of Selling.

In the following chapters we will journey all over the country to talk with many, many different types of customers to see why and how they buy. We will see for ourselves the "secrets" of the star salesmen, the selling champions, who earn fortunes and make innumerable friends, because they know the *Human* Side of Selling.

CHAPTER 5

How to Grow Wealthy Selling Retail Customers

SELLING retail customers successfully has made fortunes for many salespeople. Yet there are so many others who seem resigned to mediocrity, because they apparently believe that retail selling is

The First Time a Sales Girl Makes a Fuss Over Her and She Wants to Buy Out the Whole Store!

nothing more than taking an order or passing merchandise across the counter in exchange for the customer's dollars.

Willmark Service System, Inc., studied 40,000 retail sales transactions and reported:

Constructive salesmanship threatens to become a lost art. Too many sales persons have slipped to the status of change makers or order takers.

That survey was made by field workers in all sections of the country, in large and small retail establishments.

It is obvious that "a change maker" or "an order taker" does not understand the *Human* Side of Selling. When you become interested in customers as *human beings* you cannot possibly be just a change maker or an order taker.

Of course, some salespeople have no interest in their customers. Their only interest is in themselves—their jobs, their salaries, their commissions, the minimum number of hours they can work. Psychologists would call them "egocentric"—all wrapped up in themselves. They are the sales scarecrows Harry Hansen met when he went into several stores to buy a topcoat, the type the *Fortune* editor met when he called on drugstores, gasoline service stations, and tire dealers. Perhaps they should not be working as salespeople, particularly in retail establishments.

Retail selling is highly *personal selling*. The retail customers buy for their own use and for their families and friends. In this chapter we shall take a number of squirming little customers of various types of retail establishments and hold them gently under our microscope. Perhaps we shall see why they act, and react, the way they do. We may learn why they give all their own business, and send all their friends too, to some salesmen, and why they stay away from certain others as though they had some repelling form of psychological leprosy.

If you are a retail salesman you know that selling women customers is particularly important to your success. You have heard the *Ladies' Home Journal* slogan: "Never underestimate the power of a woman!" An experienced retail salesman might add to that: "Never underestimate the personal side—the *human* side—of a woman customer!"

In an address before a national convention of the Super Market Institute, Mrs. Charlotte Montgomery, noted writer, commentator and columnist of *Tide* magazine, spoke about this era of woman's influence and gave her audience of food retailers the inside story of women and why they buy. That inside story of the woman customer should be helpful to salespeople in any type of retail establishment. Mrs. Montgomery said:

The 1950 census, so they tell us, shows there are a million more women than men in this country. Add to that the fact that women influence a very large percentage of the family buying and you will agree that this is indeed an era of women.

Women are the most *personal* people alive! Everything that is said or done or happens, they relate to themselves. Take the things that happen in a retail store. A pleasant word or a brush-off, a thoughtless answer or a smile—those are not addressed to customers in general, but to one woman—and believe me, she takes them that way. You never hear a woman say, "That's a friendly store." Not at all. What she says is, "They are always very nice to me there."

If a woman is in a store and overhears sales clerks talking about another customer, she relates it to herself. Let us suppose she hears one sales clerk say, after a customer has left, "Who does she think she is? I can't be running all over for her!" The woman who overhears this immediately wonders what they will be saying about *her* when she is gone.

It is because of this "personal" characteristic that women like you to remember their names. I can hardly overemphasize the importance of this. I have heard women say, "I'll never go there again. I went for weeks, and they act every time as if they never saw me before!", or, "Why, I'd only been in there three times and they greeted me by name! Wasn't that nice?" This is worth working at, and I know that in a self-service market it *is* work. You have to watch names on checks cashed or packages left to be picked up. You ask friends whom you have seen shopping together or you ask children their names and so learn the mother's.

You can make women feel important by remembering the personal side of their natures and their genuine need for approval. If yesterday she said she was shopping for a dinner party or church supper, ask her today how it went off. If you have not seen her for a while, ask if she has been away and did she have a good time. *Try to really care, and show her you do.*

Make every visit a woman makes to your store important. You may say, of course it is important, because you need her business. Yes, but she is only one customer among many to you, whereas from her point of view, in relation to her whole day, that visit at your store assumes much more moment.

Look at it this way: It takes her money and involves constant choices that mean she cannot buy other things she wants. It involves the main job of her life—her homemaking, feeding her family. Perhaps, too—and this is hard for the average sales person to understand, who see women come and go in a steady stream—perhaps you and your store are her only contacts with the outside world all day!

It is true that often a woman may pass a whole day during which she speaks to no one—but no one—except members of her family, and *you*. Now suppose you don't speak to her, don't even look up as you wrap her purchase or hand over the change!

Never act as if a woman can't afford the very best! There is nothing so deflating to her ego. This business of women's pride is a subtle one—she may admit freely that she is a bargain hunter, a penny pincher, but she does not want *you* to act as if you thought so. It hurts her own pride and her pride in "her man" as a provider.

Women like success. They like to be on the band wagon, to buy what is "going over." Let your store breathe success. Never be on the negative side; never belittle. Many a retail salesman will deny he does this when he is constantly saying, "You can't get the kind of cheese you used to," or, "the quality isn't the same."

Women like to see you handle merchandise carefully. Did you ever stop to think that there is a certain psychological moment when the goods change hands—when it becomes *her* loaf of bread or *her* box of strawberries? For you to handle them carelessly, so the bread or berries crush, annoys her. If you act as if all your merchandise were valuable, fine; if *you* treat it as if it were quality—it tends to make her think so, too.

Never give the impression you are putting pressure on a woman to buy. The fact is, as we all know, that she *is* under pressure—from advertising, posters, displays. But she thinks she makes up her own mind, and you should always be on her side. Make suggestions, with the attitude that you want to save her time, money, trouble, extra trips—not just to move goods.

That's your woman customer. Understand her, cater to her likes and dislikes, create the atmosphere she finds pleasant. Then by a curious chemistry that goes on in a woman's mind, your store becomes *her* store and she will be saying to her friends, *"my* grocer says . . ." or *"my* butcher tells me." Then you know you are in!

There you have a brilliant analysis of your women customers. Whether you sell them in a grocery store, drugstore, hardware store, department store, or in any other retail establishment, make each woman customer think of your store as *her* store—and make her think of you as her own salesperson.

Dick Richard, a former schoolteacher and now owner of a $2,000,000-a-year grocery self-service market in southern California, knows that good customer relationships are a retailer's most important asset. According to the *Progressive Grocer* publication, Dick Richard started as a salesclerk in the corner grocery store and moved up rapidly in the retail grocery business until he became, in his forties, the owner of the $2,000,000-a-year Lido Market in Newport Beach, Calif.

His rapid success is a tribute to his understanding of the *Human Side of Selling*. Although 1,200 to 1,500 customers visit the store every day, Dick Richard and his salespeople know and call the majority of them by name. Those who man the checkouts are particularly careful to remember names, have a ready smile and a pleasant word for every customer.

Any customer with a sizable order is offered carry-out help in Richard's store. Dick himself frequently is seen lugging groceries out to the parking lot and is usually engaged in pleasant conversation with the customer.

From time to time Dick Richard buys out the local movie house on a Saturday morning and throws a party for the Newport kids. He sees that free candy is available for the children of his customers who see a free movie and stage show.

When a large chain announced that a new store would be opened near the Lido Market, scores of customers told Dick of their worries that the chain's lower prices might put him out of business and deprive them of their favorite store. Their worries were unfounded, for Dick Richard's sales continued to increase. When customers had a choice of buying at lower prices or continuing to buy at "their favorite store" they chose to patronize the store where salespeople recognized them as important individuals and gave them the respect, attention, and service they wanted.

Selling Hardware, Hobby Supplies, Appliances, Home Furnishings, Radios and TV

A survey among the customers of hardware stores showed that when customers change stores only 8 per cent change because of price—but 68 per cent change because of the indifference of the salespeople.

Remember the two reasons why people buy from you—(1) they think you can give them more for their money and (2) they like you. That hardware customer survey showed that 8 per cent were influenced by the first reason and sixty-eight by the second. Another example of the importance of the *Human* Side of Selling.

George Bell, vice-president of Burgess Vibrocrafters, Inc., hired a new manager for one of the Burgess hobby and handicraft stores. Within a month the sales in that store began to fall off and Mr. Bell jumped on a train and went to the city in which the store was located to learn what had happened. When he arrived at the store he was surprised to see a sign on the front door which read: "Don't rattle the door! The store opens at 10 o'clock each morning."

When he went into the store he saw signs all along the counters warning customers not to handle the merchandise displayed. One sign read: "Don't touch this!" Another: "Hands off!" Another: "You are responsible for any damaged merchandise."

When Mr. Bell asked the reason for the signs, the new store manager told him, "Everything is under control now. Customers used to wait outside in the morning and rattle the door before ten o'clock. They used to pick up the merchandise displayed on the counters and not put it back in its proper place. Now they don't touch it and we have an orderly store, as you can see. I have everything under control!"

George Bell told that store manager, "You certainly do have everything under control, but you have virtually no customers in the store. An even better method of having everything under control, as you put it, would be to lock the door and tell the customers to keep out. Then you wouldn't have to worry about anything being out of place."

SELLING RETAIL CUSTOMERS

All the "Keep off the grass" signs were removed. The customers were invited to pick up the merchandise and examine it to their heart's content, and the store's sales increased at once.

George Bell said, "A store can be too orderly just as a home can be so orderly that you feel uncomfortable in it. Keep your displays of merchandise uneven. You might even misspell a word in some

"Will it keep an old lady warm?"

minor sign. Customers will love to call the misspelled word to your attention, and they will feel just as much at home in your store as they would feel in their own home with the furniture out of place and the children's toys all over the floor."

A friend who went to a department store with his wife to buy a refrigerator told this experience with a "sales scarecrow":

When we walked off the elevator this chap reluctantly tore himself away from two companions and came over to meet us. With a let's-get-this-over-quickly smile he asked, "What can I do for you today?" I told him that we wanted to buy a refrigerator—just as plainly as that!

He said, "Step this way, please" and led us over to a General Electric box. Then he stood there, pointed at the refrigerator and made this terrific sales presentation: "We have only a few of them left. If you want one you had better buy it right now."

I told him that we were not sure that we wanted a GE. We know it is one of the best but we would like to look at one or two others that he had on the floor before deciding. My wife said that she would like to see one with shelves in the door.

The so-called salesman then led us over to a Crosley and this time his sales presentation was somewhat better. He actually opened the door, pointed to the shelves inside the door and said, "There it is!"

Then he stood there and looked mildly bored while my wife and I discussed the advantages of the Crosley as compared to other refrigerators. Finally I told him that we would like to see a Norge with the built-in clock and automatic defroster.

This time he led us to a Norge refrigerator and made a sales presentation, if you will pardon the expression, that I would not believe if I hadn't heard it myself.

When I asked him to tell us something of the advantages of the automatic defroster he said, "We haven't had any trouble with it." And that is all he said. Isn't that amazing!

Then the joker started to tell us about the store's easy payment plan. We cut him short and told him that we would think it over a little more before we decided to buy.

Actually we walked into that store determined to buy a refrigerator. That salesman very evidently had no interest in us whatsoever. He didn't find out whether we had no children, or seventeen children—whether we lived in an apartment or in a house—whether we did no entertaining or a great deal of entertaining. He didn't care what size refrigerator we needed or wanted. He was content simply to point to a refrigerator and say "There it is!" (as if we couldn't see that ourselves) and talk about time payments when we never bought anything on a time payment plan in our lives.

That salesman was a sales scarecrow who drove his customers away. These customers bought a refrigerator a week later, but at another store.

Dr. A. B. Blankenship, head of A. B. Blankenship & Associates, noted marketing and research counselors, reported that a survey his organization made of retail electric appliance salesmen showed that "Almost half the salespeople did not bother to learn what the prospect's specific needs were. Four out of ten named no customer values for the appliance. Only half the salesmen demonstrated the product in use. Only one in four attempted to close the sale."

Al Greenberg, business manager of the National Retail Furniture Association, said, "The first step in the successful selling of home furnishings is learning the customer's needs and means. And don't judge a customer by her appearance, her age or her immediate needs. Many a customer who comes in to buy a small lamp may become a thousand dollar customer before she leaves."

Mr. Greenberg continued: "Always show respect to visitors to your store, especially teen-agers who come with their parents. Some salespeople ignore them or treat them as children. That is a mistake. Treat them respectfully as adults. They can influence their parents' purchases.

"Be complimentary to customers, but don't overdo it.

"Never talk mechanical details to a woman unless she asks about them, but always do to a man. There is a classical story of a salesman who was trying to sell a stove to an elderly lady. He described the construction features at great length, talked about B.T.U.'s, thermostats and automatic damper controls when the customer interrupted him with this wonderfully human question: She asked, 'Tell me, mister, will it keep an old lady warm?'

"That," said Mr Greenberg, "emphasizes an important point in retail selling. You must sell service—the service your merchandise will give the customer, and the service you as a retailer will give her."

Fred and Ed Trage, owners of Trage Brothers Appliance Store in Forest Lake, Ill., have built a $500,000 annual volume of radio, television, and appliance sales on the philosophy that "sincere interest in the customer is the secret of successful selling."

Fred Trage said, "Ed and I figured our best chance for success was to treat every customer like out first one. We forgot about hours and everything else, except the customer's problem. We took a sincere interest in every job and gave every customer our honest advice."

In keeping with their belief that a sincere interest in the customers is the best way to sell, the partners do not hesitate to point out the features that are lacking in certain brands, as well as the good points.

When an appliance, a radio, or a television set is not immediately available, they sometimes substitute another in the customer's home until it can be replaced. As Ed said, "That is a good sales-saver, an effective builder of good will. Little things like that count up over a period of time."

Some "little things" may seem unimportant to you as a retail salesman because they mean little, if anything, from the standpoint of immediate sales volume and profit. Yet, the "little things" that indicate an interest in your customers can have a tremendous effect on your business.

Down in Kosciusko, Mo., a man walked into the Davis Appliance Company and said to William V. Davis, "My home was struck by lightning a few nights ago and badly damaged. Among other things the heating element in that electric range you sold me was burned out. What will it cost me to have a new one installed?" According to *Electrical South* publication, which reported the experience, this customer had not spent a great deal at the store, but Bill Davis realized that he probably was ill equipped to pay for the damage the lightning had caused.

"Tell you what I'll do," he told the distressed man, "I'll let you have another element with the compliments of the Davis Appliance Company." A few days later Davis made a special trip to the customer's rural home to install the element and make certain that it functioned properly.

Shortly thereafter the customer's brother-in-law purchased a washer from the Davis Appliance Company and his sister bought a new electric range. Soon after that the same customer's brother called by to say that he would purchase a refrigerator from the store and a little later a new range.

"Furthermore," added Mr. Davis, "a great many of this man's friends and neighbors dropped by our store to personally commend us for what we did. Naturally, we seized this opportunity to show them a few of our appliances."

You can never go too far in giving your customers service, because you can be sure that they will appreciate it and tell their family and friends about it. Remember that a successful retail salesman is the one who not only sells the customer but makes that customer so pleased with his service that he wants to come back and does return again and again.

Selling Men's and Women's Wear

Bernice Fitz-Gibbon, advertising director of Gimbel Brothers, New York, is one of the top authorities in retail selling in the world. She said:

Gimbels realizes that customers as well as salesclerks are human; and to encourage the little extra attentions that make happy customers, we started a "Pin-a-Rose" campaign last year. Within easy reach of every customer, we have little cards which he may fill in telling our personnel department about any sales clerk who does an outstanding job. These cards are kept on record and used in evaluating our sales staff for increases of salary and better positions. This is the sort of thing people tell us:

"I cannot let Sunday go by without sending a word of appreciation for the kind and courteous service I received in your shoe department last Friday. An old lady, lame, hot, and very tired, I was looking for bedroom slippers to fit me, which a foot defect made difficult. The young man who waited on me was not only courteous and painstaking, but genuinely kind and interested. He showed me everything possible, and when nothing suited me, instead of being irritated or impatient, invited me to come again whenever I needed anything and he would do his best to fit me. It was the one bright spot in a very hard day."

Most of the customers who fill out the cards show a kind of humble surprise in finding an interested sales clerk. Again and again, we see the words "it was so different from the usual experience with department stores"—"such a refreshing change from the usual indifference."

Now, this, I think, is all wrong. Why should it be "unusual," "refreshingly different," or "remarkable" to find a good salesperson in a department store? Simply because so many salesclerks think of customers as "sales" instead of human beings."

Read Bernice Fitz-Gibbon's words once more: "Most of the customers show a kind of humble surprise in finding an interested salesclerk." And the warm, appreciative words of the elderly shoe customer who was treated as a human being by an understanding salesman: "It was the one bright spot in a very hard day."

The retail salesman, or retail merchant, who understands the *Human* Side of Selling is far more interested in the customer's good will than in any individual sale. This experience of Stanley Marcus, head of the famous Neiman-Marcus store in Dallas, Texas, is a good example of that:

One day one of our salespersons was waiting on a man and his 16-year old daughter who wanted to buy a fur coat. I was asked to come into the fitting room to pass on a mink coat that the father had just about decided to buy. In those days a mink coat sold for two thousand dollars and the sales person was elated over her prospective sale. I discovered, as I checked the fit of the coat, that the daughter was going to a fashionable school in the East for her first year.

It seemed inappropriate for a sixteen-year-old girl to go away to school with a mink coat, and I could foresee the social ostracism she would face when her new associates first saw her in her mink coat. I tried to switch her interest to a muskrat or a beaver coat, either of which would have been more appropriate.

The salesperson shot black looks in my direction, the child pouted, and the father got mad.

I explained my position to him, whereupon he arose and walked out with his tearful daughter. For the sake of good taste, and ultimate customer good will, I had lost a $2,000 sale.

The next day, however, I was called to the fur department. The father was back, and very contrite. He apologized for his attitude the previous day and explained that when he told his sister what had happened, she had said, "Mr. Marcus was right. A sixteen-year-old girl has no business going off to school with a mink coat. Go back and buy the one he tells you to." So I sold him a muskrat coat for $295 and I made a customer for life. Six years later, when the daughter married, I sold him a mink coat.

One of the most successful men's clothing salesmen in the country is Tom Nolan of Bond Clothing Store, State Street, Chicago. The morning I called at the store for a visit with Tom I found that he had been in the tailor shop for three hours. Why? He had located and set aside 23 suits for customers who he knew would come in that day for fittings. Consequently his customers would not have to wait.

As Tom was leaving the tailor shop, he saw an exasperated customer at the will-call desk. That customer told him he had been waiting almost an hour for a suit. Tom asked the young man at the will-call desk where the customer's suit was. The young chap said, "To hell with that customer. He can't spout off at me just because he has to wait for a suit!"

That young man is no longer at that Bond Store will-call desk. Tom Nolan found the suit for the customer. He said, "If the salesman who sold that suit had been interested in the customer, he would have taken the time to be sure the suit was ready so the customer would not have to wait, just as I did this morning."

And Tom continued, "The service you give a man *after you sell him* is what makes him your customer—and your friend."

Tom Nolan looks at every man who comes into his store not as a potential sale but as a potential friend.

He said, "Some salesmen seem to have a cafeteria attitude—what the hell—here it is—take it or leave it." For instance, one salesman showed a customer a few suits and went cold when the customer said he didn't like them. The customer walked away. As he was leaving, Tom Nolan approached him with a friendly smile, found out what the customer wanted, and patiently helped him find a suit. The customer was so pleased that he bought two more suits—a sale of three suits instead of a lost customer.

Tom Nolan keeps a file card for every customer. He makes a notation of the customer's purchases and information about the customer's family, his job, and his financial standing. He always keeps informed of the status of his customer's charge or credit accounts.

When a customer comes in, therefore, Tom Nolan knows what he has been buying, what his style and color preferences are, and what he wants to pay for a suit. As he walks alongside the customer toward the clothing racks, he can say, "Three months ago you bought a brown gabardine, and six months ago a gray tweed." The customer knows Tom is interested in him and he loves it.

Then, a week after the suit has been delivered, Tom Nolan sends the customer a letter thanking him for his business and assuring him that he and Bond's Clothing Store want the customer to be completely happy with the suit.

Is it any wonder that hundreds of customers send their friends to Tom Nolan?

About 40 per cent of the men who come into Tom Nolan's department to buy a suit bring their wives, their sisters, or some other woman relative or friend. Tom checks the women's wear section of the store every morning and learns what special value or new merchandise is being featured. As he shows suits to the men he tells the women about the specials in the women's wear department.

Not only is that good business for the store, but the women appreciate the attention paid to them. They also appreciate knowing about the latest news in women's clothes. Many of them buy the featured article before they leave the store and come back to the men's clothing section to thank Tom Nolan for telling them about it.

Furthermore, as Tom said, "They have confidence in the suits their men buy here. That is another way to keep my customers and make them my friends. The salesmen who do try to make friends, instead of merely making sales, are the ones who make the big money in this business."

What a delightful contrast to the sales scarecrows whom Harry Hansen met when he tried to buy a topcoat. They were content to go through the motions of selling and just get by on their jobs, while Tom Nolan's earnings are in the five-figure bracket and he has made enough money to retire any time he wants to—by making friends of his customers instead of being merely interested in making sales.

That truly is the *Human* Side of Selling!

Selling Retail Lumber and Building Products

Selling building products to retail customers differs from most other forms of retail selling in that the product is usually sold first and manufactured later. People buy the lumber, wallboard, or other material and have it made into the finished product, which might be a play room, a new porch, or any one of many things. Few retail customers have an expert knowledge of building supplies and, therefore, the selling process, as Arthur Hood puts it, is essentially a matter of service, because it involves helping the customer buy the right materials in order to get the finished product he wants.

Arthur A. Hood, former sales training director of Johns-Manville Company and now vice-president of Vance Publishing Company, said:

> As a building products salesman you have physical products to sell—and you also have mental concepts to sell.
>
> It is true that you must have a thorough knowledge of the physical things, but it is equally true that if you concentrate on them and ignore the mental things you will never go very far in your selling job.
>
> If you think only of materials and products you will never be more than an order taker. But if you think in terms of *consumer benefits* you will become a creative salesman. Your profits, reputation and satisfaction will climb steadily through the years.
>
> To do this you must climb over the fence which separates you from your prospect. You must get the customer's viewpoint and ask yourself how he will benefit by buying what you have to sell. All successful salesmen do this consciously or unconsciously.
>
> Although the pattern of the operation varies somewhat from yard to yard, it might be broadly stated that most retail lumber and building products salesmen have three types of things to sell. These are materials, packages and ideas. The first two are physical. The third obviously is mental.
>
> The variety of materials stocked varies tremendously from one yard to another. The building products salesman should strive to know the following things about the materials he sells: (a) its ingredients and how it is manufactured, (b) its proper uses, (c) proper method of application, (d) best ways to demonstrate and display the material, (f) its selling points and *consumer benefits,* (g) features that make it superior to competitive products, (h) questions customers are most likely to ask about it—including price, terms, buying objections, etc.—and how to answer them, and (i) related items that are easy to sell in connection with the product.
>
> Not all building supply dealers have adopted the principle of package merchandising, and those that have differ in the way they handle the activity. However, the growing trend towards packaging in the building products field makes it desirable for all salesmen to understand the subject.
>
> A "package" might best be defined as "building material fabricated

into a finished unit by competent labor." Such a package unit could be anything from a new home or barn to a repair on the back porch steps. A "package" might be factory built, prefabricated, yard fabricated, or constructed on the site.

You should know as much about the packages you have to sell as you know about the individual materials which comprise them. It is wise to project your thinking along package lines because it is easier to visualize the consumer benefits in packages than in the materials themselves.

You have probably often heard the saying, "You must be sold on your products or you will not be successful in selling them to others." It's a true statement but it doesn't go far enough. You might be completely sold on the good physical qualities of your products and still fail at selling. But if you are sold on what your products will do for customers—you are on your way to success.

Successful selling is a mental process—the shaping of ideas.

Remember, however, that the idea you plant in the prospect's mind must show him clearly how he will benefit from buying what you have to sell. Basically, he is interested in himself—not you or your products.

Helping the customer get what he wants is the basis of all successful selling. In the light construction industry it involves a high type of conscientious and personalized service.

As Mr. Hood points out so clearly, being genuinely interested in the customer, and helping him get what he wants, is the *Human* Side of Selling and is sure to make a building products salesman or any other salesman more successful.

Sellng Farm Implements and Equipment

Paul Mulliken, general manager of the National Retail Farm Equipment Association, is a stanch advocate of the *Human* Side of Selling. He advises farm equipment salesmen: "Don't Sell Things—Sell Ideas—Sell Results—Sell Customer Benefits!"

1. *Don't Sell Farm Equipment.*
Sell relief from drudgery, more time for leisure, lower costs, increased production, and a higher standard of farm living.

2. *Don't Sell Tractor Attachments.*
Sell more hours of profitable use of the farm's power plant—increased use lowers costs.

48 THE HUMAN SIDE OF SELLING

3. *Don't Sell Farm Chemicals.*
Sell luscious fruit and vitamin-filled vegetables, free of bugs and other pests.

4. *Don't Sell Manure Spreaders.*
Sell greater soil fertility and elimination of drudgery.

5. *Don't Sell Barn Equipment.*
Sell more and betters cows—more easily cared for; more contented; greater producers.

6. *Don't Sell Cultivators.*
Sell properly tilled, weedless, moisture-conserving fields where crops thrive.

7. *Don't Sell Hog Feeders and Waterers.*
Sell more pork, raised at less cost and labor.

8. *Don't Sell Pumps and Water Systems.*
Sell fresh running water for the home and barn—properly dispensed if, as, and when needed.

9. *Don't Sell Fence.*

Sell rotated field crops and improved farms where livestock is properly cared for.

10. *Don't Sell Combines and Harvesting Machinery.*
Sell speed in harvesting, plus wide variety of crops handled; independence of the farm family from outside labor costs.

Here you have ten of Paul Mulliken's forty Do's and Dont's which were an outstanding feature of a popular series of articles on selling farm equipment in *Farm Equipment Retailing.* They illustrate the importance of selling what the farmer wants to get as the result of his purchase of farm equipment, rather than merely trying to sell the equipment itself.

When making a number of calls on farm equipment dealers I had an opportunity to see some remarkable examples of the importance of the *Human* Side of Selling. In one community a dealer who represents a major full-line manufacturer told me, "I am not selling a damn thing. Farmers just aren't buying. No, I don't call at their farms. They know I'm here and they can come in if they want something. When they do come in they just stand around and we argue about the political situation. I have sold only two tractors so far in the first six months this year, compared with six or eight last year when they were hard to get."

On the other side of that same town I called on a dealer who represented a smaller manufacturer, one with fewer products and not nearly so many product advantages. Yet, that dealer had sold thirty-two tractors in the first six months of the year, while his competitor across town had sold only two. How did he do it?

He told me: "I make many of my sales before seven o'clock in the morning. I call on my farmer customers while they are milking. They are out there in the barn alone and they are glad to have someone to talk with."

The other dealer just sits in his place of business all day waiting for customers to come in, while his competitor across town is interested enough in his customers to get out to their farms early in the morning when they are working alone and are glad to see him.

The second farm equipment dealer has six repair men in his

shop, but he never lets any of them answer a call for service in the field. He drives out on all field service calls himself. Why? He said, "When a farmer's equipment has broken down he is standing right there waiting while I repair it. That gives me a wonderful opportunity to tell him about new equipment I think he should buy. Also, he appreciates the fact that I come out personally, and promptly, to repair his equipment and he is much more likely to be receptive to the suggestions I make."

That dealer really understands the *Human* Side of Selling. He has bought a movie camera and he takes pictures of farmers operating the tractors and other equipment they bought from him.

When the films have been developed he takes his projector out to the farmer's home and shows him the motion picture of himself driving his new tractor, or operating his other new equipment. His customers probably have never seen themselves "in the movies," so you can imagine their feeling of pride and their friendliness for the dealer who appreciated their business enough to come out and take pictures of them.

Do you wonder why the first dealer sold only two tractors (even though he has a better line) and the second dealer sold thirty-two? What made the difference? You are right! The *Human* Side of Selling!

Selling Automobiles

The salesman who achieves the greatest success in selling cars is the one who becomes genuinely interested in his prospective customers as *human* beings. That salesman will learn what the customer wants most in a car and will sell the features and benefits of his own brand in terms of *what the customer wants to buy*.

In Janesville, Wis., back in the early nineteen-thirties there was a young man selling Dodge automobiles. One day a prospective customer told him that he had decided to buy a competitive car. Instead of crossing the prospect off his list as a lost sale, that young salesman went home and analyzed the reasons why the man preferred the other car. Putting himself in the prospect's place he decided that he would not buy the other car if he could see it along-

SELLING RETAIL CUSTOMERS

side the new Dodge and compare their features and customer benefits one by one. As a service to that prospective customer he drew up a "Comparison Chart" of the two cars and took it to the prospect's office the next day. The man bought the new Dodge.

That young salesman was Ross Roy now president of Ross Roy, Inc. By selling prospective buyers of automobiles with his "customer benefits" comparison charts, he sold so many cars that he attracted the attention of the factory in Detroit.

Soon he was asked to move to Detroit and prepare his type of customer benefit data book and comparison charts for other dealers. In a decade he became recognized as one of the leaders in sales training and sales promotion for automobile dealers and today heads a $10,000,000 business. His organization teaches thousands of salesmen the *Human* Side of Selling.

David R. Osborne, distinguished sales personnel consultant of Studebaker and other well-known companies, said:

> I have always tried to get sales people to learn as much about prospective buyers as they can, as soon as they can—and then use this information throughout the interview in making the sale *personal*.
>
> In the case of automobile salesmen, we have tried to get them to find out, in some way, within the first few minutes: how many in the family,

which members drive, and how the car is used. After this any alert salesman can find plenty of chances to bring Mrs. Hoozis and the children, and the sort of thing the family does with the car, into the sales story.

I know of some Studebaker dealerships where they have some comfortable chairs so placed that their location commands a view of every car on the sales room (not "show" room, by the way) floor. When anybody comes in to inquire about a car, the salesman is encouraged by the management to invite him to have a seat for a moment while they get a line on the model best suited for his family or business needs. When handled in the right way, most customers are quite favorably impressed by this little dramatizing of the idea of helping them to *buy* intelligently.

"Helping them to buy intelligently!" Mr. Osborne, that is indeed the *Human* Side of Selling, because it implies looking at the purchase from the customer's point of view.

One of the largest and most successful automobile dealerships in the United States is the Thornton-Fuller Company, with main sales and service headquarters in Philadelphia and three branches in outlying sections. George H. Thornton, president, learned the importance of the *Human* Side of Selling when he made his first sale.

His first prospect had said "No!" emphatically. Yet when George approached him at the right time and, instead of talking about the sale of the car, offered to be of service to the man and his wife, the prospective customer *bought*. This is a warm human interest story of George Thornton's first sale:

After I had been working for our company for about a year and a half, I was made manager of our first branch in suburban Philadelphia. I did not know anything about selling, since I had been working only for a short time, and most of my experience had been in the shop. However, shortly after I opened the branch, a friend who had been married about the same time I had, namely, a month before, called me on the phone and told me that he and his wife needed a new car. The car they had was about to fall apart, and they didn't have any money to fix it up. He suggested that I get in touch with his father-in-law, and see if I could sell him the idea of buying the bride and groom a new automobile. He also said that he and his bride did not have the nerve to ask the father-in-law for anything more, as he had been so very generous in giving them a new house and all the furniture in it as a wedding present.

So several evenings later, I got my own little roadster out, and went to call on this gentleman and his wife about six o'clock. I didn't get very far with my suggestion, as he told me he had given the children all he was going to give them, and was not going to spend another nickel on them. In fact, he was very rough with me, and ordered me out of the house.

When I called my friend the next morning and told him what a poor prospect this had been, he asked me when I had seen him, and I told him about six o'clock at night. He told me never to try to sell him before dinner, but go back and see him the next night—after supper.

In fear and trembling, I went up to call on him the next night in my little roadster, with the top down—as it was a very hot night. Before I could get out of my car, this gentleman gave me a blast—told me he was not interested in buying a car for the children, and please not to bother him.

However, I told him I hadn't stopped in to sell him a car, but I was going over to call on his daughter and son-in-law, and thought perhaps that he and his wife would like to take a ride and get cooled off. He asked his wife if she would like to go for a ride and she said, yes, so the two of them got in my little roadster, and we went over to see the bride and groom.

I left the car right in front of the house, and we went all through their home and admired the new furniture. In fact, the bride and groom were still unpacking the furniture, and some of the crates were still in the back yard.

They both came out and admired the roadster. On the way home with the older gentleman and his wife, he said to me, "Is this the kind of car those kids want?" and I said, "Yes." Then he said, "Well, you better get one ready for them and send me the bill—but," he said, "I want you to understand that I am vice-president in charge of all the freight of the Pennsylvania Railroad, and you have all your cars shipped in on the Reading. If you think I am going to pay, as part of the delivered price, a freight bill on the Reading Railroad, you have another guess coming. If you can't show me a receipted freight bill for this car on the Pennsylvania Railroad, I won't pay for it."

Of course, I did everything I could to get our company to change their procedure and have this car brought in on the Pennsylvania Railroad, but did not succeed. It came in on the Reading.

The night I delivered the car to the gentleman and his wife (as they were going to give it to the children as a surprise) he said to me, "Now before I give you the check, where is the receipted freight bill on the Pennsylvania Railroad?" In fear and trembling, I told him it came in on the Reading. He said to me, "If you think I am going to pay for that car, and pay a freight bill on the Reading Railroad, you are crazy. I won't pay for it."

Then I said, "Well, Mr. So-and-so, you wouldn't discriminate against me would you?" and he said, "No, why?" I said, "You tell me that you bought all the furniture for your daughter and son-in-law's house, and I saw the crates back of the house the other night and I noticed that some of the furniture you bought was from Lit Brothers, and the Lit Brothers warehouse is on the Reading Railroad, so why discriminate against me." The old gentleman burst into laughter, and gave me the check.

That customer said "No" twice. George Thornton could have talked about the car all day and night and would not have made the sale. However, he first rendered a service to the man and his wife and made it easy for them to see the pleasure they would get by giving the car to their daughter and son-in-law. Then, when the man refused to pay a Reading freight bill, George did not argue; he did not blame the factory; he did not alibi—he appealed to the customer's sense of fair play. He helped the customer feel important in conceding that freight bill point—and he got the order.

John O. Munn, former secretary of the N.A.D.A. and dealer editor of *Automotive News,* emphasized the selling opportunities available to the salesman who follows up the car buyer after the sale is made. In his popular book, *A Guide to Automobile Selling,* he said:

Salesmen should be keenly interested in keeping all owners as customers of the service and parts departments of the dealer from whom they bought their cars.

In the first place, about eighty-five per cent of all the new car buyers replace their cars with another of the same make. So if a dealer is successful in retaining all of his car buyers as permanent shop customers, the salesman's opportunities are considerably accelerated.

Satisfactory service establishes the confidence of the owner and makes him a customer of the house, rather than a customer for just any make of car.

John Munn has been an automobile salesman himself. He knows that a satisfied owner is your best prospect for another car—and can be a "center of influence" who will send many additional sales your way. Keep your interest in your customer alive after he gives you the order and you will make a friend as well as a customer. That is one of the many rewards of the *Human* Side of Selling.

SELLING "SERVICE" IN BANKS, RESTAURANTS, HOTELS, RAILROAD, BUS AND AIRLINE TICKET OFFICES

You've heard the expression "As cold as a banker's heart." When a customer walks up to the window to make a deposit in a bank and the teller makes him wait while he counts a stack of money, and then takes the deposit, writes in the customer's book, and hands it back to him without even looking up at him or mentioning his name or even saying, "Thank you!" then the customer begins to realize how cold a banker's heart can be.

We all have had similar treatment in some hotels and restaurants, in gasoline service stations, and in transportation ticket offices. In every case we can be sure we have met a man or woman who is not aware of, or has no interest in, the *Human* Side of Selling.

If you are selling a service of any type, here is a message for you which the Rapides Bank & Trust Company of Louisiana printed on a blotter and gave to everyone who contacted customers. It shows that every banker's heart is not a chunk of ice. You will remember this: "The customer is not a cold statistic—he is a flesh and blood human being, with feelings and emotions like your own. A customer is not an interruption of our work—he is the purpose of it! A customer is the most important person in any business and deserves the most courteous and attentive treatment we can give him."

In banks, in restaurants, hotels, or any business where the services offered by your competitors is much the same as your own, your success will be in direct proportion to your understanding of the *Human* Side of Selling.

Dan Valentine, who has been eating in restaurants for twenty-five years, said (in an article in *American Restaurant Magazine*): "I have seen large restaurants, with the best Main Street locations and good food, fail in a matter of months, while smaller establishments, without half the facilities prospered and grew. And I wondered why."

When he studied the reasons why some restaurants succeeded where others failed, he found that "It all boiled down to the fact that the successful restaurants were never guilty of the little irritating things that get on a customer's nerves."

With the help of his friends, he compiled a list of "nerve-jangling things that get a restaurant patron's goat." Notice that the list does not include even one mention of the restaurant equipment or the type or quality of food. The causes of failure are all *human* causes—principally lack of interest in the customer.

Mr. Valentine said:

Here they are, written in plain, blunt English: I hate to have to wait for a waitress to take my order. I realize that sometimes they are busy. But does that mean they can't stroll by, toss me a friendly smile, and say they'll be right there? That's all I need. Is that too much to ask?

I hate to have to ask for a glass of water. And I hate to have to ask for a refill.

I hate to have to ask for my check. There is one restaurant I never patronize any more for the simple reason I never get a check there without asking for it. It's downright irritating.

I hate to have to wait at the cashier's stand to pay my bill, especially when I have to wait for the cashier or a waitress to get through talking to some friendly fellow so I can pay my bill and get out of the place.

And here's a special peeve that not only applies to restaurants but to a lot of other places: I hate to have to scratch my change over the smooth glass of the cashier's counter. I hold out the palm of my hand, and more often than not, the cashier places the coins on the counter, ignoring my outstretched hand. This is particularly annoying—it makes me grit my teeth. And it must make a lot of other people mad, too.

I hate waitresses who have troubles—and show it. In other words, I want them to smile. I eat better that way.

I hate sloppy uniforms. There is nothing that can turn me away from a restaurant faster. I think, and rightly so I believe, that if a restaurant will tolerate sloppy help, they'll tolerate sloppy food.

I hate to have to ask for butter. I hate to have to ask for a second cup of coffee. A restaurant leaps to the top of my list when they have waitresses who voluntarily bring me a refill for my coffee.

All of Mr. Valentine's "hates" are evidence that when he studied the restaurants that had failed he found they failed because the men and women who came in contact with the customers seemed to think the restaurant business a matter of serving food and providing a place to eat it. The restaurant business is much more—it is a matter of selling and serving *human* beings, and the *Human* Side of Selling is more important than the product (food) that is sold.

If the customers like you because you make them feel really welcome and important, they will like the food you serve. If you don't treat them right, they won't like anything about your place, and they just don't come back.

Charles Loeffel, business manager of Ahrens Publishing Company, publisher of *Restaurant Management* and *Hotel Management* magazines, told me of a waitress who knows the *Human* Side of Selling so well that she is respected and admired by all her customers. It is not uncommon for her to start her day by getting dollar tips when she serves breakfast.

This waitress has been keeping customers happy in the same hotel dining room for thirty-nine years. When you come down in the morning and sit at one of her tables for breakfast, she immediately brings you three things: a steaming cup of coffee, a warm smile, and a cheerful "Good morning!"

Most of her customers are from one of two large nearby cities.

She learns which one is your home—and she brings you your hometown morning paper.

If you have a headache, she brings you an aspirin or an Alka-Seltzer.

She hurries in your breakfast order, sees that you never have to ask for a second piece of butter or another cup of coffee. She starts your day with a big lift, makes you feel important and glad to be alive. You walk out of that restaurant with a renewed spring in your step, more bounce in your spirit. All because someone treated you like a *human* being. Is it any wonder customers leave that waitress dollar tips at breakfast!

She makes them feel welcome, and important. Ralph Hitz, well-known hotel operator, made a study of hotel customers and found that they want most the feeling of personal importance. They want to be recognized by bellboys, waiters, and others. They appreciate being called by name.

As W. P. Ferguson, merchandising manager of United Airlines, put it, "When competing businesses offer essentially the same services, as is the case with the major airlines who have much the same modern equipment, the organization which attracts the most customers is the one which pleases and serves the customers best."

We have looked at many different little customers under our microscope and we have seen that some react quickly, some slowly, but all react in much the same way to cool, indifferent treatment in retail or service establishments. And we have seen how they are attracted strongly to the salespeople who show they are genuinely interested in serving them. They particularly like those salespeople who become interested in them as individuals and give them recognition, respect, and honest friendliness.

H. W. Dotts, vice-president and sales manager of Jewel Tea Company, Inc., said, "In both over-the-counter selling and home service distribution I have observed that the salespeople who are extremely successful are those who consider that the two most important phases of selling are, first, to adopt the feeling that every customer is an individual opportunity for service, and, secondly, to make the customer feel that you are interested in him or her more than in anyone else."

There you have the *Human* Side of retail selling—the way to become "extremely successful" in selling merchandise or services to customers for their own use or for their families or friends. Consider each customer as an individual opportunity for service, and make that customer feel that while you are serving him he is the most important person in the world to you.

Look at each prospective customer as a prospective friend. Treat each one as you would one of your own best friends, and you will find that they indeed do become your friends and help you move up rapidly on your way to all the success and happiness you could possibly want in the selling profession.

CHAPTER 6

How to Develop the Most Profitable, and the Happiest, Relationship with Your Dealer Customers

WHILE I was in a large grocery store one morning talking with the owner, the postman came in and handed my friend a bundle of mail. On the top of the bundle was a postcard which the grocer picked up and read. Then he looked up with a big smile and said, "There is one of the best salesmen in the grocery business! He is away on vacation but he still takes time to drop his customers a line and let us know that he is thinking about us. Furthermore, he is one salesman who never comes into the store without some helpful sug-

They Say He'd Do Anything to Sell his Dealers

YOUR DEALER CUSTOMERS

gestion about special promotions, displays, store layout or other ideas that might help me to improve my business."

I asked my grocer friend to tell me his opinion of the salesmen who call on him. He said:

There are three classifications of salesmen who call on me: the first is a nuisance, the second is the order taker, and the third I call the VIP [very important person].

A lot of salesmen come into a store and just waste a retailer's time. They tell us they have a fine product, an attractive package, the price is right, and maybe they offer me a deal. Some of them wind up by saying "You can't go wrong with this!" One said just this morning "Why don't you give me a break and put some of my stuff in?"

They are the nuisance boys and I get rid of them in a hurry. I tell them I have had no calls for their product and I am not interested in stocking any items that won't move. I remind them I can't make any money by loading up my storeroom. I make a profit only when we ring up a sale on one of our cash registers.

The second classification of salesmen—the ordertakers—aren't so bad. We need them for staple and for fast moving merchandise. You can hardly call them salesmen, however. They are more like delivery boys. They pick up an order in a store and deliver it back to the wholesaler or producer who employs them.

I call the third classification of salesmen VIPs because they are very important persons to me, or to any retailer. When they are introducing a new product, they present it to us in terms of how much of it we can sell—and why—and what they and their companies are doing to help us move a profitable volume.

Then, after they get an order, they don't stick it in their pocket and leave—like the young fellow who steals a kiss from his girl and runs away. The real salesmen know that the first order can be just the beginning of a profitable volume of repeat business and they stick around long enough to discuss displays, newspaper advertising and other promotions.

Moreover, they see that every one of my salesclerks is familiar with the product before they leave. Do you wonder why I say they are VIPs to me? I consider some of them the best merchandising counselors I could get. They know what promotion ideas are making money for dealers in other parts of town and they pass along those ideas to me. Some of them have been a big help in building up this business.

Yes, there is a big difference in the salesmen who call on us retailers. Many are just interested in the orders they can get. If they had to operate a retail store for a time and pay salaries and rent and other expenses, perhaps they would understand why the retailer's primary interest is in SELLING merchandise—in *turnover—repeat business*—and in earning, after all the bills are paid, at least some *net profit*.

There you have the dealer's point of view. Whether you are calling on grocery stores, drugstores, hardware stores, electrical appliance shops, department stores, or any other retail outlets, you can be a nuisance—an order taker, not much above the status of a delivery boy—or a respected and welcome salesman, a VIP to the retailer.

J. Sidney Johnson, merchandising manager of the National Biscuit Company, is constantly developing promotions that enable N.B.C. salesmen to help retailers move a larger volume of biscuits. He said, "I'd like to tell you of an experience that was reported to me by one of our good customers in the Northwest. Our salesman showed him one of our monthly programs for displaying bicuits with a related food. After this interview, the customer wrote me a letter. That morning, 15 salesmen called on him; 14 preceding our salesman. He said not one of these salesmen came to him with a real merchandising idea. They showed advertising, they quoted prices and they demonstrated their products, but they didn't give him a single, solitary selling idea that he could use successfully in his business. He said it was 'like a breath of fresh air' when our man presented him with the idea of displaying one of our brands of biscuits with one of his related foods."

Mr. Johnson continued: "It's important to provide our customers with better sales tools that will enable them to sell more, *more* profitably. Then we should study the entire commodity group in which our products fall to find the best location in the store, and the most attractive arrangement of the merchandise, to develop the greatest dollar sales and profit for the store owner. You and your dealer customers should be *partners for profit*."

When you think of yourself as a "partner for profit" with your dealer customer you never can be a "nuisance" or a mere "order taker." You always will be a VIP to your dealers. And they need, and want, your help.

Some time ago the National Wholesale Druggist Association

asked independent druggists what assistance they wanted from the salesmen who called on them. Of the 473 who answered, 60 per cent said they would like to have sales promotion advice, 54 per cent advice to salesclerks, 47 per cent information about promotions of other druggists, 41 per cent advice on display arrangement, 28 per cent information about items not stocked, 27 per cent assistance in getting displays, 25 per cent advice on store layout, 24 per cent assistance on display arrangement, and 15 per cent wanted managerial advice.

If you sell retail stores of any type, turn down the corner of this page and reread the above paragraph from time to time. It will remind you of the many ways you can be a "partner for profit" with your dealer customers.

You have heard the homely expression "He should have stood in bed." When you call on any retailer and simply talk about the weather or politics or your cold in the head and then ask for an order you should have stood in bed! The retailer may appear to be listening to you, but he doesn't hear a word you say *until you talk about the things that interest him*—the nine specific wants listed above and any other information, advice, or assistance that will show him how you can help him increase his sales and profits.

Carl W. Patton, merchandising manager of Jacob Miller, Inc., Harrisburg, the largest chain of furniture stores in Pennsylvania, said that many salesmen apparently have no interest in helping stores move the merchandise they buy. Too often the salesmen's only interest is in getting an order.

Here is Patton's opinion of some of the salesmen who call on him:

> They might as well come into my office and say, "All I have is a dirty circular, a desire to make a living and retire young. How about giving me an order?"
> I asked a lamp salesman whether he had any newspaper mats or at least a picture of the lamps he wanted us to buy. Do you know what his answer was?
> "But I gave you an extra 5 per cent."
> I asked him whether we should put an ad in the newspapers and tell people to come in and buy the lamps because we got an extra 5 per cent.

Mr. Patton believes too many salesmen think all they need to sell is the lowest price or biggest discount:

The salesman of a large electric appliance manufacturer offered to sell us a quantity of vacuum cleaners at a very low close-out price. I asked him for newspaper mats and circulars and he said he didn't have any. He assured me we were getting a terrific bargain in buying the vacuum cleaners at such a low price.

I told that so-called salesman that he could give me the merchandise for nothing and if it stayed in our stores it would be no bargain to us, because we can't make any money on it until we sell it.

I also told him if he had had circulars and newspaper mats and a promotion plan for dealers last year he wouldn't have to close out the vacuum cleaners now; he would have sold them all.

The guy sputtered and pretty nearly caught fire. That big vacuum cleaner order probably was the first one he had come close to in a long time. He said, "What will I tell my boss?"

Isn't that a fine thing for a salesman to say! I told him I didn't care what he told his boss. Those close-out vacuum cleaners were no buy to us, no matter how low the price was, if they didn't sell. I made it clear that I would not sign that order until he brought us the newspaper mats, photographs, circulars and other promotion material we needed.

And I didn't sign the order until he came back the next day with the promotion material he should have had with him in the first place.

We can't understand how some salesmen get by. Perhaps dealers buy the merchandise they need in spite of the salesman. You should see some of them call on our buyers. They show their product or a picture of it and say, "This is a hot item! This will sell!"

The buyer will ask, "How should we promote it?" and the salesman will say, "Well, run an ad."

They have no promotion plan, no program. Why, when we asked one the other day, "What advertising help do you have?" he said, "Look, Mac, I don't know anything about advertising."

And when we asked him, "Haven't you any newspaper mats?" he said, "I'll look!" He dug down into his briefcase and then sheepishly said, "Yes, I have a few photographs and some mats."

Salesmen should realize that every retailer has one big question in his mind when he is considering the purchase of any merchandise: *How do we sell it?*

In a small store that question is always in the mind of the store owner or manager. In a larger store or a chain, that question is always in the buyer's mind, because buyers are judged by the *turnover* and *profit* of their departments.

Whenever you call on a retailer remember that one big question in his mind: "How do I sell it?" If you don't answer that question you waste his time and yours. If you do answer it you make a sale.

Edward V. Duffy, head of E. B. Malone & Company, well-known bedding manufacturer of Miami, Fla., has a highly successful selling formula which he calls "Selling in Depth."

After he sells a store he sees that everyone who handles his products in any way is sold on them and understands them. He sells not only the buyer and the merchandise manager of a department store, but the advertising manager and the display men; he conducts a sales training course for the salespeople in the bedding department, contacts the warehousemen and deliverymen and sees that they understand and are sold on his products.

Whenever he can he tells the story of his products to salespeople all through the store. Moreover, he is constantly suggesting store-wide promotions not related to his products and he is always taking promotion ideas to heads of departments that have nothing to do with the merchandise he sells. He helps the store management in every way he can, often when he receives no direct benefit. How does he profit by that help? Put yourself in the place of the store management. If Duffy were going all out to help you, whose bedding would you push? You're right—Duffy's!

If you go further, after you have made the sale, as Ed Duffy does, and help the dealer promote the sale of your product you not only have made a sale but you also have made a customer.

The salesman who considers himself a "partner for profits" with his dealers will be particularly alert for opportunities to pass on to his customers information about successful selling methods used by other dealers.

Don Mowry, executive secretary of the National Wholesale Furniture Salesmen's Association, said:

> Salesmen frequently can assist their dealers to make better sales. One wholesale furniture salesman, who sells bedroom furniture, instructed a dealer to take the prospective customer to the mattress section, first, when such customer wanted to see various kinds of beds and bedroom suites. "The point is," said the salesman, "your customer must have a mattress anyway for the new bed under consideration. You simply say,

"Oh, here are the mattresses, and you will want one I suppose for the new bed." The woman usually will reply in the affirmative. When she selects a $59.50 or $65 mattress, you know, Mr. Dealer, that she wants a good-looking, serviceable bed. You don't have to guess. If she says she wants a $29.50 or $19.50 mattress, show her the cheaper beds and you will be right in line with her pocketbook. By understanding the *Human* Side of Selling, the salesman showed the dealer how to learn how much the customer wanted to spend without offense, and the build-up that is necessary to complete the sale has been overcome.

If in addition to helping your dealer increase his sales and profits you go still further and become genuinely interested in him as a *human* being, in helping him in every way you possibly can, then you have made more than a customer—you have made a friend.

Salesmen who do not understand the *Human* Side of Selling can starve to death in the same territory where another salesman can make a small fortune. Harold Baum, promotion manager of the Superior Sleeprite Company, told me that his company had one territory which it considered a no man's land, because salesman after salesman had tried to sell in it and had not been able to earn their expenses.

He said, "Salesmen starved to death there—until we turned it over to Nate Schaeffer. Instead of going into stores and asking dealers to buy our products, Nate Schaeffer showed them *how to sell more of our products*—and they bought all they could sell. He analyzed the business of the dealers and told them what sizes and styles they should buy for their particular trade. It wasn't long before the dealers in that 'No-Man's-Land' territory had so much confidence in Nate Schaeffer that he could come into their store and write up his own order. They knew that he would ask them to buy only merchandise that they could turn over rapidly at a good profit, and he would help them set up the promotions that would keep his products moving."

Nate Schaeffer became a VIP to his dealers. He brought an arid sales area to life with the *Human* Side of Selling and harvested some $20,000 a year in commissions where the sales scarecrow type of salesman had starved to death.

There is a hard way to sell the dealer customer and an easy way.

The hard way is to try to sell him what you want him to buy. The easy way is to *sell him what you know he can sell, show him how to sell it, help him sell it, and show him that you want to give him every assistance you can in building his business.*

When Arthur Bishop was selling department stores a line of men's suits that retailed for $100 or more, he found that many buyers thought they would not be able to sell clothing priced that high. But he was able to sell some of the biggest stores in the country. How did he do it? He knew that buyers were interested in selling a better grade of clothes and making more profit per sale, just as they were interested in selling a large volume. So he prepared a presentation to the buyers which showed them how by advertising a $100 suit of clothes they would build prestige for their men's clothing departments, attract more quality buyers and, therefore, would sell more $50 and $60 suits in proportion to their lowest priced suits.

Do you see what he did? He made his entire presentation from the standpoint of what the buyers wanted to accomplish—and they bought his high-priced line of men's clothes. He knew the *Human* Side of Selling.

Gordon Morrison, now sales training director of the Celotex Corporation, was an exceptionally successful salesman of building supplies years ago when he was a territory salesman in the eastern states. He never went into a dealer's place of business unless he had some merchandising idea to suggest or knew some way in which he could be of service to the dealer.

He studied the methods of the most aggressive dealers in his territory and was able to show others how to increase their sales. It wasn't long before he became a merchandising counselor to his dealers everywhere.

He helped lumber dealers improve their yard and store arrangement. He helped them plan their advertising, set up displays, and train their sales personnel. One time when his sales manager made a trip through the territory with him, the boss asked some of the big-volume dealers, "Who is your promotion manager?" The dealers said, "Gordon Morrison is!" That is one of the finest tributes any salesman selling to dealers can receive.

When you become the merchandising counselor of your dealer, you will make use of all the selling, the advertising, and the promotion aids your company gives you. You will assist dealers in displaying your products, in planning their advertising, in training their salesmen to sell your products intelligently.

You will assist them too, in any service problems they may have. One salesman sold a big hardware dealer by helping him repair a competitor's electric appliance. The dealer said, "You are the first salesman I have seen who knows enough about the appliances he sells to give me a hand in a simple repair like this. So I think it might be a good idea if I sold your line." The salesman was given a substantial order.

Dealers—even buyers of the country's largest stores—are human beings. Never forget that! The merchandising manager of one of the largest department stores told me that a salesman came in to see him and asked why he had not been able to sell one of the buyers of that store on whom he had been calling for three years.

The merchandising manager invited the salesman to sit down and tell him about it. He learned that the salesman represented a blouse manufacturer whose factory was in the same midwestern city as this department store. Yet the store's buyer had been ordering his blouses from New York. The salesman had been calling on the buyer about once a month for three years and had never received a single order, although his prices were right and the quality of his product compared favorably with the competitive merchandise.

The merchandising manager asked, "In all the time you have been calling on that buyer have you ever sent him a Christmas card?

"Have you ever written him a little personal note about some news item, some article in the trade press, or about something else that you thought might interest him?

"Have you ever invited him to have lunch with you?"

To each of these questions the salesman answered, "No." He added, "We are right here in the same city with you. I didn't think any of that would be necessary."

The merchandising manager said, "None of that is 'necessary.'

However, our buyers are human beings, you know, as well as buyers. Why don't you think that fact over? If you decide to do something about it, come back in a few months and tell me what happened."

The merchandising manager told me that the salesman came back a few months later and thanked him for the suggestions he had made about the *Human* Side of Selling. He had written a personal note to the buyer and had followed it up a week or so later with an invitation to lunch. During the luncheon he learned that the buyer had been ordering blouses from a New York firm because he could get certain features which he did not think he could get from the Chicago firm. The salesman told him that his company would be glad to make any changes in styling the buyer wanted and give him exactly the type of blouses he preferred. Moreover, he could save the buyer the shipping costs and give him better delivery service. He secured a large order in a short time from a buyer he had not been able to sell for three years. Why? Because an understanding merchandising manager had reminded him that "buyers are human beings—as well as buyers."

That merchandising manager told me, "I would rather see my buyers having lunch with some salesman every day than having lunch with each other or with another store employee. When they are having lunch with salesmen, I know that they will be discussing subjects of mutual benefit—and that will be good for the store as well as for the salesmen."

It isn't necessary to take every buyer to lunch, but it is vitally important to remember that every buyer, merchandising manager, department head—every retailer—is *human*. When you remember that you will be well on your way to understanding the *Human* Side of Selling.

If you are sure that you have a product, or a line of products, that a retailer should sell, never stop calling on him just because you can't sell him the first two or three times.

Perry Shupert, vice-president of Miles Laboratories, Inc., told me this story of an experience he had not too many years ago when he was calling on retail drugstores and selling Alka-Seltzer, One-A-Day Vitamins, and other Miles Laboratories products:

I had called on one particular druggist several years without any success whatsoever, in so far as interesting him in any quantities of our products other than what he purchased normally through wholesalers.

Living in the neighborhood of his store, I stopped in from time to time to purchase my own personal requirements. One evening when I was making out my sales reports I ran out of ink and was forced to go to this drugstore to buy a new supply. Now, this store was located on the edge of the campus of Northwestern University and was run in a very ethical manner. The proprietor was a stern-looking gentleman who wore the professional white coat and his store had all the earmarks of an old-time apothecary shop.

You can imagine my surprise when I learned this store did not handle ink. This is when I really blew my top and told the proprietor what I thought of him and his store in view of the excellent location. I said, "Your store is apparently run for the convenience of yourself in the manner which you feel your profession upholds, but if I were you, sir, I would open my eyes to the fact that there are thousands of university students passing your store daily who no doubt have many lessons or theses to turn in every day written in ink. Here you are in a locality of this kind, not serving your community with anything other than medicines—which is a very worthy and ambitious thing to do—but in today's era of merchandising, drugstores are becoming more and more the universal source of supplying consumers with almost anything that can be conveniently handled."

I went on: "I note you don't even carry fountain pens, cameras, and other popular items which no doubt these students, as well as the natives in this community, could purchase from you conveniently from time to time if you handled them and displayed them properly."

I felt that I had nothing whatsoever to lose in opening up to this man because he had never purchased anything from me anyway. But, much to my surprise, he asked my advice on what he should and should not handle in a locale of this kind. Naturally, I went back to my original thought when I entered the store that fountain pens and ink would certainly be logical items in view of the many thousands of students at the university close by. He asked me if I knew the representative of the pen company—which I did. And, not long after, this store carried a full line of nationally advertised pens, and ink, and was successful in selling both.

A short time later the proprietor again asked me for suggestions on various lines to handle. Knowing that I had to be careful and not lose the faith he had placed in me, I made a recommendation and followed through by helping him merchandise this product.

After about six months during which time he carried from three to four successful new items, I made my regular call on him when working in that territory. Without referring to anything that had previously happened on the items he was now handling, I went through my regular sales pitch with him. This druggist leaned back and smilingly said, "Shupert, you can write your own ticket from now on. Inventory my stock and send me what I need."

Out of all this grew an everlasting friendship and a very good customer, and I can truthfully say a successful and profitable business grew in this store. Above all, I had the satisfaction of knowing that I had helped him, as well as myself.

There you have evidence of the greatest reward that comes to a salesman who understands the *Human* Side of Selling—the satisfaction of knowing that you have been instrumental in helping your dealer customer as well as yourself, and winning a dealer's "everlasting friendship" in addition to making a customer no one can ever take away from you.

You, and you alone, can determine the extent of your success in selling dealer customers and helping them sell a profitable volume of your products.

You can decide what you want to be to your dealer customers—a nuisance—a mere order taker—or a VIP.

To be a VIP to the dealer, be sure to answer the question that is always in his mind: *"How do I sell it?"*

Help him sell your products. Help him improve his business in every way you can. Become his merchandising counselor. Consider yourself and your dealer customers "partners for profits."

See that the dealer's salespeople know you and know how to sell your products. Sell the servicemen, the delivery men, everyone connected with the store who handles your merchandise. When you "sell in depth," as Ed Duffy does, you will have a lot of people working for your success.

And remember that the dealer is a human being. Call him, drop in to see him, or send him a postcard or a note occasionally when you have nothing at all to sell him. Let him know that you really are interested in him as a person as well as a customer, and you will find that you not only are making sales but are also making friends who will go out of their way to do business with you.

When your dealer customers know you are genuinely interested in helping them increase their sales and profits and you like them personally and appreciate their friendliness to you then your success is assured, because you do indeed understand the *Human* Side of Selling.

CHAPTER 7

What Every Salesman Should Know about the Wholesale Customer—and How to Sell Him

A SALESMAN told his sales manager that he had been trying for months to sell Supplee-Biddle-Steltz, one of the country's largest wholesalers. He said, "They could buy our stuff by the carload. Our price is right. There is nothing wrong with our quality. The buyer is always friendly but I never get anywhere with him." Then he asked, "What can I do to sell that outfit?"

The sales manager asked him to tell exactly what happened the last time he called on the Supplee-Biddle-Steltz buyer. He said, "I gave him our product story the first time I called on him. He knows who we are and what we make. When I went in to see him the other day I said, 'Well, here I am again. Do I get an order this time?' He opened the catalogue on his desk and showed me that he already has six or seven other items like ours in stock. He said he has too many now and none of them are selling very well. There wasn't a lot I could say after that, so I just told him I would keep on coming in to see him and hoped he would give me a break someday."

Here's a Boatload of Orders From Your Dealers—Now Do I Get Your Order?

The salesman added: "I sure would like to get an order from that outfit. As you know, it is one of the biggest wholesalers in the whole darn country!"

The sales manager suggested: "Suppose you put yourself in the place of William George Steltz, the head of Supplee-Biddle-Steltz. If you were Mr. Steltz what would be your principal interest?"

The salesman said, "Well, I guess my principal interest would be in making a profit."

The sales manager agreed. "That is right," he said. "If you were Mr. Steltz, you would have more than a hundred salesmen calling on many thousands of dealers. There is only one way that you and your organization can make a profit—that is by selling merchandise. You don't make any money when you buy a product and store it in your warehouse. You make your profit when you sell it to the dealer. Consequently, you and your buyers think in terms of *'selling'* merchandise."

The sales manager continued: "When a salesman calls on a wholesaler and talks to the wholesaler about 'buying' his products, that wholesaler is thinking in terms of 'how much can I sell?' When you want your customer to *buy* and he is thinking *sell,* you are miles apart.

"Before you call on that wholesaler again," the sales manager suggested, "analyze the territory his men cover and determine what volume of our products they could sell. You said the buyer told you the competitive products they have in their catalogue are not selling very well. Perhaps they are not being promoted as aggressively as our products are. If you were that buyer you would not want to buy another slow-moving product, but you very definitely would be interested in buying a product that would sell in greater volume than any other of its type in the catalogue.

"The next time you call on that buyer be prepared to show him exactly what sales volume of our products he should expect, what we are doing and will do to help sell that volume. Back up your presentation with a record of the repeat sales that our other wholesalers are getting."

On the next call, that salesman secured a substantial order from

THE WHOLESALER CUSTOMER 75

Supplee-Biddle-Steltz. What made the difference? For months he had been calling on that wholesaler and talking about what he, the salesman, wanted—he wanted the wholesaler customer to *buy* from him. The wholesaler customer, on the other hand, was thinking *sell*, not buy, and they were miles apart. When the salesman went back and talked *sell*, he and the buyer had a meeting of the minds and he made the sale.

How much do you know about the wholesalers on whom you call? One salesman said, "We ought to sell the dealer direct. We could save the wholesaler's discount. After all, what does the wholesaler do for us that we couldn't do ourselves?"

At some time the management of every manufacturing organization probably asks that last question. Almost invariably an analysis of distribution methods shows that selling through wholesalers is one of the lowest cost forms of distribution. When the manufacturer sells direct he does not "save" the wholesale discount. The additional cost of doing business usually is substantially greater than the amount paid the wholesaler.

Every salesman calling on the wholesaler should understand clearly the wholesaler's importance in the distribution process. What are the basic functions of the wholesaler's business? They are: (1) buying in comparatively large quantities; (2) warehousing; (3) selling; (4) delivering; (5) financing; (6) servicing; (7) merchandising.

The wholesaler buys in large lots from hundreds of sources. He bases his selection on the needs of the many retailers in his area.

He warehouses the merchandise at points where it is available to his retail customers, and he delivers the merchandise to them when they need it and in the quantities and sizes they require.

He extends credit to the retailer and relieves the manufacturer of credit problems and of the cost of billing a large number of dealers.

The wholesaler often delivers orders the same day they are received and gives the dealer a prompt service which would be too costly for most manufacturers to provide.

The wholesaler's salesmen aid the dealer in planning his local advertising, displays, and store layouts—provide a merchandising service which increases the sale of the manufacturer's products.

Before you call on any wholesaler customer be sure you have analyzed your products in terms of the territory in which that wholesaler sells. Have a complete and well thought-out selling plan so you can show the wholesaler how he can sell a profitable volume of your products.

After you have sold the wholesaler customer, then do everything you can to help him move a profitable volume of your products. Mr. Campbell Holton, head of the Campbell Holton Company, large wholesale grocer in Bloomington, Ill., was telling me about Walter P. McCarthy, who has been selling him for more than twenty years. He said, "I would buy anything he had to sell whether I needed it or not—because I know that he would see to it that his products sold in our territory. More than twenty years ago he talked us into buying a line of feed he was selling. We bought it with some misgivings. In a few months, however, McCarthy had called on a lot of dealers, and had sold thirteen carloads for us. And he had shown our boys how to sell it. He has done that with everything he has ever sold us. So we buy whatever he wants to sell."

Most wholesalers will let you attend their sales meetings and address their salesmen. The manager of one of the larger McKesson-Robbins houses told me, "After Ed Brown of Bauer & Black came to one of our meetings and told our salesmen about the 'Miss Curity' doll promotion campaign, the men became so enthusiastic about it they went out and really stepped up their sales of Bauer & Black products."

When you attend a wholesaler's sales meeting and speak to his salespeople, be sure you have a well-planned presentation. Make it short but thorough. Give the men specific information they can use to sell your line. Dramatize your presentation. The men in your audience are human and they will appreciate good showmanship.

Would you like to know what the wholesaler's men think of you when you are standing up there talking to them? Read what one wholesaler's salesman told M. B. Massol, publisher of the *Oral Hygiene* publications:

THE WHOLESALER CUSTOMER

Too often the manufacturer's man who gets a chance to talk to us boys acts as if he believes we have nothing to think about, nothing else to sell, but his stuff. So he talks for an hour or more, going into infinite detail—including a lot of chemistry or metallurgy or engineering not too easy to understand.

He doesn't seem to realize that none of us can ever know as much about his goods as he does. We don't have time to study that much about his one line. We have plenty of other products to think about. The really smart salesman streamlines his information—sticks to really important facts so far as possible—and confines his talk to specific information we can use in selling his products.

Maybe I'm wrong, but I think a sales meeting should be similar to a cooking school. If your wife goes to a cooking school or to a lecture on cooking, she expects to learn, very definitely and very specifically, *how to do something*. She doesn't want to listen to the history of hamburgers. She wants to learn how to cook something. To be sure, she may get intangible inspiration, and that's fine. But spending the time to attend isn't worth a hoot if she can't go home and slap together a better pie or something as a result.

When we salesmen take time—often our own time—to attend a sales meeting put on by a manufacturer's representative we should be able to count on learning something new about selling the man's products—something specific and definite—almost as specific and definite as the recipe our wives would expect to learn in a cooking school.

Your wholesaler's salespeople are human. Think about them as human beings and treat them as you would want to be treated if you were in their places. See that they understand your products and know how to sell them. And be sure they have reason to respect you and like you. They can move a tremendous amount of merchandise when they are enthusiastic about it, when they like the man who sells it in their territory.

Many wholesalers will permit you to travel with their salesmen and call on prospective customers. Be sure to treat the wholesaler's salesmen with respect. Keep your appointments with them promptly. Show them how they can help their dealers sell your products and they will be selling for you long after you are gone.

Whenever you call back on the wholesaler who is selling your products, see to it that you are of service to him in some way. Don't be like the salesman who called on a wholesaler and said, "How about a little order for my cutlery today?" The buyer told him, "I am overstocked now. Business is bad. We are cutting down on the lines we handle, and we are eliminating lines that don't sell."

The salesman said, "Well, business is tough everywhere," and he left. He considers that wholesaler a customer. He doesn't know that he has lost that customer. A manufacturer may have a thousand wholesalers on his books, but only fifty may be buying regularly. He may think he has a thousand wholesale customers, but actually he has only fifty. They are customers only when they are selling your products regularly. Bring them promotion suggestions every time you call.

You know that some wholesalers—grocery, drug, and hardware wholesalers, for instance—sell thousands of different items. No one in the wholesaler's establishment can be an expert merchandiser of every product his company sells. You, however, should be an expert merchandiser of the particular products you sell, and you should consider yourself the merchandising consultant of your wholesaler.

Make it your business to help him plan his promotion program of your products, plan dealer cooperative advertising, displays, and other promotion activities. Be alert for opportunities to be of service to your wholesalers.

Remember that your wholesaler customers are human beings, just as you are. They have a job to do and they will appreciate your help. When you call on them think in terms of what they want and need, rather than in terms of what you want, and you will have little difficulty in selling them.

When you are introducing a new line of products, or opening a new territory, how do you select the wholesaler that you want?

Do you first make a list of the specific qualifications you want your wholesaler to have?

In a Marketing Conference of the American Management Association, Laurence C. Hart, vice-president and general sales manager of the Building Products Division, Johns-Manville Sales Corporation, discussed the selection of building products distributors:

THE WHOLESALER CUSTOMER

The highly perfected techniques utilized in modern market analysis and distribution surveys will provide any manufacturer with a list of accounts in each trading area in direct order of their desirability. Qualifications of a building products merchant can be measured in terms of:

1. Responsibility and standing in the community—moral and financial.
2. Contractor and consumer acceptance.
3. Warehouse inventory and service facilities.
4. Attractive merchandise display.
5. Conference rooms for customers.
6. Adequate sales and estimating personnel.
7. Application-contractor clientele.
8. Local advertising and sales promotion activity.
9. Adequate local banking connections for deferred-payment financing.

I cannot very well give specific examples of success and failure without mentioning names or location. But I can say this—in going over a list of many, many hundreds of accounts selected over the period of the past 25 or 26 years on the basis of that list of qualifications, I had difficulty in finding more than three or four which have not turned out satisfactorily—both from our viewpoint and from theirs.

Selecting the wholesalers or distributors you want to sell your products is an important step. Check each one you consider with the list of qualifications you set up.

The presentation of your proposition is the next step and one which wholesalers tell me many salesmen do poorly. They say that salesmen frequently merely ask for an order and don't tell the buyer "why" he should give them an order.

The Johns-Manville method of making the presentation to the prospective distributor may be helpful to you. It suggests the thoroughness of planning that should precede your call on the prospective wholesaler customer you have selected. Mr. Hart said:

> After the account has been selected, the job becomes a matter of development and of getting right down to the point of final negotiations. One of our most successful district managers developed a technique which has now been broadened for wider use throughout the country, by making a printed presentation to the prospective distributor. To give you an idea of the amount of material included in that survey and the amount of information given to the prospect about his own business, which undoubtedly he had never had before, I want to list some of the

items covered. This is a presentation to an account in Shrevesport, La.:
—A statement of the basis of our proposition.
—An analysis of the distributor's market by counties. (In this case, these happen to be in Arkansas, Louisiana, and Texas.)
—The number of retail dealers, the number of customers, and a listing of our sales of J-M products in the previous year.
—The approach to the market, and what our company offers in return for the services required of the distributor.
—The operating principles of our merchandising plan.
—The type of service which we are able to provide through our district offices and through our personnel.
—A complete outline of our advertising and sales promotion policy with specific examples.
—A description of the Guild form of sales training.
—Technical services provided by our company on construction work.
—Factory service provided from our 17 factories.
—Functions which the wholesaler is to perform.
—Responsibilities which the wholesaler owes to his retail customer as well as those to his source of supply.
—Finally, a practical partnership report of the type of manufacturer-distributor relations which we are constantly endeavoring to maintain.

Notice that Mr. Hart referred to a "practical partnership." Consider yourself a partner of your wholesaler customers. In your partnership the interest of each partner is the same—selling a profitable volume of your products to the dealers in the wholesaler's territory, and through those dealers on to the final consumer.

Never again think of a wholesaler customer merely in terms of a "buyer" of the products you sell. Always think of him—talk to him—in terms of a "seller" of your products. Then you and the wholesaler will be talking the same language.

If you know the wholesaler and respect his importance in our economy—and in the distribution of your own products—if you are aware of his methods of operation and are genuinely interested in helping him, you can become a Very Important Person to your wholesaler customer.

Remember that every official, every salesman, and every buyer in the wholesaler's establishment is a human being. Each one is interested principally in his own success and in the success of his company. If you will help him succeed in his job you can be sure that he will do everything possible to help you succeed in yours. When you realize that, you understand the *Human* Side of Selling and are sure to be an exceptional success selling the wholesaler and helping the wholesaler move a profitable volume of your products.

CHAPTER 8

How One Word Can Help You Sell More Insurance — and Move Up Rapidly into the Million Dollars a Year Class

SELLING insurance can be one of the most rewarding careers in the selling profession. As an insurance agent you have the satisfaction of supplying something everyone needs, and you have an opportunity to earn a fortune.

Countless men and women have become wealthy through their success in selling insurance. Many thousands of others sell enough to earn a fair-to-good living. Each year there are some who fail.

It is becoming increasingly difficult to fail as an insurance agent because most companies today have so many aptitude and other screening tests that the men and women they select have a better than average chance for success. Moreover, almost all insurance organizations now give new agents at least basic insurance sales training. And the men and women who follow the instructions they receive during the training period are reasonably sure to sell insurance.

"Remember Yesterday When my Husband Told You Jokingly What You Could Do with that Fire Insurance Policy..."

HOW TO SELL MORE INSURANCE

Why, however, will some become outstanding stars, who seem to sell so easily, while others apparently work much harder but sell very little?

The answer might be in their knowledge of insurance or the mechanics of selling it. Both are important. Yet Jack Lacy, one of the country's greatest salesmen, spent five solid months studying intensely every factor connected with the selling of life insurance before he made a single call—and he did not write even one policy during his first selling month. He soon found the reason why, and then went on to top a million dollars his first year.

You might say, "The answer is simple—some people are just 'born' salesmen!" Yet a farmer, whose wife's illness forced him to move to the city, sold insurance so successfully that in twenty-five years he had built the largest automobile insurance company in the world. That man was George Mecherle.

"Ah!" someone might say, "both Jack Lacy and George Mecherle were more mature men when they started to sell insurance. Perhaps prospects have more respect for an older person." Yet Don Markham, a young Navy veteran, still in his twenties, easily tops a million dollars a year.

How do they do it? One, a star salesman in other fields before he became an insurance agent, one a farmer, and one a young Navy veteran. Is there any one thing they have in common? Is there something they have that the run-of-the-mill insurance salesman does not have? There must be something—what is it?

There is one great quality these men have in common. It is the reason for their magnificent success. And it can help you sell more insurance than you ever dreamed you could sell. Those men *think completely in terms of how much good they can do for their customers.* They not only *think* that way, but they *feel* they must help people, and they *act* in their contacts with customers and prospects as though they genuinely want to help them, instead of simply wanting to make a sale.

One word describes this terrifically magnetic quality that draws people to you—and draws sale after sale your way. That word is "attitude."

The dictionary defines "attitude" as "the way you think, act and feel." If the way you think, act and feel is completely in terms of your customers, and how much good you can do for each one, you are bound to make better use of your training in prospecting, programing, record keeping, and all the other selling skills you have acquired. But, above all, you will approach each prospective customer with the determination that you are going to try your darnedest to do some real good for that customer. He will see it. He will feel it. And you will find that more and more prospects will *want to do business with you.*

The attitude of the Lacys, the Mecherles, and the Markhams is the *Human* Side of Selling insurance. Smart Alecks and birdbrains will say that "attitude" can't be so important, and they will go blundering along calling on prospects and thinking only of "selling policies" and the "commission" they can make. While they scramble to earn enough each month to pay their bills, you will see that your "attitude" toward your customers is right, and you will shoot right by them to the top of your organization.

When Jack Lacy sold insurance he led the salesmen in his company with more than a million dollars a year in annual volume. He was almost sure to be a success as an insurance agent. After all, he had been a star salesman for years, and had taught salesmanship to many others. During his first selling month, however, he didn't write a single policy. What was wrong?

Because he believes in knowing all about the service or product he sells, Jack Lacy had spent five long months studying the types of policies his company wrote, studying federal and state inheritance taxes, and acquiring other information that would help him give his customers the most complete service.

At the end of that period of intense study Jack was convinced that he could analyze any prospect's insurance needs and recommend the correct type of insurance for him. He knew, furthermore, that he definitely could save money for most of his customers with his knowledge of state laws, inheritance taxes, and other information that he had acquired.

HOW TO SELL MORE INSURANCE

So he started out in his native city of Boston full of enthusiasm, eager to use his rather thorough knowledge of insurance. On the first day he met a friend he hadn't seen for a long time. The friend said, "It is good to see you, Jack. I have missed you. Let's have a good long talk. By the way, what are you doing these days?"

Jack Lacy answered, "I am selling insurance." As soon as he had said that, the friend looked at his watch and remembered an appointment. He was late, it seemed, and perhaps he had better hurry. He would see Jack some other time.

For a whole month, whenever Jack Lacy told people he was "selling insurance" he found that they remembered some appointment they had to keep, were very busy, or weren't interested.

After a month of hard work without selling a single policy, Jack decided that it would be a good idea to review his own salesmanship course. Then he analyzed his work during these first discouraging weeks and found that he had been approaching prospective customers thinking in terms of what he wanted—to sell insurance. The prospective customers, however, did not want to buy insurance—they were interested only in the benefits they would get from insurance. Furthermore, most of them had been buying insurance from some other salesman. Why should they want to give their insurance business to Jack Lacy?

The answer to that question was easy. Jack's intensive study of all types of personal insurance and the laws and regulations affecting federal and state inheritance taxes had convinced him that he could save substantial amounts of money for his customers. In effect, he would be helping customers find money. There was the customers' point of view!

One morning after he had reached that conclusion he was walking down the street in Boston when he met another friend he had not seen for a long time. The friend asked, "What are you doing these days, Jack?"

Jack Lacy said, "I am in the business of finding money for people." The friend immediately said, "Good, maybe you can find some for me!" and Jack Lacy had a perfect opening to tell how he might "find money" for him—by reviewing his insurance policies and helping him select the right policy for his family and his estate objectives.

The first month Jack Lacy sold insurance from the standpoint of what he could do for the customer he wrote policies totaling $77,000. And he soon moved up into the leadership of his company with sales topping a million dollars a year.

One of the greatest successes in the insurance business is the success of George J. Mecherle, founder of the State Farm Insurance Companies. Mr. Mecherle was an Illinois farmer. When Mrs. Mecherle became afflicted with arthritis, George decided to lease his farm and move to town, where she would be near medical care. He began to sell tractors and within a year he had set a new sales record for the company. He decided that the farmers needed insurance protection that was not available to them at that time, so he started his own insurance company—the State Farm Mutual Automobile Insurance Company—in March, 1922. Twenty-five years later George Mecherle's company was the largest automobile insurance company in the world.

This message from George J. Mecherle to his agents shows that his understanding of the *Human* Side of Selling—his "attitude" toward policyholders—is the reason for the phenomenal success of his organization:

Friendship is known as the highest degree of perfection in society. So, when we call on our policyholder, let us carry that feeling of friendly helpfulness and neighborly kindness in order that each will have a clear understanding of the friendly policy of the organizations we represent. The desire of any service organization is to give that service in full completeness.

From year to year we are learning that *service* carries with it its own reward, and to the extent and manner in which our service is dispensed compensation in every form will flow to us.

The past few years have taught us that a new philosophy of life is in the making. Old standards have been swept away. Success and attainment are no longer measured solely by material acquirement. We have truly learned that *what we really keep is what we give,* and the returns are immediate. Therefore, under this new philosophy the standard of success will eventually be the measure of service given.

The standards of success will be the measure of service given, Mr. Mecherle said, and the far-reaching success he has achieved in his own life is proof that the measure of service given can indeed determine the measure of success.

Donald Markham, a young Navy veteran, is one of the most successful salesmen in the Chicago area. After only thirty-six months in the insurance business his annual sales top a million dollars. How does Don do it? He thinks, feels, and acts in terms of giving his customers "superservice." You really enjoy selling insurance as Don Markham does when your "attitude" toward your customers is right, when you understand the *Human* Side of Selling.

Donald Markham said:

I often feel that I really don't have a job at all—it is too much fun to be work. Guess I just like people. I get a boot out of knowing them, learning their ambitions and problems, even though we may never do business. Frequently I am able to help them with a problem out of which I get only nervous indigestion immediately—but five have helped me for every one I have helped.

Fortunately, and singularly, I am able to pick my own prospects. Nobody tells me that this week I'll call only on lawyers, or ship-fitters, or college presidents. So it seems up to me to determine those people whom I'd most like to know. The chances are that, if I enjoy their company, if they are the type of guy that I'd like to know socially, we'll eventually do business, *because I'm interested in them and they know it.*

Everyone can do the same thing I have done if he really wants to. I am not a supersalesman. As a matter of fact, I feel a distinct weakness in the science of selling as it usually is defined. Therefore, my efforts have been to become a super servicer, and let the service do the selling. It seems to have worked and I have had a lot of fun doing it.

There you have the *Human* Side of Selling—the essence of success in selling insurance, or in any other type of selling.

Remember that your customer is a *human* being. He resents indifference. He will put on his boxing gloves when you attack him with "sales arguments." He will resist "high pressure." *But,* when you can say, as Don Markham did, *"I am interested in them and they know it,"* when you "get a boot out of knowing them, learning their ambitions and problems and helping them," when you "become a super servicer and let the service do the selling," when you realize fully that "what we really keep is what we give"—you will find that you soon stand far out from the crowds as a star salesman.

It is that one word "attitude" that makes the difference. If your attitude is right, you too can move up rapidly to the million dollar a year class. You will achieve all the success that you care to achieve, and you will say, with Don Markham, "I have had a lot of fun doing it."

CHAPTER 9

How the Customer in the Medical and Dental Professions Wants to Be Sold

WHILE visiting Dr. Ralph Kreisberg, prominent physician in midtown Manhattan, I asked him to tell me what he thought of the salesmen who called at his office. "What is the reason," I asked, "that some are respected by members of the medical profession and are successful in selling them while others barely sell enough to stay on their employers' payrolls?"

Dr. Kreisberg said:

You should have been here at noon yesterday. You would have met the type of salesman doctors like to see. This chap has been calling on us for some time and I invited him to have lunch with me yesterday.

I took him to lunch. I like him, because he is always cheerful, friendly, and considerate. When he sees that my nurse and I are busy, with a reception room full of patients, he shows that he respects our time.

He leaves his card and phone number so we can call him for special service.

Does He Get the Order?

He calls regularly. We can count on seeing him at the same time and same day, so we plan our orders for his products accordingly. And he never fails.

He is always pleasant. He will do anything to be of service to us.

He is sincere and honest. You might say he is an all-around nice person. We like him and give him as much business as we can.

That salesman knows the *Human* Side of Selling. He knows how doctors want to be sold. And there are many salespeople who call on the medical and dental profession who are like that man. What a contrast, however, to some of the other salesmen who call on doctors and annoy them so much they refuse to see them again. If the obnoxious salesmen represent prominent companies with exclusive products, the doctors do business with them reluctantly—and buy as little as possible.

Here are some of the reasons why a number of salesmen get little or no business when they call at Dr. Kreisberg's office. One always keeps his hat on and is so sloppy in appearance that the doctor and his nurse and receptionist prefer not to see him. If his company did not have a particularly good product, he would get no business at all. As it is, the doctor buys only his minimum requirements.

Some salesmen come into the doctor's office smoking a cigar, cigarette, or pipe. They show lack of respect and besides some foul the air so much that the office must be aired out before the next patient is admitted.

Some salesmen put their sample cases on the doctor's upholstered furniture. Those sample cases may have come in contact with a sidewalk that was not exactly clean or with the floor of a streetcar or bus. When the salesman picks his sample case up off the doctor's upholstered chair or couch as he is ready to leave he may find that he has left a dirty smudge on the nicely covered furniture.

Never put your briefcase or sample case on the furniture or desk in a doctor's office. Put it on the floor.

A doctor's time is valuable. He has appointments with patients in his office. He has outside calls to make. He must be at the hospital or clinic at certain hours. He is always subject to emergency calls.

MEDICAL AND DENTAL PROFESSIONS 91

Yet some salesmen have so little respect for the doctor's time that they come in poorly prepared for an interview. They open their briefcase or sample case and fumble around in it. Sometimes they find that they forgot to bring the very thing they wanted to discuss with the doctor. Don't let that happen to you. Always plan your calls so that you know exactly what you want to discuss and have all your samples and literature arranged in your case so that you can reach everything you need quickly and in proper sequence.

A major pet peeve of all doctors is the salesman who says "I'll only take thirty seconds, doctor," and then stays for fifteen or twenty minutes. One doctor told me, "When a salesman asks for thirty seconds and then stays for twenty or thirty minutes, the next time he calls I don't want to see him."

If you plan your call, you should know exactly how much time you need with the doctor. If you need ten minutes, don't ask for thirty seconds. You must win the doctor's confidence in your integrity, and show him that you respect him, before you can get him to buy from you.

Doctors have no time for salesmen who argue with them, who do not try to understand the doctor's problems or the doctor's point of view. One doctor told a salesman who represents a prominent drug company that the penicillin he had sold to the doctor clogged his needle. The salesman claimed, "We have never had any other complaints about it."

The doctor's reply to that was "I don't care whether you have had any other complaints. It clogs my needle. I can't use it, so take it back."

The salesman said, "We have more orders than we can fill."

The doctor told him, "All right. So you have more orders than you can fill. Don't do me any favors. Just take it back. No matter what you say, I don't want it."

That doctor was fair, and he is human too. He thought that probably his shipment of penicillin just happened to be a faulty batch. Yet he didn't believe the salesman's statement that the company had had no other complaints, because he knows that other doctors use the same type of needles that he uses and, consequently, would have the same clogging trouble. He changed to another company's penicillin and it has not clogged his needle at any time.

He told me: "If that salesman had said, 'I am sorry that you had any difficulty with our product, doctor. Let me take it back to our laboratories and have it examined. I will replace it with another supply and I am sure that you won't have any trouble with it clogging your needle. You know our reputation, doctor, and you can count on our product and our desire to satisfy you.' If that salesman had said something like that to me, I would still be buying his company's products.

"By arguing with me, the salesman implied that after twenty years of medical practice I didn't know how to use a hypodermic needle. He may think he won the argument, but he certainly lost my business."

If you call on members of the medical profession, read the *Journal of the American Medical Association* and other medical and surgical publications. If you call on dentists, read *Oral Hygiene*, the *Journal of the American Dental Association*, and be sure to read *Proofs*, the dental trade journal. By reading these publications you will keep informed about the latest developments in the professional world. You will know what your customers need and want.

When you have learned something about the practice of each of your customers you can bring him, or send him, clippings of articles you think may interest him. When you do you will find that you are stepping out of the rank of ordinary salesman in his estimation.

In one of his editorials in *Proofs*, Merwin B. Massol, publisher of the Oral Hygiene Publications, reported a study of the actual time salesmen calling on dentists spend face to face with a customer or prospective customer each day. Mr. Massol said:

Many a statement about selling problems must be accepted at face value. Often there is no way to check it. But it is easy to check for yourself the following statistics regarding sales-exposure time.

Hack Deeley has compiled some startling statistics. He found that Deeley Company salesmen who travel in country communities average

MEDICAL AND DENTAL PROFESSIONS

only one hour and 58 minutes sales-exposure time in an 8-hour day. City salesmen average only 69 minutes a day. (Hack discovered that his salesmen, on this basis, had time for only 50 actual sales words per call.)

You don't have to agree with Hack. You can compute your own statistics. You likely won't get precisely the same answers that Hack did. But the chances are the answers you do get will astonish you.

If you are calling on the medical and dental profession, analyze your day's work. Determine how many minutes each day you actually spend selling your products face to face with a customer or a prospective customer. You probably will find that your actual selling time is so short each day that you will have a new realization of the importance of whatever you say and do during each selling interview.

Dr. Rolland B. Moore told the readers of *Proofs* why he wanted to throw some salesmen out of his office and why he bought from other salesmen continually for twenty-five years:

For many years, I have patronized a certain large dental supply company that has several branches. I am considered one of the company's oldest customers. In college I bought my freshman laboratory tools, later my college operating instruments, and upon graduation I had them equip my office.

About five years ago, a new salesman for the company called on me for the first time. He antagonized me on his first call. He was one of the fresh, know-it-all kind. That first day, without invitation and within a few minutes after he came in, he walked into my operating room, looked around, and then, indicating my chair, said, "Well, well! One of the old-timers, eh! Why don't you throw it out and get one of the new models?"

"This suits me fine. I can get any position with it you can get with yours," I said. He subsided. Then he herded himself over to my X ray.

"One of the old residenters, I see! Do you know you couldn't get $50 for that now?" he said.

I was beginning to get sore. "It takes good pictures even if it isn't the latest model. I didn't ask you what it is worth and I don't care," I replied.

He noticed an old cabinet I use for storage of extra chair supplies, large bottles of drugs and medicines, my office coats, and forceps. "Would you take ten bucks for that? I might buy it for a museum piece," this fresh mullet laughed. I was getting just sore enough by that time to order him out of the office.

Although he was representing my favorite supply house, I wouldn't give him an order. He called on me three or four times after that but I wouldn't have bought anything from him to keep him from starving.

Then I had a call from a former salesman who had just rejoined the company. He was a graduate in dentistry but had let his license lapse while serving in the Dental Corps in World War I. When he went on the road, I became one of his customers and bought hundreds of dollars' worth of supplies from him. On his first call after rejoining the company, I again gave him a nice order—some of which I could have gotten along without, but I was just that glad to see him again. I asked what happened to the other man.

He just grinned and said, "So many customers wrote in to the manager that if the fellow called again, they would throw him out and quit buying from the company. So the young fellow was canned and is now down in Texas."

I had always liked to buy from this dentist-salesman. He knew just what I wanted and often gave me tips on better methods.

Then there was the pharmaceutical salesman who called on me to sell dental pharmaceuticals. Invariably when he came, he would come into the reception room whistling.

He was always smoking a Turkish cigarette that smelled like a pot of boiling glue. In a minute or two, my reception room simply reeked with that vile-smelling Turkish tobacco. When he'd leave, I'd have to open the windows to air out the office.

Finally, I just quit buying from him. I myself formerly traveled on the road for a pharmaceutical manufacturer, calling on physicians. I never under any circumstances entered a physician's office while smoking. First, it is bad manners. Secondly, professional men do not want their offices smoked up. If patients do it, that is different.

There are times when practice is poor and not many supplies are being used. During those times, dentists do not need much of anything. No dentist likes to turn down a salesman completely. I know how it goes myself, having been on the road.

Two supply salesmen used to call on me regularly. One of them I had been buying from for a long time; the other one was new in the territory. They always called about three days apart and the older man was the first. Month after month, the newer one called on me and I'd have nothing for him. He was a nice young fellow and a persistent guy. When he'd leave he would say, "Perhaps next time, eh, doctor?"

One month I divided my order and gave him half of it. He knew I had done so. Every order I gave him was properly filled and shipped sooner than I expected it. In time, he got the greater part of what I bought. He wasn't just an order-taker. He was a real salesman and he knew his line. The other man just took orders.

Sometimes salesmen for small supply houses call on a potential customer and oversell him. It is worse for future business than to undersell. It is still worse to withhold information on a product—state its good qualities and not mention its bad ones. One supply salesman who called on me had a reliner for acrylic dentures. He told me all of its good qualities, but not its bad points.

I had been using a reliner that blistered the gums and I was much dissatisfied with it. This salesman assured me the one he had wouldn't do so. So I ordered from him and a few days later the reliner came. Only after receiving it did I find that it took a week for it to harden. He hadn't told me that. I sent it back by return mail. Misrepresentation to make sales creates distrust. Business is founded on mutual trust.

A salesman from whom I had bought supplies for at least 25 years called on me during the latter part of last war. I was short of sharp burs at that time but had about 1,500 dull ones stashed away. I told him I needed a gross of assorted burs. He said he had them but that the steel they were made of was so soft they wouldn't cut cheese and he was ashamed to sell them. He asked if I had any pre-war dull burs. I told him I had. He advised me to have them resharpened and use them until the War was over. Then better steel could be bought and good burs made from it. He'd gladly write my order then.

Although I am not living in this man's territory now, I am buying from another branch of his supply company. But if I ever go back in his territory again, I'll buy from him. I can trust him, so he'll get my business.

Salesmen who sell the medical and dental profession are calling on some of the finest professional men and women in the country. They have a wonderful opportunity to build long-lasting friendships if they are honest and unselfish and have a sincere desire to be of service to their customer.

Helen MacDonald Webster, who prior to her retirement was with Edwards Dental Supply Company in San Francisco for many years, said, "Do you ever ask yourself questions like these: How strong are my business friendships? Do I tend them as carefully as I should? Do I value them as 'business getters' only? Many salesmen, sharp, upstanding chaps as they usually are, know perfectly well that business friendships are valuable to them. But in common with the rest of mankind they often take for granted those things to which they are accustomed—that taking-for-granted is the crux of the whole matter.

"Friendship is too complex a thing to be taken for granted or neglected. It is as delicate as a rose leaf, and yet it can be as strong as a steel cable if it is forged of the right materials; and of those right materials unselfishness and honesty and a sincere desire to serve are probably the strongest."

The customers in the medical and dental profession want to be sold by salesmen who respect them, who show they appreciate the importance of their time, who are considerate, friendly and cheerful, sincere and honest—salesmen who will try to understand the doctor's point of view and do everything they possibly can to make the work of the doctor, his assistant and nurses easier. When you are that type of salesman you understand the *Human* Side of Selling. And because you do you are sure to be one of the most successful salesmen and will make many lifelong friends among your professional customers.

CHAPTER 10

Who Are the Institutional Customers— and How Do They Want to Be Sold?

IF someone were to ask a salesman, "Who are your institutional customers?" he might say, "Why, they are schools and hospitals, hotels and restaurants, clubs, public and private institutions."

Could I Interest You in One of Our New Upholstered Seats?

That answer would be correct, with this exception: a school, hospital, hotel, restaurant, club, public or private institution can buy nothing at all. Someone—a man or a woman—a human being must decide on the purchase and authorize, or give, the order. The customers, therefore, are the men and women in these institutions who purchase, or influence the purchase of, your products.

You might say, "Of course, that is so. Everyone knows that. What point are you making?"

The point I am making is this: to sell the institutional market successfully, the salesman who understands the *Human* Side of Selling will learn *Who is Who* in each institution—*who* can buy his particular products. Then he will learn all he can about each "who" so he will know how that man or woman wants to be sold.

Fred Bradley, who represents the *Nation's Schools* publication, told me an experience which illustrates the importance of knowing the Who's Who in institutional selling. One day while he was talking to the sales manager of a weather strip manufacturer he asked, "Why aren't you getting more school business?"

The sales manager said, "Our men are calling on schools, but they just aren't buying our stuff. I can't understand it, because we had a special sales manual prepared showing the men how to sell schools. A promotion man we had who claimed to know the school market prepared it."

Fred Bradley said, in his forthright way, "Let me see that manual." After he had read it he turned to the sales manager and told him: "No wonder your men haven't been selling any weather stripping to schools. This manual tells them to call on the school janitor and sell him. The janitor can buy as much weather stripping as the man in the moon. As a rule he doesn't even buy the soap he uses. The man your salesmen have to sell is the school administrator, the superintendent. He is the only one who can buy your products or authorize their purchase."

Those salesmen were calling on the wrong man. Perhaps they thought they were doing a good selling job because they were following instructions. They were making calls on schools and reporting the calls.

INSTITUTIONAL CUSTOMERS

If they had been interested in the *Human* Side of Selling, however, they would have learned *who* in each school could buy their weather stripping. Then they would have learned all they could about that man (or woman)—his background, experience, plans for the school or school system, why he might want to buy weather stripping. After that investigation they would have called on the right person, and they would have sold him the way he wanted to be sold!

In some communities the law specifies that competitive bids must be secured by the school system for some major purchases. How would the *Human* Side of Selling influence the school administrators who must accept the lowest price? The superintendent of schools in one of the largest cities said, "The law does not say we must take the lowest price. Sometimes we take the fourth, fifth or sixth bid, because we believe it provides the best dollar value."

There you have it. Even on competitive bidding, if you have convinced the superintendent that your product or service "provides the best dollar value," you can get the order although your price may not be the lowest.

What influence do school board members have on school purchases? Usually school board members are primarily interested in community relations, in curriculums that fit the needs of their communities, in finances and budgets and the policy-making facets of the educational system.

The full-time school administrator is the "general manager" of the schools. The board of education is his "board of directors." As one school authority put it: "The school superintendent or administrator meets with the board and tells them what they have to do to get their kids to measure up to the kids in other school systems. He submits a prepared plan, the board approves it, and leaves the details of material selection and purchases to him."

Larger city school systems may have business managers and purchasing agents. In colleges and universities the nonacademic aspects of administration may be headed by a business official and a staff consisting of assistant business manager, purchasing agent, superintendent of buildings and grounds, and director of feeding. This structure varies according to the size of the institution. In small institutions the president is sometimes the business official as well as the academic head.

When you are calling on any school, college or university, first learn *who* is the official who can buy your products. Then learn all about him before you see him.

When you become interested in the business official as a *human* being, you will learn how he wants to be sold—what you can do to be of the greatest possible service to him—and you will make many more sales than you ever thought possible.

When you are selling hospitals, again the Who's Who is important. As a rule, you must sell the hospital administrator. According to *Modern Hospital* magazine, the hospital administrator "may be a businessman with little or no medical background. He may be a doctor with a business turn of mind. He, or in some cases she, may be a registered nurse with a sound business sense and superior ability."

In a booklet entitled *So You're Going to the Hospital,* which every salesman who calls on hospitals should have, *Modern Hospital* gives you this picture of the hospital administrator:

Whatever his professional or business experience, the Administrator is pretty likely to be a normal human being. With slight variations in character due to the nature of hospital administrative duties, he is subject to the same appeals that will sell any other businessman. By nature he is likely to be somewhat conservative. The health of his community, responsibility for the life of the individual patient and a close association with scientific medical procedure tend to make him deliberate rather than impulsive.

You will find that he depends for much technical guidance upon the heads of his various departments—his surgical, nursing and obstetrical supervisors, dietitian, housekeeper, pharmacist, laundry manager, comptroller, mechanical superintendent. He may delegate specific administrative duties to a business manager or purchasing officer.

He is everlastingly alert to new products that will save time and money and increase general efficiency. Necessarily, he must give a hearing at least to everything that is new and sift from the new that which is worthy of full consideration. He is concerned with long range costs and

INSTITUTIONAL CUSTOMERS 101

efficient performance as well as with original cost. He dare not ever close his mind.

He will see salesmen and will welcome those who have something of genuine value to him and his institution.

He prefers that all salesmen clear through his office, or the office of his purchasing officer, before they take the time of his department heads.

In the nature of his responsibilities to his community and his governing board, he reserves the final right of approval on every purchase.

In other words, his position is very comparable to that of the head of any progressive commercial enterprise of similar size. His authority is a little broader, his responsibility is a little deeper, his impulse a little weaker, his judicial nature a little stronger.

Under the hospital administrator are the professional staff and the executive staff. Professional staff members—medical and surgical—are interested in buying the equipment and supplies they use themselves in their practice within the hospital. The professional equipment of a hospital is available to all the doctors and must satisfy them all; therefore, the administrator and the medical staff usually decide jointly on expenditures for equipment within their budget.

On the executive staff of the administrator of the larger hospitals there will be one or more executive assistants. One of these assistants may be a business manager, who may be in charge of purchasing, or a purchasing agent, whose specific responsibilities are the purchasing of supplies and equipment. The business manager or purchasing agent works closely with the administrator and all department heads. When a hospital does have a purchasing agent or a business manager in charge of purchasing, this executive should be contacted first by the salesman and all purchases cleared through him.

The superintendent of nurses is interested in nursing and educational supplies and equipment. As a rule, her purchase recommendations are followed but must be approved by the administrative office.

As surgical and obstetrical supervisors are responsible for the efficient operation of the surgery and delivery suites, their opinion is considered by the purchasing agent or administrator when there is a choice to be made between brand A and brand B, or between type A and type B.

The hospital dietitian is important in the routine purchase of foods, particularly in the selection of perishable foods. She is the executive of the kitchen and is directly concerned with the food preparation. The salesman selling food products or food service equipment certainly should see the dietitian, but he should remember that the influence of the administrative office on the purchase of these products outweighs that of the dietitian. In the several thousand hospitals that do not have full-time dietitians, the dietary departments are usually supervised by the administrator.

It is the housekeeper's responsibility to select the cleaners, soaps, the linens, bedding, draperies and upholstery, and many other items needed to maintain a clean and attractive hospital. As the budgets are always a factor in hospitals, the housekeeper's recommendations are usually made in consultation with the administrative office.

The laundry manager should be contacted by the salesmen who sell soaps or other laundry supplies and equipment. The administrative office invariably must approve price, quality and delivery, so the experienced salesman will always contact the purchasing executive.

While the hospital pharmacist usually specifies the products to be purchased for his department, the selection of many proprietary items is the result of a conference between the pharmacist and the administrator and the professional staff.

The salesman experienced in selling hospitals knows that the various department heads are influential in the purchase of consumable products. They also influence the selection of furnishings and equipment. When price, delivery, and long-range maintenance problems and costs are factors in the purchase—as they invariably are in most items of capital investment—then the administrator or the administrative assistant usually is the one who decides on the purchase.

Bessie Covert of *Modern Hospital* said:

> In my discussions with manufacturers in our fields I have many times been told that it is of great advantage to be familiar with the customer's problems and to express an interest in them rather than only in the sale of the products.

INSTITUTIONAL CUSTOMERS

An interest in and understanding of the customer's problems sells more products in the long run than concentration upon sales alone. For instance, one of the very successful salesmen in the hospital field told me that he spends quite a bit of time and thought in working up ideas that will be helpful to the hospital people he sees—quite apart from the product he is selling.

He has developed in this way several ideas which have proved valuable to hospitals to the point where they have been adopted by the hospital. And the ideas have had nothing to do with his product—but they have had a great deal to do with the hospital administrator's regard for him and with developing the administrator's interest in what he *is* selling.

He told me that he never goes into a hospital without having a helpful idea or suggestion to pass along to the administrator or to a department head.

There you have the *Human* Side of Selling the hospital administrator, his assistants or department heads, the school administrator, managers of hotels, clubs, or any institutional buyer. When you sell the institutional market, remember that your customers are *human* and that they prefer to buy from the salesman who is genuinely interested in helping them in every way he can.

If you sell to hotels, clubs and restaurants you will soon learn that the manager is the principal buying influence. In the larger hotels (with 200 rooms or more), in the large clubs and restaurants, the various department heads become important in the buying, or at least in the selection, of the products you sell. Generally the restaurant owner is also the manager and has complete control over all purchases.

Some hotels and restaurants set specific hours for salesmen to call. Unless you are a local salesman who can call at the hours specified, it is well to telephone for an appointment. Never call on a hotel or restaurant manager during any meal period. Experienced hotel and restaurant salesmen say the best time to see the manager is shortly before lunch, directly after lunch, and just before the dinner hour.

The booklet *Selling to Restaurants and Hotels,* prepared by the Ahrens Publishing Company, Inc., gives this advice to salesmen selling to hotels and restaurants:

Know as much as possible about the manager's experience before you contact him—and you will be able to conduct your sales talk accordingly. Tradesmen in the town, as well as employees, can usually help with this information.

Give the most careful consideration to the selling of the manager in that he is the man that must be reached in some way before the sale is consummated—perhaps not in the case of unimportant purchases—but very definitely when the yearly purchases mount up. Where they mean a change in methods or policy—where they require capital investment—remember the manager must always be sold!

If you are calling on hotels and restaurants you should have a copy of the Ahrens Publishing Company's booklet. In it are many valuable statistics about these institutions and the volume of their purchases, and selling suggestions such as the following "Hints in Selling the Manager":

1. Always make an appointment.
2. Carefully choose your location to deliver your sales talk to the manager. Obviously the hotel lobby is a poor spot for your talk in that the manager's attention is divided between your sales talk and the activities of the hotel.
3. Are you selling soap, towels, sheets, etc.? Then the manager's office is a good place for an interview. Still better, in the case of some hotels, is the salesman's own room if he happens to be staying at the hotel and it can be arranged that way.
4. Are you selling food products that must be tested? The kitchen or store room, in the presence of the restaurant manager, steward or chef, is your best location. It offers you an opportunity to sell more than one factor at the same time.
5. Never attempt to sell food products just after the manager has had a meal of any kind. It probably is the last thing he wants to think of. Approach him just before lunch or dinner.
6. In hotels, terminology deserves considerable attention. Your prospect's hotel is his "house"—his front office and departments in conjunction with it are the "front of the house"—and the steward's department, kitchen, engine room are the "back of the house."
7. Make your approach cordial—but not lengthy because these executives are busier now than ever before in their business experience.
8. Is your product advertised through general advertising mediums? Then make reference to it but emphasize the special advertising being done in the manager's own business publications such as *Hotel Management* and *Restaurant Management*. Otherwise, he

may draw the inference that you do not consider the restaurant and hotel market important.

The steward, chef-steward, and chef are three of the most important department heads in the larger hotels, because well over half the hotels' revenue comes from food and beverage sales.

It is the steward who usually buys food supplies and is responsible for all departments that handle foods. You will usually find him at the market in the early morning hours buying perishable supplies and in the hotel kitchen during mealtimes. Unless you make an appointment with him, the best time to see the steward is during the two hours immediately before noon.

The manager and the steward invariably consult the chef in the purchase of food, beverages, and kitchen equipment. The chef is often in the kitchen early in the morning, hours before the dining room opens, and seldom has time for salesmen except during a few hours in the afternoon.

The larger hotels usually have an executive housekeeper and the medium and smaller hotels a working housekeeper, most of whom live in the hotel. In the large houses the housekeeper is sometimes responsible for the actual buying of supplies for her department, whereas in the smaller hotels the housekeeper is an adviser to the manager on purchasing supplies. Housekeepers are consulted by the manager on the purchase of furnishings, room supplies, and redecoration and modernization.

Hotel engineers, electricians, and maintenance department heads are important in the selection of mechanical equipment and frequently are consulted by the manager or purchasing officer.

When you call on a hotel or restaurant manager, put yourself in his place. What would you want to know about the product or service you want to sell? Of course you would be interested in learning about anything and everything that has a bearing on how you can increase your business and your profits. You would give serious consideration to devices that save time and save labor, that will improve your service to the public, that will attract more profitable business to your establishment.

If you represent a manufacturer selling the institutional market you will find in many cases that you can sell the largest number of customers through wholesalers or institutional supply dealers.

In selling schools you will want to consider the school supply and equipment distributors, whose salesmen contact all schools, many at a lower enrollment level than would be profitable for you to contact if you were selling a single product or a restricted line.

In selling hospitals you may find it profitable to sell through the large national hospital supply firms or through the local hospital equipment and supply distributors.

In selling restaurants, clubs, and hotels you will find that they buy most of their new and replacement equipment from restaurant and hotel supply houses and from the contract departments in department stores. You may make the original sale to the hotel, club or restaurant yourself and rely on the local equipment and supply house for repeat and replacement business.

If you are selling grocery products you will find that many wholesale grocers have special contract departments which specialize in institutional business. You will also sell the institutional market through provision houses, meat wholesalers, and wagon jobbers.

Whatever your product, you will find dealers or wholesalers that sell the institutional buyers in your area—paper jobbers, janitors' supply houses, specialty supply jobbers, and the hardware dealers who may have contract departments that sell kitchen and restaurant equipment, dining-room and sundry supplies to the institutional market.

There are various outside influences which can determine the purchase of the product you sell to the institutional buyer, but these outside influences depend on the type of product or service you sell. They may be architects, building contractors, consulting engineers, interior decorators, or the institution's advertising or public relations counselor.

As a salesman who understands the *Human* Side of Selling, you will first of all learn specifically *who* is the particular customer you have to sell in each institution on which you call. While that customer may be the administrator or the manager, in most cases you know that the various department heads are influential and in many cases are the actual buyers. No two institutions are exactly alike in management or department head influence, so you will be sure to learn *who is who* in each case.

You will determine whether your product or service can be sold most effectively directly to the institutions or through the institutional supply house. If you sell through the supply house you will cooperate with that wholesaler or dealer. You will help familiarize his sales organization with your products and give his salespeople every assistance you can in selling their institutional customers.

By all means, you will read the leading hospital, school, hotel, restaurant, and club magazines. By reading these publications you will keep yourself familiar with all modern trends in the institutional market. Moreover, you will find many articles and news items that will be of interest to your own institutional customers. Your customers, particularly the administrators and managers, are busy men and women. They will appreciate your bringing to their attention articles and news items that you think might interest them.

Remember your institutional customers are *human* beings! They like the salesman who shows that he likes them as individuals and is genuinely interested in being of service to them. Charles Loeffel, business manager of the Ahrens Publishing Company, Inc., said, "We do not look for 'high-powered' salesmen in our business. What we want are *good servicemen*—men who can take an active interest in the customer's problems and who will honestly make an effort to fit their services into the customer's picture so the salesman, the supplier and the customer can all grow together."

The salesmen who achieve the greatest success in selling the institutional market are what Mr. Loeffel calls "good servicemen," men who win the customers' respect by taking an active interest in the customers and doing everything in their power to help them. That is the *Human* Side of Selling the institutional customer—the sure, happy way to earn your fortune and a host of admirers and friends.

CHAPTER 11

*What the Industrial Customer Will Buy—
and How To Sell Him*

A SALESMAN in the Special Products Department of the Kellogg Switchboard and Supply Company asked Carl Megelin, his sales manager, to go with him to see the treasurer of one of the largest industrial organizations in the Chicago area. He told Mr. Megelin, "I learned in the Purchasing Department that the treasurer is the man who would have to decide whether the company could use our type of equipment. I called the treasurer and made an appointment for ten o'clock tomorrow morning. Can you meet me outside the main office of that plant about ten minutes to ten? This is a big prospect and I would like to have your help in selling the top men."

Carl Megelin drove up to the main entrance of that plant at ten minutes to ten. The salesman was waiting for him. They sat in Megelin's car and discussed the prospective customer before they went in to keep their appointment.

Mr. Megelin asked the salesman, "What are we going to sell this company? What equipment do you intend to recommend?"

The salesman replied, "I don't know, Carl, but look at the size of that plant! They certainly can use some of our stuff!"

Carl Megelin was surprised, to say the least. He said, "We can't go into that treasurer's office and say, 'Here are all the things we make. We hope you want to buy some of them.' That executive is a very busy man with a great many things on his mind besides intercommunication and telephone systems. We know something about the products his company manufactures. Our experience with

What a Salesman—He Saw All the Sweater Girls in the Plant and Sold the Boss Blinders for Our Safety Goggles!

similar organizations should tell us approximately what they might need. Let us analyze the facts we have and then go in and make certain specific recommendations."

Before you call on an industrial customer put yourself in the place of the man you are going to see. If you were in his place, what would you need, what would you want to buy?

The general manager of a large manufacturing organization said, "Many of the salesmen who call on us have a one-track mind. They are thinking only of what they want to sell. They don't even take the trouble to find out what we make so they can determine which of their products we might need and what we might be interested in buying."

The first step in selling the industrial customer should be learning all you can about his business, so you can determine *what* that customer needs and which of the products that you sell will fit his needs. When you determine *what* he needs and can buy, then the next step in selling the industrial customer must be learning *who* can authorize the purchase.

Mr. Megelin said, "In every large industrial organization there are ten men who can say 'No' for every one that can say 'Yes.' The salesman must learn *who* is the man who can say 'Yes.' He must not overlook the men who can say 'No,' but finally he must see and sell the man who can say 'Yes' if he is to close his sale."

According to John K. Wilson, vice-president of *Production Equipment* magazine, "Too many salesmen selling to industry spend all their efforts on the purchasing agent. The salesman who directs his efforts only to this individual is selling mechanically, for the purchasing executive usually buys what is requested by those higher up. The salesman who understands the human side of selling calls on and sells the plant executive who is personally concerned with the operations of his plant. That man is human. He has problems the salesman can help him solve."

Mr. Wilson added, "Some salesmen selling industrial products through wholesalers and supply houses simply drop in and look over the want lists—another type of mechanical selling. Want lists do not always reveal the possibilities for sales if the human side of

THE INDUSTRIAL CUSTOMER

selling is followed. The salesman must reach on to the potential users and bring his products to their attention. When you do this, the want lists of your wholesalers and supply houses will soon list the products you want to sell."

If you represent a manufacturer who advertises in business publications you will find that your advertising is helpful in reaching and selling the man in each industrial organization who can say "Yes," as well as the many others who might say "No," if they are not sold on your products and your firm.

For instance, if you were selling Illium, a corrosion-resistant alloy, and were calling on the American Machine and Foundry Company, your Illium advertising in *Materials & Methods* publication would be reaching the works manager, production supervisor, project engineer, tool designer, heat-treating foreman, master mechanic, and a number of other key men who might influence the use of Illium in the products manufactured by their company.

If you were calling on E. B. Badger & Sons Company, your *Materials & Methods* advertising would be carrying the story of your product to the vice-president, the chief metallurgist, the estimating engineer, and the plant superintendent—all men who might influence the selection of Illium in some application where corrosion resistance is important.

McGraw-Hill, publisher of *Business Week,* and *Factory Management and Maintenance,* makes this important point to salespeople who sell industrial customers: "The Man you never heard of may be the one you will have to sell."

According to McGraw-Hill:

> Behind the man you see is often a man you never heard of, whose "No" can stop you, cold. Or his "Yes" can change the mind of the man who has been saying "No" to you.
> Maybe he sits in the office just beyond, behind a door without name or title. His desk may be Up Front or Out in the Shop—or he may be the guy who is Always on the Road selling to others what you sell to his firm. And that goes whether your product is an article for resale, or a material, or a piece of equipment for making your customer's product.
> In the organization of a big user or a big distributor there may be dozens of such men.

For example, in one typical, moderately-large, midwestern industrial plant there are 27 people who have a common interest in the selection and use of equipment that goes into that company.

They are:

- 1 Manager of Manufacturing
- 1 Assistant General Factory Manager
- 1 Production Manager
- 3 Plant Engineers
- 1 Assistant Plant Engineer
- 10 Superintendents
- 2 Assistant Superintendents
- 1 Chief Industrial Engineer
- 1 Materials Handling Engineer
- 1 Chief Electrician
- 1 Master Mechanic
- 1 Supervisor
- 1 Manager of Quality Control
- 1 Assistant Head of Operations, Planning Department

If you sell the type of thing these men work with, any one of them can block the sale of your product to this company. Or any one of them can start the ball rolling your way. Win all of them to a belief in your product and you are solid with a multi-million dollar concern. This type of organization is important to you—and you have to reach correspondingly large numbers of men in it.

Your company's advertising in *Business Week* and other business publications may reach all the executives and department heads in the industrial organizations on which you call. That advertising will help you sell, even if you never see all the men it reaches in any one organization. Study your firm's advertising. Show it to prospects and customers. Use it to help you sell.

If you have an important industrial prospect you are trying to sell, no doubt you could get the names of the key men in that prospect's company who are subscribing to the publications in which your products are being advertised. Ask the publisher's representatives to get their subscribers' names for you. They will not give you their entire subscription list, but often will give you the names of subscribers in the important companies you want to sell. When you have the names of those key men you can call on them confident that they have been reading about your products in the publications to which they subscribe.

After you have analyzed your prospective industrial customer and have determined *what* he needs and can buy—and when you have learned *who* is the man who can say "Yes" and the many others who can say "No" if they are not sold—then *plan* your sales presentation, and plan it in terms of *what* your prospective customer wants to hear about your products *and their benefits to him.*

C. Edward Augsbach, management consultant and head of Industrial Budgets, Inc. said, "Many salesmen don't seem to realize that purchasing agents, department heads, and executives of industrial organizations are busy men. In a manufacturing business today anyone in a position of responsibility may have fifty things on his mind at one time. Yet, salesmen will call on us and expect us to put everything aside and find out where and how the salesman's products can be useful to us."

Mr. Augsbach continued: "Salesmen who call on industrial organizations and fail to sell usually fail because, first of all, they don't know the customer and what he needs. Secondly, they fail to get to the right man. Next, they not only have no planned presentation of their proposition, but many times they can't even answer questions about their products. Finally, many salesmen who sell one product to an industrial customer seem to be content to take orders for that same product over and over and never try to sell other items which their firm may produce or distribute."

The head of the purchasing department of a manufacturing concern told me of a salesman who had been selling his company abrasives for years. One day that salesman happened to be in the purchasing department when a requisition came in for bandsaw and hacksaw blades. He heard the requisition discussed and told the purchasing agent, "Why, we sell saw blades." The purchasing agent said, "Why didn't you tell us? Your service has been good and you could have had at least part of our hack and bandsaw blade business all along."

That salesman had been missing business he could have had from that company simply because he was content to take orders for just one of the products that his firm sold.

The successful industrial salesman analyzes every customer to determine his potential purchases of every product that he sells. *Industrial Distribution* magazine recommends that the industrial salesman analyze his customer—and keep a record of his calls and sales to each customer on a customer analysis sheet or card.

According to *Industrial Distribution:*

Through such an analysis, the salesman can determine among which specific customers there are opportunities to improve sales coverage. It will save him time and direct his own efforts.

If the sales to any one customer are low, the salesman can examine sales of each major line to see which one has dropped off and is pulling the total down.

It is probable that the salesman may already know the reason or reasons for the decline if he has been calling on the account steadily. Again, he may ascertain the reasons by inquiring about them on his next visit.

Nevertheless, the situation can stand a review of the salesman's selling efforts. Was his coverage of the account adequate preceding the decline? Were the lines in question discussed sufficiently? Was his sales presentation convincing? Is the customer aware that his purchases of these lines has lessened? Could the salesman use a little more training on knowledge of products and applications? Would a visit by a factory man help? The answers to these and other questions suggested by the circumstances, can be most valuable in maintaining maximum volume in each line for each customer.

Reginald Jerman, salesman for the R. C. Neal Co., carries his customer analysis book in his car as he makes his daily round of calls. He checks over previous sales to each customer before starting out. There may be a pump manufacturer on the list whose purchases of screw products may have fallen off; he will have to find out why. His sales of cutting tools to a metal working plant may be holding up, but his sales of related items such as abrasives, grinders, precision tools, etc. may indicate room for improvement.

Mr. Jerman does not keep actual figures of potentials, but he has developed the habit of thinking in these terms. For instance, his records showed his previous year's sales of abrasives to a casting firm were $4,200 which seemed, at the time, a fairly substantial amount of business. Nevertheless, from what he knew of the company's plans, and prospects, Mr. Jerman started the new year with a revised estimate of

THE INDUSTRIAL CUSTOMER 115

this plant's potential for abrasives. His new estimate was double the previous year's figures. At the end of the first six months of the new year, his sales of abrasives to this plant were $7200!

Without the sales analysis record, Mr. Jerman doesn't think a salesman can possibly know where he stands, line by line, with his customer.

The value of a customer's monthly record of purchases by lines can be used as evidence of the salesman's interest in his customer's business. In many instances, the customer does not know how much of each line he is buying from a single distributor. This often results in a divergence of orders to different sources of supply, much to the discomfiture of the salesman who is expending sales effort on the lines which are diverted.

This may happen only occasionally, but the salesman without a customer analysis record is at a disadvantage. More and more orders may be inadvertently diverted, and he continues to lose business without becoming aware of how or why. Many salesmen approach the customer with the analysis record and prove the point. Invariably, the buyer is impressed with the details, and pleased with the knowledge that the salesman is appreciative of the business.

Analyze your territory. Analyze each one of your industrial customers, and keep a customer analysis record.

Don't hesitate to let the customer know that you are interested enough in him to study his business and determine how the products you sell can be useful to him. Your industrial customer is a human being—he will appreciate your interest, particularly if you back up that interest with service.

There is a one-syllable word that causes more trouble for some salesmen than any other word in the English language. That word is "price." Yes, some salesmen are so price conscious that they think they can't sell unless they have the lowest price, or at least a lower price than their principal competition.

Furthermore, they assume that the industrial customer buys at the lowest price he can get. This is not so. The general manager of a large industrial organization told me: "Certainly we are interested in price. But price is not our first consideration by any means. Generally, we want the answers to three questions before we consider the price. Those questions are: (1) how will it increase production efficiency or improve the salability of our products? (2) what will it save us? (3) in the case of new equipment, how long will it take to pay for itself?"

Down in Panama City, Fla., Dave Robertson, head of the Dave Robertson Electric Company, sells electrical contracting jobs at two or three times the price quoted by competitors. And, although he is comparatively new in northwestern Florida, he is getting some of the largest electrical installations in his section of the state.

How does he do it? According to *Electrical South* magazine, the entire secret—if it is a secret—is wrapped up in "selling future expansion" in every commercial installation. As Mr. Robertson puts it, "Find out what is needed for immediate operation—for the next two years increase in business—and then double that amount." He sold an ice plant an 800-ampere circuit when the owners had planned to have a 400-ampere circuit. That plant has enough electrical capacity for ten years of expansion and the executives of the company are extremely proud of their foresight.

To achieve the greatest success in selling the industrial customer, put yourself in that customer's place. Determine *what* he needs, *what* he will buy, and *how* he wants to be sold. Then find out *who* in the company can say "Yes" and how many can say "No." Be sure to make your selling presentation most thorough to the man who can say "Yes!"

Respect your industrial customer as a busy man. Carefully *plan* your sales presentation to him—and be sure that your presentation is planned in terms of *what the customer wants to hear about your products and their benefits to him.*

Analyze your territory and your customers and keep a record of their needs and of your sales to them. In that way you can be sure you are not overlooking any opportunity to be of service to them.

Keep a well-balanced perspective about price. If men like Dave Robertson can get two or three times as much as their competitors for a job by giving the customer more of what the customer wants, so can you.

Finally, when you have sold the customer, let him know that you appreciate his business, and go all out in giving him more service than he could get from anyone else.

Remember that your industrial customer is *human* and he will prefer to give his business to the salesman who shows that he understands the *Human* Side of Selling.

CHAPTER 12

How to Make "Cold" Purchasing Agents Good Customers and Warm Friends

WHILE waiting in the reception room of a large organization one day I could not avoid overhearing the conversation of several salesmen. Evidently they were waiting to see the purchasing agent or someone in the purchasing department. I had picked up a magazine and had started to turn the pages when I heard one of them say, "Look at that sign over the table. Isn't that a laugh! Listen to this: 'Whether you are a customer or a salesman, while you are in this plant you are our guest and we will do everything possible to extend our hospitality to you.' They ought to make the purchasing agent read that. I'll bet he has never seen the damned thing!"

One of the other men asked, "What's eating you? Has he been giving you a rough time, too?"

The first salesman said, "Yeah, the old boy sure is a hard man to sell. He has a hunk of ice for a heart and ice water in his veins. I have been waiting nearly half an hour for the old buzzard and,

Purchasing Agents Are Easy to Reach When You Know How

when I do get in to see him, he will probably say he is not interested in my stuff and give me a quick brush-off."

The second salesman nodded his head sympathetically. "I know what you mean. Purchasing agents are cold customers all right."

Another man sitting in that reception room had been smiling as he listened to that conversation. He asked the first salesman, "Did you have an appointment with the purchasing agent? If you did, I can't understand why he has kept you waiting nearly half an hour . . ."

The salesman said, "No, I didn't have an appointment. What good would it do? I have been dropping in on him on and off for nearly a year and I have never gotten to first base."

The smiling man said, "I suspected that you didn't have an appointment. You see, I have been selling him for years and I know many boys who call on him. I have an appointment with him in about two minutes (I always get here early) and I'll bet you that he does not keep me waiting!"

Just then the receptionist called the name of the man who had just spoken and he turned to the other two as he started up the stairs and said, with his big friendly smile, "Do you see what I mean? He really is a prince when you get to know him!"

That salesman was right. The purchasing agent happens to be a friend of mine. In fact, we had lunch that day with another executive of the company. During lunch I told him I had heard that he was a hardhearted monster—just another cold purchasing agent who delighted in making life tough for salesmen.

He laughed and said, "There's no such thing as a cold purchasing agent. Certainly we are busy. If a salesman could sit at my desk for one day he would have some idea of the problems we have and the work that goes through that department. Then he might have more respect for our time and, I think, would try to be more cooperative than some of the salesmen are today.

"Don't misunderstand me," he added. "I am not criticizing all salesmen. We couldn't get along without them. And a number of the salesmen who call on us are among the best friends I have. We need salesmen. We want them to call on us. We want to buy from them—but some of the so-called salesmen who call seem to do everything they can to keep us from giving them an order.

"Why, there was one man who came in to see me just before lunch. He said he had been waiting nearly an hour. He didn't have an appointment and I was sorry to keep him waiting, but I was in a meeting with the plant superintendent and engineers, and I had another appointment, so he had to wait. It happens that we could use some of the stuff that he sells and I asked him about various sizes and prices. You may believe this or not, but that chap couldn't even give me that basic information. He said he would have to get it from his factory.

"That is one of the main criticisms that we purchasing agents have of salesmen today. So many of them don't know what they are selling. They seem to be little more than errand boys. They apparently think their job is to make a certain number of calls—to get in to see the purchasing agent. Then they have to run back for the information they should have had when they called. Some don't even know what we are making, although they could find out easily and then determine before they call how their products could be of use to us. Many seem to think we should drop everything and visit with them. They come in and light a cigarette, or even a cigar, and sit back as though they intend to spend the whole day.

"Fortunately, however, there are many salesmen who have more respect for a purchasing agent's time, who understand his problems and responsibilities, and seem sincerely interested in being helpful. They are the boys who get the lion's share of our business."

Jokingly I said, "Why, you haven't got anything to do all day long. Why don't you have a private bar built into your office and invite the salesmen who call to come in and have a drink with you?"

He laughed. "I would like that, with many of the men at least. But I will give you an idea of one day in the life of a purchasing agent and you will understand why we may seem impatient or even grouchy at times.

"We receive purchase requisitions from all departments. They all come to my desk and I distribute them to my four assistants.

Those purchase requisitions have to be processed. Salesmen must be called in or orders must be sent on to the suppliers.

"We have meetings with the plant superintendent, with the boys in the engineering department, and with various department heads. We may have a session with the controller.

"This morning I received a memorandum from the general manager, who wanted to know why we are paying 20 per cent more this year for one of the thousands of items we buy. I looked up our total purchases during the last year and found we had bought a total of $67 worth of that particular item. Yet, I have to answer the general manager's memorandum promptly. Perhaps I am answering it at the very moment my telephone rings and the reception desk tells me some strange salesman wants to see me. What sort of humor would you be in?

"We constantly are concerned with the movement of supplies we have ordered into our plants. Strikes in the factories of our suppliers or breakdowns in their machinery, transportation tie-ups, supplies received damaged in transit, claims for shortages or faulty material—all makes a purchasing agent's job a complicated one.

"Then we periodically have the problem of model changes which require new types of materials, new tools, new patterns.

"In our particular organization I have the problem of getting our people to order far enough ahead so we can maintain a constant flow of materials. Everyone is inventory conscious these days and the tendency is to order at the last minute and not enough. Consequently, we are tangling with the cost control department.

"Then there is pressure from the advertising and sales departments who need their promotion material overnight. To top it all, we have the irritating experience of having to see salesmen who don't even know their own products, who obviously have no understanding of the purchasing agent's job, and who evidently assume that every purchasing agent is going to be antagonistic. Their attitude often suggests that they think selling is merely a matter of matching wits with a prospective customer."

There you have a behind-the-scenes view of your purchasing agent customers.

The salesman who thinks of purchasing agents as cold and unfriendly simply does not understand the *Human* Side of Selling. Purchasing agents are human beings—men and women who have complicated and important jobs. They want to buy from you. They must buy from salesmen. And they need your help.

You can make purchasing agents your friends by respecting the importance of their work, by making it your business to learn all you can about their companies and their specific requirements, and then determine how you can be of the greatest possible service to them.

Look at yourself as a potential "partner" of every purchasing agent on whom you call. When you have learned everything you can about his company, so that you can be sure he will be interested in products of the type you are selling, then *plan your call* so that you will be prepared to show the purchasing agent specifically how his company can use your products and how you can best serve him.

Some salesmen seem to think that the purchasing agent's only interest is in buying at the lowest possible price. That is not so. The purchasing agent is interested in getting the best possible value, not necessarily the lowest price.

The purchasing agent is responsible for the buying of so many different types of supplies and equipment that he cannot be an expert in the selection of everything his company needs. He relies on the various department heads in his organization, his engineers and laboratories—and on the experienced salesmen who call on him.

As a salesman you should be an expert on the products or service you sell. If you are you can be of great help to your purchasing agent customers, especially if you are genuinely interested in helping them rather than in merely getting an order.

Some salesmen are afraid to "go over the head" of the purchasing agent when necessary to secure the interest or approval of the plant manager, department head, engineer, or other officials for their products. If you ever think of "going over the head" of a purchasing agent you can be sure that you have the wrong attitude toward that customer. Never ignore the purchasing agent. Of course, his influence does vary. In many companies he is one of the top officials;

in some he may simply issue the orders for materials selected by others. In any case, he is the purchasing agent for one reason—his company relies on him to represent the management in dealing with suppliers. Make him your friend—go through him, or with him, to other department heads in his company, and he will help you sell your product or service if he believes that it will be useful to his organization.

Purchasing agents are *human*—and they prefer to buy quality rather than price alone. Sometimes it is necessary for a salesman to help the purchasing agent sell quality to his management. William Wood, now president of the Heinn Company, helped many a purchasing agent sell the high quality and higher priced Heinn looseleaf binders to management when he was a salesman. He contacted every department head, and even members of the board of directors, where necessary, either personally or by mail. Consequently, he sold many unusually large orders for his top quality loose-leaf binders. The purchasing agents who bought these binders were proud of the fact that they purchased binders that gave many years of service and were a credit to their companies—not low in price, but high in value per dollar.

Purchasing agents appreciate good service, and they prefer to buy from the salesman who they know will personally follow orders through and see that his products are delivered according to specifications and on schedule.

The head of an industrial supply house told me that his salesmen had built up the largest business among industrial concerns in their community because they would rush delivery of equipment out to a plant in their own cars, if necessary. They have given purchasing agents their home phone numbers and any purchasing agent or maintenance man can call them in the middle of the night for some emergency supplies or vital piece of equipment, and they will gladly go out to their shop, pick up the needed item, and deliver it to the customer.

Those salesmen not only go all out in giving 24-hour service to their customers, but they know the great value of showing their appreciation for an order. When an order comes in by mail, invariably they phone the purchasing agent and thank him for it. They know the *Human* Side of Selling.

R. S. Wilson, vice-president in charge of sales of the Goodyear Tire & Rubber Company, recently made an interesting study of purchasing agents' opinions of salesmen. He had a postcard mailed to five hundred leading purchasing agents. The postcard asked this one question:

> Think specifically of the best salesmen representing any company who calls on you and tell us briefly why you consider him the best.

Mr. Wilson said:

That the purchasing agents were interested in the subject was evidenced from the fact that over 30% replied—a very satisfactory return. I purposely made the question broad so that the purchasing agents could use their own words.

It wasn't hard to classify the answers in broad categories, and here is this significant thing: Over 50% of the reasons given as to why the best salesman was "Best" centered on the man himself. Not knowledge of the product—not service—not entertainment—but the man.

Such adjectives abounded as "Dependable," "Sincere," "Honest," "Friendly," "Considerate," "Intelligent," "Loves-his-Job." To anyone who has lived selling for any period of time, these answers are no surprise. But as I leaf through these revealing replies, I wonder again at all the fol-de-rol that used to be taught on Salesmanship. Remember the catchphrases about "Creating the buying attitude," "Controlling the prospect's mind," and "Forcing action"?

Mr. Wilson's survey is further evidence of the fact that purchasing agents are *human* beings, and they prefer to do business with the salesman who understands the *Human* Side of Selling.

If you make it your business to learn all you can about each purchasing agent on whom you call, and his responsibilities, if you will show that you respect him and are genuinely interested in helping him—if you will go out of your way to be of service to him whenever you have the opportunity—and treat him as you would want to be treated if you were in his place—then you will find that there is no such thing as a "cold" purchasing agent. Those on whom you call will appreciate you—they will buy all you want to sell them—and many will become your warm friends. That is the *Human* Side of Selling.

CHAPTER 13

Why the Buyer of Advertising Is Never Tough When You Sell His Way

PERRY LABOUNTY, Advertising Director of one of the middle west's most progressive newspapers, *The Bloomington* (Illinois) *Pantagraph,* told me, "When I started to sell advertising I didn't know anything at all about selling. I had been a printer. Yet I sold eighty-five new advertisers in my first three years, some of whom had never bought newspaper advertising before. How did I do it? Well, as I had never sold anything in my life, I didn't know a thing about selling technique—about the best way to open an interview, ask for the order, and so on. So I decided to start out by asking myself how our newspaper could help my prospects increase their sales. Then I called on them and told them why advertising in the *Pantagraph* would be good for their businesses. Mine was a simple straightforward story, because I didn't know any better. Moreover, I told my story to clerks in each store, to the secretary and assistants of the big advertisers because I learned they are interested and could sell their employers better than I. Advertisers are human I found, and many who had never bought from the high pressure salesmen who had called on them bought advertising from me when they

How Was I to Know He Was Sensitive about his Media Selections?

saw that I was really interested in their primary interest—increasing their sales and profit."

An advertising salesman who does not understand Mr. LaBounty's humanness took his hair down one day and said, "Selling advertising certainly is a hard way to make a living. Why is it that advertisers and advertising agencies are so tough? Why are they so difficult to sell?"

That man had just come from a meeting with Howard Lampman, Executive Director of the Wheat Flour Institute. The next time I saw Howard Lampman I told him about the incident and asked whether he agreed that all advertisers are tough buyers. This was his reply:

Yes, and I'll tell you why. In my own case I am responsible for spending as much as a million dollars a year for various forms of advertising. While I rely on our agency for media recommendations, I do see publishers' representatives and many others who would like to sell us some form of advertising.

Of course, I am busy—have a full schedule every day. The fact that I am busy, however, does not make me tough. What burns me up is this: so many advertising salesmen who call on me evidently have made little or no specific preparation for the call. The lazy so-and-so's come into my office and take up my time talking in generalities about the thing they want to sell and they don't seem to care about our problems, our advertising objectives or the sales objectives of our organization.

Advertising salesmen ought to be the best salesmen in the world. After all, advertising itself is a form of selling. Of course, many advertising salesmen are tops. But others, believe it or not, come in to see me and can't talk about anything but circulation, the rate per page or per thousand copies, the latest survey of secondary readership which shows they are a better buy than competition—or if they are radio men, they talk about the time availabilities or programs they would like to sell.

So many of them aren't salesmen at all. They are like an advertising cafeteria. They spread out what they have to sell before you and want you to decide whether you can use it, how much and when and then give them an order. We advertising buyers are sometimes tough with that type of so-called salesmen. However, we are never tough with advertising salesmen who sell us the way we want to be sold.

You might ask how do we want to be sold? Any salesman could answer that question who will just put himself in the place of an advertising manager long enough to think about the advertising manager's job. In my own case this organization has certain policies which I must keep in mind when I buy advertising. Those policies have been in effect a long time and any salesman could learn them easily.

Of course I work closely with our advertising agency. A salesman can easily learn who the agency is and who in the agency is responsible for our account.

The advertising salesmen I am always glad to see are those who first learn what we are trying to do and then come in and show me how whatever they want to sell will help us accomplish our distribution and sales objectives. I am only human and I like the salesman who is interested in helping me rather than merely selling me something.

Yes, advertising executives, sales managers, and advertising agency men are human. They are always glad to see the salesman who is interested in helping them, who will go out of his way to be of service to them, and they are tough, or appear to be tough, only with the "advertising cafeteria" type of salesmen, the lazy salesmen, the "big shot" salesman, the "wondering" salesman, and the salesman who gets the order and then forgets all about the service he promised to give and doesn't.

What do I mean by "lazy" salesmen? An advertising agency space buyer called the representatives of 14 national magazines. He told each representative that the agency was making up an advertising schedule for a manufacturer of a product sold to business executives. He described the product, told how it is distributed and asked each man to make up a presentation of the reasons why his publication could help sell the advertiser's product.

Most of those men simply wrote a letter to that space buyer giving him information of a general nature and their own opinions about the merits of their publications. Some attached brochures or other literature which told a general story about their publications.

Only one of the fourteen thought enough about this prospective full-page advertiser to submit a thorough presentation of the specific reasons why his publication would be a profitable advertising medium for that particular manufacturer.

That advertising salesman documented his presentation with reports of market analyses, copies of testimonial letters from manufacturers of similar products, and other data. His publication was the first one selected of the four that were recommended. Some of the ten who were rejected may think that space buyer tough, hard to sell, whereas they might have missed a good-sized order by being too lazy to help the buyer make an intelligent selection of their publications.

Some publishers' representatives think it smart to by-pass space buyers in advertising agencies. One of them told an agency account executive, "I know that you decide what publications are going to be used. Your media department just places the order." The account executive assured him that was not so, but the "big-shot" salesman didn't believe him.

That publisher's representative did not know that the media manager, or space buyer, of that agency resented his condescending treatment so much that he would include his publication on a schedule only if he absolutely had to. The media buyer in an agency is human. He too likes to do business with the salesmen who respect him and show that they are genuinely interested in helping him do his important work well.

In many agencies the media buyer is one of the top executives and is constantly searching for more effective ways of selecting scientifically the right media for each advertiser's specific marketing objectives. The advertising salesmen who show that they are sincerely interested in giving the media buyer the greatest possible assistance in his media selection will always be welcome in the buyer's office.

Perry Shupert, vice-president of Miles Laboratories, Inc., told me the type of advertising salesman who irks him most is the "wondering" salesman. He said:

Occasionally, fellows come in here who are the wondering type of salesman. They wonder if we can use their product, they wonder how our business is and how many salesmen we have. In fact, they wonder around so long I never really know the purpose of their call.

To give you a more exact idea, a young fellow came in here not long ago who works for a wire manufacturing company down in the southern part of the state. He was a snappy looking individual, but his approach was that he was wondering if he could be of service to us in designing a display, which he more or less described by motions of his hands. He went to a great deal of explaining as to the type of drug stores he called on that would use the display and of his conversations with different druggists. He concluded by saying he had never seen anything like this display in the drug stores and wondered if we would be interested if his company could make it for us.

A funny thing happened, for on the opposite side of my office sat the very display he was describing and there are approximately 40,000 of them in use in the retail drugstores in the United States. I was amazed when he discovered the display and said, "That is what I am talking about. We could make that very display for you, only ours would be constructed differently."

He finally "wondered" out without really giving me much information about his company or the type of displays they furnish and he left me wondering if he really knew what he was talking about in the first place.

I realize this is an individual type, but the incident is fresh on my mind. I doubt very much if this individual will ever come back, because I think I discouraged him when I told him there are 40,000 of the displays he described in the drugstores and that he must not have looked very hard, for there are 18 of them being used in our local drug stores in Elkhart.

The top advertising and sales executives such as Perry Shupert, who directs advertising expenditures totaling many millions of dollars each year, are never tough with the salesman who has a carefully thought-out presentation and knows specifically how he can be of service. Mr. Shupert continued:

Here is the type of salesman I like to have call on me. First of all, I like for the salesman to call up, whether he is in the locality of our offices or out of town, and state his objective. After making his objective clear and finding out whether or not his idea is in line with our type of work, I like a salesman who sets a date and is prompt in keeping it. Then after he gets here he doesn't have to go into a song and dance about the train being late, or something to that effect.

Second, I like the fellow who opens his briefcase and starts telling me about the idea he mentioned on the phone and has some knowledge of the construction, the potentiality of the display, and changes that could be made, all accurately thought out before he arrives.

In the particular field of display advertising I also like a man who, after the idea is submitted and he finds it is not practical for our company, asks the simple question, "Are there any problems now existing in your work where our company can be of service in either designing or creating something to fit that need?" I say this because so many fellows who almost have something we can use become discouraged if they can't sell what they have brought with them.

In conclusion, I dislike to see a salesman, after he has completed his sales message, lean back in the chair and enjoy the air conditioning of our office for another half an hour with additional conversation about the weather, current news, etc. I like the fellow to fold up his tent and go on to the next customer.

I always say it isn't what he is selling, but how he is selling that makes a salesman a success.

"What" you are selling is the material side of selling. "How" you sell is the *Human* Side of Selling. The salesmen who are interested only in the material side of selling are the ones who find advertising buyers "tough."

When a Chicago advertising agency recommended a half-hour television program to a client, it selected a certain television station because the salesman had promised that a studio seating 100 people would be available for the show. The studio was large enough to seat 100 people. The salesman did not tell the agency, however, that another show was scheduled for the same studio shortly before and another immediately after the agency's show and consequently it would not be possible to have any audience in that studio. The sets for the other shows and the cameras, microphone booms, lighting equipment, and wire stretching across the floor made a studio audience impossible.

After the agency had signed the 13-week contract and the advertiser had invited dealers to the studio for the first television show, it was learned that the studio could not be used for the audience as the salesman had promised. The contract could have been canceled but the promotion plans for the show were too far along.

During the thirteen weeks the television show was on that station, the station's salesman never called on the agency nor on the advertiser—until renewal time. He did not get the renewal order. So he thought the agency and the advertiser certainly were "tough"—and they were. They told him bluntly that they were moving the show to another television station, and they told him why.

The salesman who represented the other television station kept in touch with the agency and the advertiser week after week. Although the show was televised from 9:00 to 9:30 each evening, he frequently was at the studio to help with the rehearsal and with the production of the show itself. When the advertiser had important distributors or dealers who wanted to see the show, the representative of that television station stayed in town to see that his customer's guests were shown every courtesy.

He can walk into that agency or into that advertiser's office any time and he is always welcome. The very same people who were "tough" with the first salesman are never tough with him.

The advertising manager of a large company told me that the publishers' representatives who get a full-year schedule of advertising from him, and never come back to see him until renewal time, irk him, because, he said, "I know there are various services they could be giving me. However they spend their time working on prospects and don't pay any attention to me, because they think they will get a renewal of their contract automatically. Some of them are going to be fooled. When I have a choice to make between two publications, the salesman who has been calling on me all year long and going out of his way to be of service to us is the man who is going to get the order."

Are advertising buyers influenced by the *Human* Side of Selling? Listen to Victor Fabian, for thirteen years advertising manager of the Palmolive Company and its successor Colgate, Palmolive Peet, and now media director of C. Wendel Muench & Company:

There was a *Saturday Evening Post* representative who was one of the most welcome salesmen who called on me. Why? Because he never came in without a merchandising idea, a report of some experiences he had had with our jobbers or retailers, or some promotion suggestion that might help me. He was always unobtrusive and gracious—never placed me under obligation to him. But he showed he was interested in me and in my company.

We had been using one column and page ads in the *Post,* not giving it much of our twelve million dollar advertising budget. One day, however, I phoned that *Post* representative and asked him to come to my office. When he arrived I told him I had heard that an automobile advertiser had not renewed his contract for thirteen center spreads in the *Post*. And I gave that man an order for those thirteen center spreads. He could hardly believe his ears—it was the largest order he had ever received.

It is a pleasure to help guys like that. If salesmen only realized that buyers of advertising are human, they would find it a great deal easier to get the orders they want.

Buyers of advertising are never tough when you sell them the way you yourself would want to be sold if you were the customer. The most successful advertising salesmen invariably are those who understand the *Human* Side of Selling.

CHAPTER 14

How to Impress and Sell the Management Customer

ONE of the most successful salesmen of heavy industrial equipment told me, "The higher up I go when I call on a prospect, the easier it is for me to see an executive. Often the top man in a company is the easiest one to see. Why? Because the boss, as a rule, is quite HUMAN—that's why he got to be the boss!" That is one man's opinion. Another salesman said, "I can't get in to see the top executives I have to sell. They're always too busy! Everyone is too busy—or their secretaries say they are in order to keep salesmen away."

The first salesman understands the *Human* Side of Selling. He has no trouble reaching the executives he wants to see. The second man, a paper salesman, knows his products well, but he makes a lot of fruitless calls for he evidently does not remember that the prospective management customers he wants to see are *human*.

Every executive is busy. If you find one who isn't busy you may

By the Way, J.K., Don't You Think You Ought to Make that Order Two Carloads Instead of One?

THE MANAGEMENT CUSTOMER 135

learn there is something wrong with his business. No matter how busy they may be, however, there are few men and women at management level who are not interested in hearing about products or services that might benefit their organizations.

A friend of the paper salesman asked him why he wanted to see one of the top executives of a well-known manufacturer. The salesman said, "I have been trying to sell the purchasing agent, but he tells me he is satisfied with his present source of supply. I can't get to first base with him. So I have worked out a plan which I believe will save that company at least 15 per cent of its production costs. I want to tell my story to the general manager, but I can't get to see him."

His friend asked, "How have you been going about it?"

The salesman said, "I have asked for an appointment. Each time I do, however, his secretary or his assistant asks me who I am and whom I represent. When I tell them I represent a paper company, they refer me to the purchasing department. Mr. Swanson, the general manager, they say, has nothing to do with the buying of paper."

The friend suggested that the salesman tell Mr. Swanson's secretary next time he called for an appointment that he wanted to talk to her boss about a plan which might cut the company's production costs 15 per cent. That might help her decide to get the salesman a date with Swanson.

The salesman agreed to try that approach. It did not work. The secretary told him again that she was sorry but he would have to see the purchasing department.

The salesman's friend was not discouraged. He suggested, "You must remember that secretaries are human too. When a salesman tells a secretary that he wants to see her boss, his attitude sometimes implies that he does not consider her at all important; his message is only for her employer—and will she please get off her lazy seat and announce him. Secretaries, and receptionists too, soon develop a subconscious antagonism toward some salesmen." That antagonism usually is the result of their experiences with salespeople who did not know or had no interest in the *Human* Side of Selling.

The friend asked the salesman to go back to that company and tell the general manager's secretary that he would like to get her advice. Because he realized that she could tell quickly whether her boss would be interested in knowing a simple way to cut the company's production costs, he would like to explain the whole proposition to her.

The salesman went in to see the secretary. He told her the complete story of his proposal, just as he would have told it to her boss. He did not talk down to her, nor did he appear condescending or insincere. He had reached the point where he was so full of the cost-cutting plan he had developed for that particular company that he had to tell it to someone. As he put it, he gave that secretary the "full treatment." When he had finished the story, she said quietly, "I am sure Mr. Swanson would be interested in talking with you." She looked through her appointment book and arranged a conference with her boss.

When the salesman walked into the general manager's office, Swanson greeted him with "My secretary tells me you have a very interesting proposal that could save us quite a bit of money."

Do you see what had happened? That general manager had been presold by his secretary.

In the beginning the salesman had made two mistakes which kept him from seeing the general manager. First, he had phoned for an appointment and had simply identified himself as a representative of a well-known paper house. As the prospective customer was a large user of paper, the secretary of the general manager knew that paper was bought by the purchasing department. Therefore, she referred him to that department.

Secondly, the salesman had treated the secretary as though she were merely an office intercommunication system which he expected to carry his name into the inner office.

When he was reminded that secretaries are *human,* too, and when he took the time to tell that secretary his whole proposition and asked her advice, then she decided her boss would want to see him and she made an appointment for him.

One of the most successful salesmen I know always learns the

THE MANAGEMENT CUSTOMER 137

name of his prospective customer's secretary—and calls her by name when he asks to see her boss. Later he writes the secretary a short note in which he thanks her for her courtesies. He has no trouble getting appointments anywhere.

That salesman is a master of the *Human* Side of Selling. His sales to big business total many millions of dollars annually. One of the key secrets of his great success is this: *Before he calls on an executive for the first time, he learns everything he possibly can about that man as a human being!*

He secures all the information he can about the man's education, his family, his hobbies, his friends, his clubs, his bank, his past business connections, his politics, his church, his likes and dislikes. When he calls on that prospective customer he knows him much better than do many of the prospect's own associates.

Quite often the personal information he gathers about the prospective customer discloses the fact that they have some mutual friends or business acquaintances. In that case he arranges to meet the important executive through a friend or acquaintance. You can see why he invariably is a welcome visitor to his prospective customers.

Remember that top management men are human. Consequently, they do appreciate the salespeople who are interested in them as human beings, not merely as "prospective customers."

They are busy. They have meetings scheduled all day with department heads, or with attorneys, bankers, government officials, and many other people. At the time you call they may be preparing a report for a board of directors' meeting, or may be in a meeting discussing a major change in company policy, or any one of a hundred other problems.

They like the salesman who knows his own products, but also makes it his business to know their companies, their position in the industry, their policies, and the products they sell.

They appreciate the salesman who does not merely tell them about the product or service he would like to sell, but shows how he can save money for them, increase their sales and profits, improve their employee relations, their customer relations, or their community relations.

One salesman who called on George Bell, vice-president of Burgess Vibrocrafters, Inc., took more than a half hour of Mr. Bell's time to talk about the product he wanted to sell. When he had finished his sales presentation, Mr. Bell asked him, "How do you think we could use your product?" The salesman replied, "I don't know. I thought if I told you about it you might find some place to use it." The interview was politely but firmly brought to an end. That salesman will not be able to sell many executives if he expects them to do his thinking for him.

Busy management men appreciate the salesman who comes prepared, who has his presentation organized so he can go through his complete sales story with little lost motion.

Executives admire salesmen, and prefer to do business with those, who are never guilty of the following seven sins against the *Human Side of Selling*:

(1) They do not like salesmen who do not phone themselves but have their stenographers call and try to make an appointment. The executive vice-president of a large manufacturer told me, "You'd be surprised how often some salesman's secretary calls and tells me she wants to make an appointment for her boss. I ask her why he doesn't call and she usually tells me that he is busy and she is making his appointments for him. I tell her that I happen to be busy, too. I never see those men. I never will."

Several executives have indicated that they are irritated by salesmen who have switchboard operators or stenographers put through phone calls for them and say, "Mr. Jones is calling you—just a minute please," and make the customer wait for the salesman. One sales manager, a busy man, hangs up. A number of other executives have all their calls come through their own secretaries to be sure that the caller is on the wire when they pick up the phone.

(2) Executives dislike salesmen who are late for appointments, or who say they want "just ten minutes" and stay for a half hour. Remember that the management customer's daily schedule is crowded and he has little regard for the salesman who does not respect his time.

(3) They don't like salesman who can't answer questions intelli-

gently. Tom Tanis and John Wentz of the Tanis Company, Management Counselors, spend many hours preparing for a call on a prospective management customer. They take turns putting themselves in the customer's place, anticipating all the questions he may ask. Consequently, they do not waste the executive's time. They have the answers ready.

(4) Management customers do not like salespeople who are not neatly dressed—or who are overdressed. Because they are human, they are influenced by a salesman's appearance. There's no reason why a salesman can't be clean and neat, no matter what he wears.

A salesman who knows the *Human* Side of Selling will always consider the type of customer on whom he is calling and will dress accordingly. For instance, he will not wear a loud "race track" suit when he calls on an ultraconservative prospect.

It certainly is worth while to know something about the clothes habits of your prospective customers. I put on a double-breasted sharkskin suit which had just come from the cleaner one morning before making my first call on a prospective customer, the president of a large New York Company. The suit had been pressed so beautifully that I probably looked like a clothing store dummy when I walked into that president's Park Avenue office. He had called one of his vice-presidents in for the meeting. They both had spent the weekend in the country and were relaxing comfortably in baggy tweeds. During our discussion their eyes occasionally would run up and down the carefully pressed edges of my suit as if they were running a mental finger along each edge to see if the crease was sharp enough to cut. Somehow they both were a bit cool and I did not get the order.

If I had learned in advance that they were the "tweed suit type" and had worn tweed myself that day, perhaps I still would not have been able to sell them. At least I would have been more "at home"—less a stranger to them. The dignified president of a large company told me, "I am always a bit suspicious of salesmen who overdress. Perhaps they give me an inferiority complex."

One Saturday morning I had come to the office in loafers, slacks, a tieless sports shirt, and a sport coat. Our office is closed on Saturday and I expected to spend a few hours writing reports. While I was sitting at my desk leisurely smoking a pipe, the telephone rang. To my surprise the caller was the president of a prospective customer, who said, "We are having a board of directors' meeting this morning, and I would like to have you come right over if you can and present your proposition to our directors."

What could I do? I didn't have time to go home and change into a business suit. I knew they were all dignified executives, and we were going to discuss a proposal that would involve more than a quarter of a million dollars. I hurried over to that meeting "as is."

It was one of the hottest days in August. The meeting room was not air conditioned. The directors sat around that room looking stern and uncomfortable. After I was introduced to each one of them, I decided that perhaps they would take off their coats and relax a bit in that hot room if I took off mine. So I asked the chairman of the board whether I might have his permission to take off my coat and roll up my sleeves before discussing our proposal. He said, "That's exactly what we need in this organization—more people who take off their coats and roll up their sleeves!" And he took off his coat, too. Before that meeting was over, I got the order.

When you call on top executives it doesn't matter what you wear so long as you are clean and neat. However, they will have more respect for you if your clothes are on the conservative side.

(5) Executives don't like salesmen who do not respect their subordinates. A printing salesman lost the hundred thousand dollars of business he had been getting each year from the advertising director of one company. When that advertising director delegated the buying of printing to an assistant, the salesman snubbed the assistant. The assistant would ask for quotations and he would give them condescendingly. He would tell the assistant, "Here are the quotations. Give them to your boss." Within a few months the assistant would have nothing to do with the salesman and the advertising director refused to interfere with his assistant.

Many salesmen find it necessary to "go over a buyer's head" to his boss. There is nothing wrong in that if you do not ignore the buyer.

Remember that buyers, assistants, secretaries, all are *human* beings. Unless you treat them with respect, they won't like you and their employer won't like you either.

(6) Executives have no use for salesmen who are insincere. A general manager told me that he would like to do business with a certain salesman because he is a fraternity brother, but he can't believe him. He knows the salesman exaggerates and he hasn't the time to find out just how many of the man's claims are true and how many are exaggerations. Executives must do business with people on whom they can rely.

(7) While executives are *human* and usually appreciate a good joke, the salesman must pick the right time to tell a story and the right type of story to tell. One salesman lost his chance of getting an order by telling an off-color story to the vice-president of a company who happened to be the deacon of his church and a very religious man.

Another salesman wonders why the general manager of a large company will not see him. He is always making wisecracks about the company's products in a belittling way. He thinks it is funny. The general manager does not.

Watch out for those seven sins against selling the management customer. Avoid them and you are sure to be more successful.

The industrial equipment salesman who found that the higher up he went the easier it was to see an executive said, "The boss is *human*, that's why he got to be the boss." Remember that fact and it will help you impress and sell the management customer.

One of the top executives in this country, K. S. Adams, president of Phillips Petroleum Company, has a selling formula which has enabled him to sell his ideas and his enthusiasm throughout his career. Listen to Mr. Adams:

> One of the important musts in making a sale is to put yourself in the customer's place, answer all the questions he will have in mind in a way that will make him know that you are interested in helping him get as much as possible for his money.

A salesman who evidently is more interested in making a sale than in his customer has two strikes against him. Even a salesman with a pleasing personality and an excellent knowledge of his products will lose many sales if he doesn't remember that he must have his customer's problems and interests foremost in his mind.

Find out what your customer wants to know, tell him, and, above all, make him know that you are on his side.

A. M. Hughes, vice-president of Phillips Petroleum Company, told me, "Those of us who have seen this plan of selling in action know that it works."

It's bound to work for you—it is the *Human* Side of Selling!

Learn everything you can about your management customer before you call on him. Study his business. Learn his policies, position in the industry, his sales objectives. Plan your call carefully. Then put yourself in his place and treat him the way you would want to be treated if your positions were reversed.

Show his secretary, his assistants, and his department heads that you respect them and they will all help you sell the boss.

When you understand and are guided by the *Human* Side of Selling you will show your management customer that "you have his problems and interests foremost in mind"—that you definitely "are on his side"—then you cannot miss. You are sure to impress the management customer favorably and sell him successfully.

CHAPTER 15

How to Find Prospective Customers

DO you remember the story about the man who had lost a horse? He asked himself where he would go if he were a horse, and he went there and found his horse. That story is not an infallible way

Now Where Would I Go if I Were a Horse?

to find a lost horse, but it does illustrate three steps that every salesman must take to find prospective customers.

Step number 1: You must *want* to find prospective customers.

Step number 2: You must *think* about the places prospective customers can be found.

Step number 3: You must *go* out and find them.

If you are a salesman in a grocery store, drugstore, or in any retail establishment where you sell over-the-counter merchandise, you may have no interest in finding prospective customers for your store. You may assume that your job is to sell the customers who come into your place of business—and of course you are right. Nevertheless, if you are interested in growing in value and importance to your employer you will want to help him increase his business, and one way to do that is to help him find prospective customers.

If you work in a retail establishment, how can you find prospective customers? You can tell your friends about your store. You can tell your neighbors about the store and about new services or merchandise which you think they might like. They will be glad to know about the friendly atmosphere and other advantages of coming into your store.

When you have made a sale to a regular customer who seems particularly pleased with her purchase, you may say, "If you think any of your friends would be interested in that item, tell them to come in and see me, I will appreciate the opportunity to be of service to them."

If you are an outside salesman for a retail establishment you will be given the names of prospects who came in for information about some product, or called to inquire about an advertised item. These prospects will not be enough for you if you want to reach your maximum success in selling.

How can you find additional prospects?

The most effective methods will depend on the products or services you sell, but generally you will find all the prospects you want (1) by making house-to-house calls; (2) by telephone solicitation; (3) by getting the names of prospects from old customers; and (4) by calling on people whom you may have crossed off your

FIND PROSPECTIVE CUSTOMERS

prospect list because they did not buy the last time you contacted them.

Many salesmen do not like to make house-to-house calls, sometimes described as "cold" calls. However, millions of dollars worth of merchandise is sold each year by salesmen or women who sell only by ringing doorbells and selling from one house to another down the street.

Your success in finding prospects by making house-to-house calls will depend almost entirely on your attitude. If you are convinced you can be of service to the prospective customer—if you ask yourself just before you ring that doorbell, "What can I do for this prospective customer to be of the greatest service to her?"—you will be more likely to get a friendly reception and find a prospective customer.

When you telephone a possible prospect to see whether you can interest him in the product or service you sell, put yourself in his place. Are you telephoning at the most convenient time? Or are you telephoning when your prospective customer is having lunch or taking a bath?

Remember that the person you are telephoning is human and is interested primarily in his own affairs, so don't start your conversation by talking about the things that interest you. Talk about the prospective customer's interests and why you believe you have something that will interest him.

If you were given his name by a neighbor or friend, be sure to mention that fact at the beginning of your telephone conversation, because it will help to establish a friendly atmosphere.

One of the most effective ways of finding new customers is to get the names of prospects from old customers who like you and are satisfied with your service. If you have sold a television set to a customer, don't hesitate to say, "I bet some of your neighbors and friends would like to have a set like that!" When the customer is enthusiastic about his own set and exclaims, "They certainly would!" that is the cue for you to suggest that he give you their names so that you can show them a similar set.

When you contact those prospects and tell them their friend or neighbor is so happy with the television set he bought from you that he suggested they might like to see a similar set, you usually will get a friendly, interested reception.

It is human for a salesman to become discouraged when prospects do not buy after a number of calls and decide that they never will. Conditions change, however, and people are changing continually. Go over those old prospect lists. Take out the names of people on whom you haven't called for months. Go see them. You may uncover a surprisingly large percentage of live prospects and make a nice profit on your earlier work in cultivating them.

If you sell for a wholesaler you know that your prospects generally include every retail establishment which stocks your type of merchandise. Your own prospects will include every retailer in your territory whom you do not already sell.

If you really are interested in increasing the number of accounts you sell you will analyze the retail outlets you do not sell. Perhaps you will have a card file with a card for each outlet which might be considered a prospect, either an immediate or a long-range prospect. You will know, of course, that you probably never will sell everyone. It will be important, therefore, to analyze each one to determine which you believe can be sold now or in the immediate future, and then concentrate on them.

If you sell for a manufacturer and have a section of the country assigned to you, your prospects may be wholesalers as well as retail outlets. When you decide that it is necessary to replace a wholesaler, or when you must appoint one where you don't have any wholesale outlets, you may find the best wholesaler in a number of ways. First, consult the advertising manager of the local newspaper and the local radio station and ask them to tell you which wholesalers have the qualities that you want. Then call on as many retailers as you can and ask them to recommend the wholesaler with whom they prefer to do business.

You probably will get a number of recommendations. By checking with dealers, newspapers, and radio stations you will be likely to find the best wholesalers for you, and you will appoint the one who will be most likely to produce the sales volume you want.

FIND PROSPECTIVE CUSTOMERS

If you sell to retailers you may find it profitable to discuss prospective retail outlets with local newspaper and radio station managers. They can tell you which ones are the best merchants.

If you sell insurance, prospecting—continually searching for new prospects—is one of the most important phases of your work. Don Markham, who in his third year as an insurance salesman topped the million-dollar annual mark, finds his prospects this way: "I see at least seven people every day—on a 7-day-a-week basis. Actually, these calls are limited to six days each week, so I see eight or nine each day. Of these calls, at least three every day are calls on new people, ones I have never called on before."

By calling on eight or nine people a day—at least three new people every day—Don has been finding enough prospective customers to enable him to become a great insurance salesman.

If you sell advertising you probably have been given a list of companies who might be prospects for your publication, or outdoor medium, or car cards, or your radio or television station. Do not assume that the list contains all your prospective customers. In fact, do not assume that the list of prospects given to you by your company is even up to date.

A large advertising agency each week is receiving mail from some of the largest publishers in the country, addressed to people who haven't been with the company for ten years, and in some cases even addressed to people who are dead. Obviously, these publishers and their sales representatives have not been keeping their prospect lists up to date.

A prospect list must never be a static thing. Keep your list of prospects alive. Keep adding to it by searching for companies or individuals who might someday be prospective customers.

Do not assume that a prospect is not worth cultivating further because he has said "No" to you a number of times. Before you decide that he is no longer a prospective customer turn him over to someone else in your organization and let him try a solicitation. Perhaps you have been going about selling him the wrong way.

If a company is a logical prospect, never give up and decide that he cannot be sold. Leonard Woods, of McIntyre, Simpson & Woods, publishers' representatives, had a prospect in Detroit on whom he had not called for five years. He would not even call him a prospect. Yet he kept the name on his prospect list.

One day when he was in Detroit Leonard Woods was caught in a storm. As the rain poured down he ducked into the doorway of an office building he happened to be passing and waited for the rain to stop. After five or ten minutes he decided that it would be raining for a long time, so he took out his cards to see whether he had any prospects in that building.

The only prospect in the building was the tough old advertising agency man who had never given him an order. He had not called on this man for five years. He decided that a call now probably would be a waste of time, but it would give him a good opportunity to practice his sales presentation and make some use of his time while waiting for the rain to stop.

As he sat in the reception room of this man's office, he remembered his earlier calls. The man was an expert in his field and he knew almost as much about the various business publications as Leonard Woods did. Nevertheless, Leonard said that he decided he was going to make that advertising agency man listen to his complete sales presentation, every bit of it.

When he was ushered into the executive's private office he took every exhibit out of his portfolio one by one, went over every feature of the publication, every advantage it had over competition, described every reason why it would produce a profitable return for this man's client. He talked on and on and when he had finished—when he had "given the man the works"—he said, "Well, that's it. What do you think about it?"

The agency executive asked Mr. Woods for the advertising rates of the publication. He studied them for a minute, and then said, "I will take six pages in color." He continued: "I have just been making up a schedule for this client and I have been wondering what to do in your field. I thought I knew all about the various publications which we might consider, but you have told me some things today which I have not known before, and I saw immediately that your publication is the one I should use."

Leonard Woods said he almost fainted—and he learned a lesson that he will never forget. Never again will he assume that a man is no longer a prospect just because he has never been able to sell him. Ever since that experience he asks himself, when he does not make a sale, "What have I missed? What haven't I done? What information haven't I given this man that would convince him that he should be a customer of my publication? Have I given him the works?"

Everyone who should be a prospective customer, of course, is not a prospect. A good salesman learns how to *qualify* a prospect by asking questions which, in the first place, show the prospect that you are genuinely interested in him and, secondly, gives you the information that you need to determine just how much of a prospect he is.

When Arthur Witzleben was manager of the wallpaper department of Gimbel Brothers in New York, he found that some of his salesmen were wasting a lot of time with people who came into the department. In some cases the people were not prospective buyers at all; they were just "looking around." In other cases they were prospects for a certain type of wallpaper, but the salespeople did not know what the prospect wanted and lost the business by showing samples of a type of wallpaper that was of no interest to the customer.

Mr. Witzleben taught his salespeople to qualify these prospects by asking three questions: (1) What rooms are you thinking of papering? (2) Approximately how much did you have in mind spending? (3) How soon do you need it?

If the prospective customer said she wanted to repaper her living room, in reply to the first question, the clerk would know generally what type of paper to show her. Obviously he would not show her bedroom wallpaper.

If she said that the paperhangers were already in her house and she needed the paper the same day, certainly the salesman would show her wallpaper that was in stock and could be delivered immediately, and not paper that might not be available for two or three days.

In any form of selling you must qualify your prospects just as the salespeople in the Gimbel wallpaper department did. You can determine, first, whether they are prospects and, second, what they are likely to buy.

When you have a qualified prospect, then you can determine the most effective way to sell them what they need, in terms of what they have indicated they want.

Remember that prospects are people—human beings—and they are all around you waiting to be found. You can find all the prospects you want—if, first of all, you *want* to find them and secondly, you *think* about *who* they are and *where* they are likely to be, and then go out and get them.

If you will organize your prospects, take at least as good care of your prospect lists as you do of your inventory of merchandise—if you never take prospects for granted but continually reexamine them and—if you *qualify* them so you know just what they are likely to buy and when—you will find that you have a live and growing group of prospects who continually are becoming customers—profitable customers—of yours.

CHAPTER 16

Never Let a Customer Forget You!

WHAT is a "customer"? Let's take another good long look at one.

We have seen that the customer is a human being, even as you and I are human. We know that the customer, regardless of his position, is a little person and, at least subconsciously, is aware of his

Just Stopped By to Ask Whether You're Completely Satisfied with Those Vitamins You've Been Buying for Your Husband

unimportance in the vast universe. We know he dislikes anyone who emphasizes his unimportance, and loves those who single him out as an important individual.

We have discussed the customer as the "man behind the dollar"—the man or woman whose purchases actually pay our salaries or commissions.

What change takes place in a man when he becomes a customer of yours? Why, he decides he wants to buy something from you, and he does buy from you.

Because he has bought from you once or more, we may assume that he is predisposed to buy from you again—if you treat him right.

The salesman who is interested only in the material side of selling—the commission or salary, the sale, the job, the product—often will forget about the customer as soon as he makes the sale. After all, he got the *things* he wanted from the customer and is no longer interested in him.

We are all self-centered to some extent at least. And many a salesman has his mind so full of his own problems that he hurries through his breakfast in the morning, and rushes out of the house without kissing his lovely wife. Then, on the way to work, he sees some pretty young woman with trim ankles and pleasantly contemplates her possibilities, even though she may never be a prospect.

That salesman treats his customers in much the same way. He neglects them, because he thinks they are "sold" and need no further cultivation. He forgets that every customer at one time was a prospect, just as his wife at one time was his sweetheart. With the proper attention, customers give you much more business (with less expense, less time and sales effort) than the best prospects. And any customer, like a lonely wife, can be lost by lack of attention.

The salesman who understands the *Human* Side of Selling will be more interested than ever in the man or woman who becomes his customer. He will be interested in the service he can give that customer, in doing everything he can to make that customer a friend.

John W. Mock, well-known sales consultant, emphasized the service opportunities in selling when he said, "And after the sale is made, what then? Service, of course. But there is something

NEVER LET A CUSTOMER FORGET YOU! 153

more: *continue to sell them after they're sold!* I mean good, old-fashioned, sincere, honest-to-goodness *appreciation* and thoughtfulness which holds your customers against all competition, and *makes them salesmen for you.* They tell their friends that doing business with you is a pleasant experience, and such selling is beyond price. Yet it costs only a few minutes of your time with an occasional hearty 'Thank you.'"

Tom Nolan, the Babe Ruth of men's clothing salesmen, the man who earns more in one year than most other retail clothing salesmen earn in five, never forgets a customer and never lets any customer forget him.

Tom Nolan has an individual card for each customer in his personal file in the Bond State Street Store in Chicago. On that card is a record of every suit the customer has bought, his preferences for color, material, style and price, his sizes, and information about his work and his home and family. When a customer comes in, Tom can ask him, "How did your family like that brown tweed suit you bought two months ago?" Do his customers like that? Wouldn't you?

And Tom Nolan keeps a ledger at home in which he writes the name of every customer and notes the date of his last purchase. If a customer has not returned to the store within a reasonable time, Tom calls him. Do they like that? Wouldn't you?

When a customer sends a friend to the Bond Store to see Tom Nolan about a suit, Tom writes the new customer's name on one side of that ledger and the name of the customer who recommended him on the other side. A week after the new customer walks out with his suit, Tom writes him a letter, thanking him for the opportunity to serve him and reiterating his assurance that he and the store want the customer to be completely happy with his purchase.

At the same time Tom sends a letter to the man who recommended the new customer and thanks him for sending the new man in. Do you think customers appreciate Tom Nolan's sincere gratitude and thoughtfulness in writing them? Wouldn't you?

Do Tom's customers like it? Well, they sent more than a thousand friends in to see Tom last year. And when Tom and Mrs. Nolan went over the customer ledger one evening they found that one well-satisfied customer had sent Tom more than a hundred new customers. Remember Tom Nolan—and you will always remember that it pays, and pays well, to never let a customer forget you, and never to forget a customer.

Because customers are little people it seems they are almost accustomed to being ignored, forgotten, even mistreated. When one salesperson shows them that he believes they are important by remembering to show his gratitude, by thanking them for sending friends to him, by writing or calling them, they will go out of their way to help him succeed.

How would you like to operate a comparatively small grocery store across the street from one of the largest supermarkets in town? The giant supermarket is part of a great national chain. It has the widest selection of groceries and meats and its prices usually are the lowest in the shopping area.

What could possibly make you successful in that midget store in the shadow of a goliath? You are right—the *Human* Side of Selling.

Ben Rubins, who owns that small grocery store, is genuinely interested in every customer who comes into his store. His interest makes him a friend. He knows the family, asks how the boy is doing in fifth grade, how the daughter likes boarding school. And he never forgets a customer!

When he learned that my mother had not been in his store because she was ill, he telephoned to ask, "And how is the momma today?"

Ben has never lost his thick accent, and he has never lost his love for his neighbors.

His prices may be much higher than those of his modern contemporary across the street and his assortment of grocery products may be limited, but the customer in Ben's store is never a mere statistic forgotten as soon as she walks out the door. Ben never forgets, and his customers keep coming back, happy to crowd into his store and wait for Ben or his friendly salespeople to say, "Hello there, Mrs. Moore, and how is the momma today?"

Whatever you sell—groceries, men's clothing, television sets, locomotives, sheet steel, cosmetics, or insurance—remember that you

NEVER LET A CUSTOMER FORGET YOU! 155

are not selling *things;* you are selling *people.* Yes, it is a *human* being who buys what you want to sell. And we human beings are forgotten so often, even by our family and friends, that we can't help becoming fond of those who do not forget us. The salesman who remembers us soon becomes our friend and we are happy to recommend him to everyone who might be interested in his services.

Don Markham, the friendly young man who sells insurance, becomes so interested in his insureds that he never forgets them and never lets them forget him. He subscribes to all the newspapers in the Chicago area and his stenographer goes through them every day looking for photographs of his customers or news stories about them. She cuts out anything she thinks one of Don's customers might like to see. Don sends the newspaper item to the customer with a short note. Do they appreciate his thoughtfulness? Wouldn't you?

When Jack Lacy, president of the Lacy Sales Institute, sold insurance he, too, topped a million dollars a year. How did he do it? He became so interested in his customers that they became his friends. And he never forgot them. After he had sold them all the insurance they needed and could buy, he still telephoned them or called on them from time to time to see how he could serve them.

He told of one occasion when he called on a doctor three or four weeks after he had sold him a large policy. The doctor said, "I'm glad you called. I told another doctor, a good friend of mine, about you and I promised him I would ask you to see him, but I've been so busy I've forgotten to call you."

That friendly call alone resulted in the sale of a large amount of insurance to the friend of Mr. Lacy's customer. It does indeed pay never to forget a customer, and never to let a customer forget you.

Gunnar Young has built one of the most successful florist businesses in the country. How? There are three other florists within two blocks of his place. But he gets most of the business, because he likes his customers—and never lets them forget him. He makes a note of birthdays, wedding anniversaries, and other special events and his customers receive an attractive bouquet or plant from

Gunnar Young on those occasions. Do they appreciate being remembered? Wouldn't you?

Charles Mitchell, Pacific Coast sales manager of Oscar Mayer & Company, writes a personal note to his customers from time to time. When he is in Phoenix, Ariz., and sees something that might interest a customer in San Francisco, he sends that customer a postcard or a short letter. Perhaps he finds a souvenir that would please a customer's wife or children. He sends it to them. Do his customers appreciate his thoughtfulness? Well, they give him carload orders and help him top the whole country in sales.

Some firms forget customers until they lose them. And if enough new customers keep coming in they do not care about the customers they lost. When sales volume starts to drop, however, someone asks, "What's happening? Why are the customers staying away?" And perhaps then a letter will be mailed asking the lost sheep why they haven't been in lately. Often such a letter is "too little and too late." The customer is lost—frozen out by poor service, chilled by being ignored, mistreated, forgotten.

I have received such a letter from an automobile dealer. Why haven't I come in for service lately? Never did I receive a letter from anyone connected with that dealer during the year I took my car in regularly. Never did I receive even a phone call from the salesman who sold me the car. I was just another "unit of sale," a number on the service department work schedule.

Suppose a Tom Nolan or a Don Markham had been the salesman I knew in that dealer's organization. Why, I would still be a happy, satisfied regular customer and I would be suggesting to many of my friends that they take their cars there to be serviced or go there to buy new cars. Instead of a cold, lost customer, that dealer would have an enthusiastic customer-salesman who would be delighted to sell for him without compensation because someone was interested in him and did not forget him.

John Walsh, midwestern sales manager of *Drug Topics,* never forgets a customer, even though the former customer is no longer in a position to give him an order. Why? Simply because his interest in his customers is genuine. Consequently, Johnny Walsh, as he is affectionately known throughout the country, has scores of men and women in the drug industry and in the advertising business boosting him wherever they can. Some may not be able to give him an order, but perhaps they influence others who can. An important reason why John Walsh sells far more advertising space than any of his competitors and has innumerable friends.

Harold Strobel, sales manager of LaCrosse Breweries, Inc., said, "I am more interested in a customer after I sell him than before, because then I have an opportunity to make him a friend by helping him make a darn good profit on our product. A salesman who forgets a customer after he sells him must be just a plain fool."

Doesn't that make sense? Yet some salesmen who sell wholesalers or retailers still think it smart to "load 'em and leave 'em." The salesman who understands the *Human* Side of Selling will never "leave" a wholesaler or retailer customer. He will consider himself a merchandising counselor who will help plan and execute the promotion activities that will sell his merchandise to the final user.

The biggest asset a salesman can have is a satisfied customer. You may think of your own assets as the money you have in the bank, your automobile, your home, your merchandise. But you can get all that, and more, from the profit your customers will bring you if you do not let them forget you.

Keep a record of your customers. Remember what interests them. Show them that you remember, even at times when you can't sell them anything—or especially at those times! Go out of your way to show your gratitude for favors. Two of the most profitable words in a salesman's vocabulary are "Thank you!" Appreciation is not a common art. Cultivate it.

If you sell to wholesalers or retailers, consider them as your partners in the sale of your merchandise. Never neglect an opportunity to show them you are constantly searching for ways to help them move your merchandise and earn more profit. Stop in to see them with helpful suggestions even when you know they are not ready to give you another order. Send them suggestions for improving any part of their business. When you remember to help them, they will never forget you.

No one is more important to your success as a salesman than your customers. Show them that you appreciate their importance by never forgetting them. Go all the way with your customers and they will go all the way with you—to make you an outstanding success on the *Human* Side of Selling.

CHAPTER 17

Your Customers Need You

MORE than three million people have read Dale Carnegie's magnificent book *How to Win Friends and Influence People*. It seems that every one everywhere is hungry for friendship.

You can be thankful that you are a salesman or saleswoman, for you need never be without friends. It is not an exaggeration to say that a salesman has more opportunites to win friends than anyone in any other profession or business.

Why do you have so many opportunities to win friends? Because you meet so many prospective customers and so many customers—and *your customers need you.*

Some salespeople, who spend most of their time selling behind the counter in a store, consider themselves and their saleswork unimportant. The customers walk up to the counter, ask for the merchandise they want, hand over their money, and leave. How can those customers *need* the salesperson who serves them?

Thank Goodness, a Salesman!

Of course, if the salesman or saleswoman behind the counter acts like a slot machine, the customer might as well buy in a self-service store or from an automatic vending machine. However, customers are *human* beings and they prefer to do business with *human* beings. They are gregarious; they need to be with people—friendly people. They need, sometimes desperately, the friendly smile, the word of recognition, the feeling of importance that you can give them when they come to your store to make their purchases.

The only salesperson behind a counter who will feel unimportant is the one who goes through the day with a mental mirror hanging before his eyes. He can't see across the counter—he can't see his customers as human beings and realize their need for friendly attention—because his mind is focused on that mirror and all he can ever see or think about is himself.

If you work in a retail establishment where customers are coming in all day long, please remember their need for you. You have a glorious opportunity to make them your friends, to give them a mental and spiritual lift by your attention, your recognition, your respect, your enthusiasm for serving them. Their life will be better because of you, and you will be happier because you have an opportunity to make so many friends and to serve them so well.

In *Man Alive* I discussed the many reasons why the profession of salesmanship is the greatest profession in the world. Why is it the greatest profession in the world? Because every one of us needs salesmen. We are all customers of some salesman and it is true that life as we know it today simply could not exist without salesmen.

To illustrate how vital salesmen are to every one of us, I drew this picture in *Man Alive* of the United States without salesmen:

Imagine what would happen in this country if overnight all the salesmen were liquidated and selling in any form forbidden! Tomorrow morning your bread and milk salesmen would not make their usual deliveries. Your grocery store would be closed, because there would be no sales clerks to serve you. Your gasoline station could not open because there would be no one to sell you gasoline. Department stores, specialty shops, and other stores would board up their windows. Retailers and jobbers everywhere would frantically cancel orders. Factories might store their products for a while, but soon bulging warehouses and complete lack of demand would force them to close and throw millions of people out of work.

Without salesmen our entire economy would come to a standstill. Food would rot on the farm while thousands of families starved. Overnight we would sink into the blackest depression you could picture in your worst nightmare.

Salesmen are vital to our complex modern civilization. And salesmen become more and more important to our way of life as we find new ways to market food (for instance, by quick-freezing and dehydration), as we develop new industries (television and synthetic rubber, for example), as we improve established products and services, discover new medicines (such as the sulfa drugs and penicillin), as we cross great new frontiers of modern science.

The miracle of splitting the tiny atom has opened new vistas of a more abundant life for all. We are on the threshold of the atomic age. Our salesmen and saleswomen will be the guides who lead us into the mighty promised land of atomic energy.

Yes, salesmen are essential to every family, to every business. Whether you sell atomic-powered airplanes or animal feed, *your customers need you.*

If you sell consumer goods, the customers need the merchandise you bring to them. If you sell products to retailers or wholesalers for resale, the customers need the opportunity to make a profit and build up their business that you bring them. If you sell industry or institutions, your customers need the savings and the improved service you can make possible.

Above all, your customers need *you!*

Regardless of the type of customer, he needs your interest in him. When he sees that you are genuinely interested in him, and want to help him in any way you can, he will respond by giving you all the business he can give you, and by giving you something even more valuable than his business—his friendship. When you have his friendship, when that friendship is based on your eagerness to be of service to him, he will become *your* customer and you will know that he will buy everything from you that he possibly can use.

For many years the Campbell Holton Company had received almost no business from the southern part of Illinois. After a new man was assigned to that territory, however, it became the largest volume producer of all.

What made the difference?

Is the new man a "supersalesman"? Yes, he is—in one important respect: he likes people and is constantly looking for ways to be of greater service to the people who are his customers.

When he goes into a grocery store he greets every one of the salespeople in the store by name. Although he seldom spends more than twenty minutes in any store, he has a friendly word for every employee. Instinctively he recognizes the *human* need for attention, recognition and friendliness and he fills that need whenever he walks into a customer's place of business.

There is nothing too much that he can do for a customer. One day the owner of a large grocery store told him that he had a lot of bills to pay and he hated the task of making out a check for every one of the invoices stacked on his desk. The salesman offered to sit down at the desk and write all the checks for him. Ever since that day the grocer has been saving his invoices until the salesman calls.

When he comes into that store he walks right back to the desk, sits down, goes through the invoices, and writes all the checks. Once when he came in, the salesman of a competitive wholesale grocer was at the counter, talking to the proprietor of the store. As usual, he walked right back to the desk where the stacked invoices were waiting for him. As he passed, the proprietor waved to him and said, "I'll be back with you in a few minutes." By the time he had finished writing the checks the grocer was standing at his side with an order.

He told him that the other salesman had been wasting his time for more than a half hour talking about the weather, politics, and trying to sell some of the products of his wholesale house. He gave that other salesman an order for only three items, specialties which the Campbell Holton Company does not sell. He gave the check-writing salesman an order for forty-four different items. And, including the time he took to write the grocer's checks, that man was in the store less than twenty-five minutes.

Does it pay to understand that your customers need you—to look for additional ways that you can be of service to them—and then go all out to provide the service that your customers need? It paid for that Campbell Holton Company salesman. He took a territory that was barren of orders and turned it into the richest section of his company's entire system.

If you sell to wholesalers, your customers need the sales volume and the net profit that you can bring them. They need a salesman who understands them and who is sincere in his determination to help the wholesaler make a profit.

The salesman whose only interest is in selling to the wholesaler is a sad creature. He thinks that selling his product is the wholesaler's job. It is, of course. Nevertheless, the salesman who sells the wholesaler should know more about his products than his customer possibly can and, consequently, should consider himself a merchandising counselor of the wholesaler.

Campbell Holton spoke of some salesmen who go through the motion of appearing to be interested in helping the wholesaler move the merchandise he purchases. He said. "They come into our Saturday morning meetings and talk about their products in an unenthusiastic way, as if they are doing it because they have to. It would be better if they had stayed at home."

Mr. Holton, now past his 80th birthday and recognized as one of the deans of the wholesale grocery business, then made a remark about the *Human* Side of Selling which reveals great insight into the deep need the customer has for the salesman. He said, "It is not enough to give the customer the service that he needs; you must *want* to serve him and your wanting to serve him must be a warm, friendly, enthusiastic desire. You can't fool the customer by just going through the motions. He knows. He can sense your real interest in him."

Does it pay to recognize the fact that your wholesale customers need you? I know other salesmen whose customers have so much confidence in them that they check the wholesaler's inventory when they call and write their own orders.

Put yourself in the wholesaler's place. Wouldn't you be delighted with the salesmen who had your interest so much at heart that they would do everything possible to see that the merchandise they sold you turned over rapidly and made you a respectable net profit? Of course, you would! You would *need* salesmen of that type and you would buy all of their products you could possibly sell.

Harold Baum, promotion manager of Superior Sleeprite Company, said:

Perhaps the most vital picture for a salesman to form is what his customer needs and what the salesman can give him. Obviously the customer needs more than just the product the salesman wishes to sell.

Take bond paper, for instance. Each of five salesmen may have a different brand. All of the brands may be closely comparable in quality and price. All may be available for immediate delivery. Yet, I must choose one brand—or one salesman, which amounts to the same thing.

It is apparent that the salesman is part of the value that I can get as a customer. What part of that value is the salesman?

Mr. Baum's reply to that question indicates the customer's *need* for a salesman which is above and beyond his need for the product the salesman sells. Mr. Baum explained:

The salesman's presence makes goods conveniently available; that, rather than the wish to get an order, should be the justification for calling on his prospect.

His intelligence helps the customer select the right goods, because the salesman can see and analyze uses and adaptations to the needs of the customer. Some times he can honestly show the prospective customer that he can sensibly do without one or more of the salesman's commodities. If the salesman exercises his intelligence and ingenuity with integrity when he calls on a prospect, he will do more than merely get an order—he will build a customer instead.

The salesman's value to his customer may include authoritative facts about delivery, shipping routes and assistance in expediting rush deliveries when needed. It may encompass datings on bills, advantageous alternatives of packing, or economies in utilization. It may embrace engineering advice, laboratory tests, work analysis, and sales promotion assistance.

If a radiant love for his fellow man is included with all that service for his customer, you have a salesman to whom the customer prefers to give his business. When five salesmen call, all selling essentially the same product, one of those salesmen will recognize the customer's need for so much that he can give personally, that the combination of his product and himself will be such an outstanding value that the customer will have no choice but to give him the order.

An unhappy young wife went to see a psychiatrist. She was convinced that her marriage was a failure and there no longer was any reason for her to live. Friends had advised psychiatric treatment.

After hours of soul-searching psychoanalysis, this unhappy wife suddenly turned to the learned psychiatrist and said, "Doctor, do you know what I want more than anything else in the world, what every woman wants—it is to be needed."

She said she had a feeling that her husband didn't need her; her friends didn't need her; her family didn't need her. What purpose did she have in life? Why should she go on living?

The psychiatrist talked to her husband, to members of her family, and found, as he knew he would, that they needed her very much. They needed her affection, her companionship, her interest in them. When the psychiatrist convinced her of their great need for her, she went away happy.

Why did that young wife think she was not needed? The psychiatrist put it this way: "She had been turning her thinking inward instead of reaching out with her mind and her heart to those around her. When I told her 'Your husband needs you' and convinced her that he does, you should have seen the look of peace and happiness that came over her face!"

Many a salesman who is unhappy in his work may be somewhat like that young wife. His thoughts may be turned inward too often. He may be thinking of the order *he* wants; the commissions that *he* will earn; the hours that *he* will work; the increase in salary that *he* hopes to get; the products that *he* hopes to sell.

With his thoughts turned inward he is uncomfortable with the prospective customer, or at least indifferent; sometimes subconsciously belligerent. He may have the feeling that he wants to take something away from the customer and instinctively feels that the customer will resent it.

Salesmen who are suffering from "ingrown" thinking probably could benefit by a visit to the psychiatrist, just as that young housewife did. The psychiatrist would recommend that they turn their thinking outward—to a healthy interest in the customer. He would assure the salesman that his customers *need* him, and when the salesman finds himself thinking of the customer's need for him and of the many ways that he can serve the customer and contribute to the customer's happiness and well-being, he will be an entirely different person.

His self-respect will mount. He will start his day thankful for another whole day full of opportunities to serve the customers who need him.

When you understand the *Human* Side of Selling, you know that *your customers need you.* Your customers no longer are vague figures across the counter who hand you money which you transfer to the cash register. They no longer are merely names which you hope to have on the dotted line. You become interested in them as fellow human beings. You reach out to them; you are friendly, you want to serve them—and they become your friends!

There is no profession or business in the world where you will have more opportunities to make friends than you have as a salesman. The doors to your customers' homes and their places of business will be wide open to you when they see that you are genuinely interested in them as human beings and sincerely anxious to serve them in any way you can.

Far beyond the income that you can make as a salesman—and your income virtually is unlimited—is your magnificent opportunity to make countless friends and be one of the most popular and most loved and needed men or women in the world.

PART III

Salesmen Are Human, Too— What To Do About It

CHAPTER 18

How a Salesman Is "Born"

YOU will find that the star salesmen continually are studying themselves, as well as their customers. They know they are human beings, and they are going to make mistakes of some sort all their lives. The unsuccessful salesman goes on making the same blunders day after day. The star analyzes himself, improves his selling methods, continues to grow in his understanding of his own human qualities, which have so much influence on the *Human* Side of Selling.

You have heard many times that some man or woman is a "born salesman." That expression seems to imply that the individual described has an irresistible personality which enables him to sell without much effort. There are people who believe that salesmen are "born"; they think you must be a "born salesman" or you can't be taught to sell.

Others contend that salesmen are made—by education and training—not "born."

Guess He's Going To Be a Salesman When He Grows Up

HOW A SALESMAN IS "BORN"

It is my belief that every one of us is born with the instincts that can make us successful salesmen. In other words, we all are "born salesmen." But something, many things in fact, happen to us as we grow up that dull or suppress our natural selling instincts, and keep them from developing.

Here are the reasons why you and I, why all human beings, are "born salesmen" . . .

Human beings are naturally gregarious. We are born with the herd instinct. We want to be with people. We want them to like us. We want to get along with them.

We have no inherent prejudices against any race, creed, or color. We like everyone, until our elders put blinders on our minds and hobbles on our gregarious feet.

Your instinctive desire to be with people, to be liked by them, to get along with them, if developed naturally, would make you one of the best liked salesmen, one who knew and profited by the *Human Side of Selling*.

We come into a strange world with a lively curiosity about it and the people in it. You have heard children repeatedly ask their parents, "Why, mommy? Why is the grass green? Why is the sky blue?" or, "Who is that man, daddy? Does he have a little boy, too?" And innumerable other questions.

Developed naturally, that childhood curiosity about everything around you, and every person you meet, would be one of the most valuable assets you could have as a salesman. You would learn everything you possibly could about the products you sell and how they benefit customers. You would know your company, its policies and principles, your boss and his objectives. And you would be constantly studying your customers and finding ways to be of greater service to them.

You are born with a healthy ego. You want to stand out, to be recognized. If developed without hindrance, that instinctive desire to be above the average would make you work harder, study harder, try harder to please your customers, and would help you become a star salesman.

You are born with certain needs which make up the strongest

instinct in your life—the desire to survive. That simple desire expands to include financial security, a comfortable home, clothes, food, and many other needs. Those needs, those desires of yours, if not satiated or dulled, would keep you sizzling with ambition, driven by determination to be a successful salesman.

Every one of us, you might say, is a "born salesman." But, what happens to us?

As we grow up we have much of the mental and spiritual life pounded out of us by the bigoted, militant mediocrity of our elders, who themselves are the victims of the generation that preceded them.

We learn that we are not supposed to like certain people. We learn that we should associate with "our own kind." That frustrates our natural gregariousness. Instead of reaching out to people with the warm trusting "I-like-you-won't-you-take-me-in-your-arms" smile of a child, we draw back, don't want to have anything to do with people we don't know. We are faintly hostile, or at least indifferent, until the other fellow proves he wants to be friendly.

We are told repeatedly, "Don't ask so many foolish questions!" Many of us, in fact, never are told why the grass is green or the sky is blue. Our parents or older relatives probably were not told when they asked those same questions. Their natural curiosity became dulled and they never did find out. As so many of our eager childhood questions draw impatient rebukes or evasive replies, we gradually ask fewer and fewer, and our bright-eyed curiosity fades into stereotyped complacency.

You remember what happened to your inherent ego. Unless yours was an unusual family, you were told not to "show off." In too many cases family life seems to be designed to make children feel they are not important. I once saw a mother slap her boy (he must have been about five) on the street before several of his playmates and cry, "I'll teach you to come when I call you."

And I saw another boy, perhaps three, who ran into the house one evening to show his father something he had just made. He was bubbling with pride. He had made something himself. What happened? His mother said, "Don't disturb your father while he is reading his paper!"

HOW A SALESMAN IS "BORN" 171

And the father, looking up from the sports page for a moment, said, "Yes, son, you just run along and play. Daddy's tired tonight."

They might as well have said, "You're not important, little man. Don't bother us, please!"

Those unfortunately are not isolated cases. They indicate the "conditioning" given our inborn egos in the process of making us comfortably mediocre men and women who will think and act pretty much as everyone else does.

Of course, our instincts are part of us. They never die entirely. We can revive them, just as we learn to walk again after a broken leg or an operation has kept us off our feet so long we forget how to walk.

If every one of us is born with the instincts that would make a successful salesman, then certainly anyone who wants to be a salesman can learn to sell successfully. As a matter of fact you may learn to sell successfully, and after many years forget everything you learned—as many salespeople do during war years and the shortage years immediately after the war. But even if you forget how to sell you can relearn, if you really want to.

General Electric invested a half million dollars in an elaborate theatrical production called *The Birth of a Salesman* in order to teach thirty thousand G.E. dealers and their salespeople how to sell electric appliances. An important part of the performance was the "rebirth" of a dealer who had forgotten how to sell during the World War II postwar rush.

It had been so easy. He didn't have to sell. Customers begged for refrigerators, washing machines, and other G.E. products. When the hard-selling days came back, he soon became discouraged, seemed defeated—until his "rebirth" as a salesman.

How was he "reborn"? His wife and his G.E. distributor reminded him how before the war he really had been interested in *people*—in helping them enjoy all the labor and timesaving advantages of G.E. products. Since the postwar buying rush had ended, his only interest had been in "business," and in thinking and talking about how bad it was.

When he stopped thinking about "business" and began to think once more about *people* (and the G.E. appliances they needed and should have) his whole attitude changed. He no longer was a defeated man. He told his wife, "I remember how I followed the ice wagon down the street and sold electric refrigerators. Now I'm going to follow the laundry truck and find the people who need our new automatic washers."

That dealer was reborn as a salesman when he began to think and talk about *people* and their needs—when he came back to the *Human* Side of Selling.

If you're an "old-timer," discouraged by the return of competitive selling, remember salesmen are "born" and can be "reborn."

Yes, every one of us is born with the instincts—the natural inclinations—that can make us star salesmen. Bring those natural inclinations of yours back to life! Particularly, keep your natural gregariousness vigorously alive. You were born with the desire to be with *people,* to be liked by them and to like them. Get back that childlike faith in people, that eager, friendly interest in them, and you will be a star—on the *Human* Side of Selling.

CHAPTER 19

He Knows His Stuff—Everyone Respects Him

A THIN, intense young man got a job selling lithography in New York City in one of the bitterly competitive years of our major depression. There were too many lithographers, too many salesmen, not enough business. Price cutting, expensive gifts, offers of lavish

He's Worn that Cap and Gown Outfit Ever Since He Finished that Sales Training Course

entertainment had made buyers completely sophisticated. It was a tough situation for a young salesman who represented one of the lesser firms, with no price or product advantages.

What did he do? Joe Leigh found that most salesmen knew little about lithography. They were pleasant-mannered "contact men." They could contact a prospect, learn what he wanted to buy, and bring the specifications back to their shops. Then they would get quotations and sketches if necessary and take them back to the prospect and try to sell him.

That was not enough for Joe Leigh. He learned everything he possibly could about the lithographing business. He studied every type of lithographed display being produced. He investigated new processes, found ingenious die-cutting and construction possibilities. Before long he knew so much more about the business than most competitors that he was welcomed and respected wherever he went.

He did not stop when he had acquired an unusually thorough knowledge of his own product. He studied the sales and advertising programs of his prospective customers and showed them how he could develop lithographed displays that would help them increase their sales.

Joe Leigh got the big lithographed display orders—and at his own price. Moreover, because he knew how to use this sales promotion medium so effectively, his customers found it profitable to pay him more, because they got a bigger return in increased sales.

Joe moved up rapidly in his company as he sold rings around most competitors. It wasn't many years before he was elected president. Today Joe—Mr. N. J. Leigh—is chairman of the board of Einson Freeman Company, Inc., which has grown under his direction to be one of the leaders in the industry.

The experience of Joe Leigh is a splendid example of the American way of life. There is nothing so vital to our American Free Enterprise System as salesmanship—and nowhere are there so many opportunities for advancement as there are in the profession of salesmanship.

The salesman is "free" to make his own future as big as he wants it to be. And the salesman who knows the meaning of the word

HE KNOWS HIS STUFF

"enterprise" will be enterprising enough to learn everything he can about (1) the products or service he sells, (2) his customers and their needs, and (3) how his products or services can benefit his customers.

How can a customer respect a salesman who hasn't enough respect for himself to become acquainted with the products he sells? Yet the head of the purchasing department of a large manufacturer told me that most salesmen who call on him and his buyers are not even good order takers. They know so little about their products they have to take his specifications and go back to their factories for quotations and confirmations. Not much different from the army of lithographing salesmen who were scrambling for the meager business when Joe Leigh decided to step out of the chorus and become a star!

Yes, knowing your products can go a long way toward making you a star salesman. That same purchasing department head gives a large volume of business to one salesman. Why? In his own words, "He knows his stuff. He knows what we need and sees that we get it." The same salesman happens to sell the products his firm produces to virtually every company in that industry. He is respected and admired everywhere he goes. No door is closed to him. Purchasing agents, production executives, sales managers, presidents—all are glad to see him. Why? He has made himself an authority on his type of product and the industry he sells.

You may say you sell in a retail store and knowing the products you sell can't be so important. People come in and buy what they want. And besides, what has product knowledge to do with the *Human* Side of Selling?

Knowing the products you sell—and how they benefit the customer—is important to your success in any selling job. And that knowledge is important because it has a definite effect on the *Human* Side of Selling.

I walked into a drugstore to buy a tube of shaving cream. As I waited at the counter, I saw a display of hairbrushes next to the cash register with a sign advertising "Sensational Value—Nylon bristles, plastic brushes, only 98¢." I asked the salesclerk who wrapped up my tube of shaving cream, "What was the regular price of these brushes?"

He said, "I don't know. I think it was about a dollar and a quarter." And he gave me my change and started to walk away.

The brushes were well designed. I picked up one and as I looked it over I noticed a copy of a newspaper advertisement describing the brushes taped to the cash register. The headline was: "Sensational Value—Formerly $2.50, now only 98¢."

That sales clerk was not interested enough in the merchandise his store was featuring to read the advertisement. He was little more than a human slot machine. I asked for a tube of shaving cream, put my money "in the slot" and got the shaving cream. That was all. No interest in serving me, in selling me more. By his indifference in his merchandise and his customer he lost a sale—and a customer.

By contrast, another drugstore salesman—and he deserves to be called a "salesman"—knows so much about the products he sells that he tells me and my family about them in detail—and we're glad to see him and listen to him—and our purchases in his store of everything from razor blades to exotic bath salts represent a substantial amount.

The first drugstore salesclerk's attitude suggests that he isn't interested in his customers enough to know what he is selling. And consequently few customers will be interested in him. Actually he is a "sales scarecrow" who drives customers away.

The second man's attitude is one of keen interest in everything he sells—and in the needs or interests of his customers. When he receives something new which he thinks one of us might like, he tells us about it and demonstrates it if he can. We are *human*. We appreciate his interest and respect his knowledge—and we *buy*.

Richard Stone, leading authority on successful restaurant operation, once asked a hundred and fifty waiters and waitresses if they knew why "corned beef" was called "corned beef." Not one of them knew.

He asked them about other foods they served. They had never thought much about them. And then he made a statement which went to the core of the *Human* Side of Selling. He said, "If you want your customers to respect you, you must first respect yourself and your work. And if you respect your work, you will study it and know what you are serving and why. Try it, and watch how you go up in the estimation of your customers, and yourself!"

A farmer was brought into a sales meeting to tell the salesmen how to sell farmers. He said, "before you can sell a farmer, you must take enough interest in his needs to learn something about them, so you can tell him how the products you sell can help him. As a rule he is too busy to listen to a lot of generalities and figure out what it all might mean to him in the operation of his particular farm."

For many years the Chrysler Corporation has sent out to its thousands of dealers a series of sound slide films showing dealers' salesmen why Chrysler products give the car owner all the style, comfort, and performance he wants. Every month dealers receive new films and hold meetings with their salesmen to be sure they know the automobiles they sell.

The training films, produced by former automobile salesmen of Ross Roy, Inc., Detroit, show the Chrysler dealer salesmen how to present their cars to prospective customers in terms of customer benefits instead of product features alone. More and more customer-conscious organizations are increasing the efficiency of their salespeople with continuing sales training programs.

If you want your customers to respect you, make it your business to know as much about the products or service you sell as any other salesmen in your field. Learn how the things you sell benefit the customer. Learn everything you can about the customer himself, his needs, his preferences, his ambitions. Become an authority in your selling job. Your confidence in yourself will increase with your knowledge. With confidence will come more pride in your work, in yourself, in the service you are able to give your customers.

Keep your inborn curiosity about everything around you, about the people you meet, vigorously alive. You will feel more alive yourself. And you will be welcomed by customers everywhere, because they respect you as a salesman who really is interested in serving them the way they want to be served, and knows how to do it.

CHAPTER 20

An Honest Joe—He Gets Our Business

ONE of the most valuable assets a salesman can have, probably *the* most valuable asset, is a reputation for absolute honesty—unvarying integrity—complete reliability.

Nate Schaeffer had that reputation to such an extent that he could walk into the furniture stores of customers in his Ohio territory, look over their stock, and write his own orders. The dealers signed—because they knew that Schaeffer would never oversell them or sell them a single piece of furniture they could not move in a reasonable time at a good profit. Moreover, they knew that Nate would see that the order was delivered when promised, even if he had to take a train to the factory in Chicago and personally see that the furniture was shipped.

When a competitor tried to sell one of Nate's dealers, he shook his head and said, "We buy from Schaeffer. He's an honest Joe—he gets our business."

A reputation for personal integrity pays big dividends in selling. When a customer knows he can trust you absolutely, his sales resistance drops at once. Unfortunately, many salespeople seem to think it necessary to exaggerate. Some misrepresent. Others make mistakes through ignorance or neglect in handling a customer's order, and don't tell him, hoping he will not notice the error. Some will sell merchandise a customer can't use, or sell too much. To them, the order is the important thing, not customer satisfaction and good will.

Salespeople of that type make prospective buyers wary. In the buyers' minds is the warning "Let the buyer beware." It keeps flash-

That Used Camel Salesman Told Me It Was Just Like New—
Had Been Driven Carefully by a Rich Suburban Family

ing a red danger signal—until you turn it off by showing evidence of your sincerity and honesty. It pays to be completely honest with your customers. For instance, don't pretend to know more than you do. If you need the help of a customer, ask for it. When he sees that you are sincere he will be glad to give you a helping hand.

A young man in his first job, with a corn products company, was told to go out and sell crude corn oil. He didn't know anything at all about the product. But he was a straightforward young fellow and he was honest enough to ask questions. His first question was, "Who buys this crude oil?" His boss told him that soap manufacturers use it in making soap.

He looked up the names of soap makers and decided to call on the National Soap Company in Detroit. At the National plant he was shown to the office of a Mr. Kramer. After exchanging greetings, the honest young salesman said, "Here's a letter from my company about our product. Frankly I don't know a darn thing about crude corn oil. If you decide to buy it, you will have to tell me why."

Mr. Kramer read the letter and then silently studied his caller. He soon was convinced the young man was sincere for he arose from his desk and said, "Come with me." He took the eager salesman on a tour through the soap plant and pointed out how crude corn oil was being used, in competition with other oils.

Back in his own office he said, "That's why I buy crude corn oil. Now ship me a few barrels of your product."

As the enthusiastic salesman wrote his first order, his mind raced ahead of his fingers. He thought, "I've made one sale. Now what do I do about the next one? He looked up from his order book and asked his customer, "Mr. Kramer, would you mind calling some executive in some other soap company and telling him the advantage of using crude corn oil?"

That young salesman found his customer responded to his honest and straightforward approach. He didn't mind calling other soap companies and helping Clarence Francis off to a fast start on a momentous career.

AN HONEST JOE

That young salesman was Clarence Francis, now Board Chairman of General Foods Corporation. Mr. Francis learned when he made his first sale that customers are indeed human. They respond warmly to a salesman who shows by his honesty and sincerity that he respects them.

Mr. Francis still proudly considers himself a salesman. In the opinion of all who know him, he typifies the *human* side of American business.

You can profit by the example of Clarence Francis and other stars in the selling profession who invariably find that being a square shooter and earning a reputation as an honest Joe is a powerful aid to success.

Never under any circumstances lie to a customer. Once you do you might as well fold your tent like the Arabs and silently steal away. You're through with that customer. He will never believe you again.

Never promise a delivery you know your firm can't make. That is lying, but some salesmen do it when they think it necessary to get an order. Of course, it is possible to promise a delivery you honestly believe can be made, and find out later that circumstances beyond your control make the promised delivery impossible. Notify the customer as soon as you can. He may resent the delay, but he will respect you for telling him about it in advance.

Delivery dates too often are taken lightly. I heard a salesman say, "Sure, we promised to have it there Friday, but they won't mind if we don't get it there until Monday or Tuesday."

I asked him if he had told the customer that the work was delayed. He said, "No, it won't make any difference." It is making a difference. That customer told me, "We can't rely on him any more. We're giving him less and less of our business."

Chicago is one of the most competitive drug wholesale markets in the United States. Yet, with some of the biggest wholesalers in the country there, one small independent jobber has built a multi-million-dollar business. He sells the same supplies, the same nationally advertised products sold by other wholesalers, yet many hundreds of druggists prefer to buy from him. Why?

The retail druggists who do business with him know that when he makes a promise it will be kept, regardless of cost or inconvenience.

One of his truck drivers came into the office one afternoon about four and reported that a druggist in Joliet had complained that a dozen tubes of tooth paste he had ordered for delivery that day had not been delivered. Without hesitation, he told the driver, "Get the dozen tubes out of the stock room and drive right back to Joliet with them."

The driver protested, "But that's sixty-five miles each way! Why drive that far just to deliver a dozen tubes of tooth paste? The cost of gas—" That was as far as he got. The jobber said, "When we make a promise to a customer we keep it, regardless of cost. That's one reason why we keep our customers."

Put yourself in the place of your customers. Can they rely on you? Can they believe you, or do they think everything you say is "subject to keystone"?

In the jewelry trade, prices are quoted to dealers at list, less "keystone," which is 50 per cent. There is one jewelry salesman who has such a reputation for exaggeration and carelessness with the truth that his customers say, "Everything he tells you is subject to keystone, keystone, and keystone!" That reputation doesn't help him sell. He is low man on the totem pole of sales volume in his company.

A clothing store salesman assured a customer that his suit was a perfect fit." The customer wore it home. His wife looked it over and said, "Why, dear, it's all wrinkled across the shoulders!"

That clothing salesman lied to his customer, probably because he didn't want to be bothered with an additional alteration. He had made the sale and he couldn't make any money on alterations. Well, he lost that customer. He had made the customer feel like a fool before his wife and he said he would never go back to that store.

The manager of one of the largest chains of clothing stores in the country told me, "One of our major problems with our salespeople is getting them interested in satisfying the customer with a real fit. They want to make the sale and get rid of the customer as soon as possible. The most successful salespeople are those who are interested in making customers instead of merely making sales."

Someone has said, "It's only human for a salesman to be interested in the sale instead of the customer. After all, his salary or commissions depend on his sales."

That is not true. It is not human to be interested in the sale and not the customer. In the first place, it is another example of "man's inhumanity to man" and, in the second place, it is bad judgment.

The customer is the *man behind the dollar*. Without the customer there would be no sale. Furthermore, the customer is the source of additional sales. So, satisfying the customer is not only good ethics, it is good basic business judgment.

You lay a sound foundation for customer satisfaction when you demonstrate your honesty, your trustworthiness. Moreover, you show the customer that you have his interest at heart.

You will have a distinct advantage over many other salespeople when you show your customers they can trust you under any circumstances. As the clothing store executive said, there are not enough salespeople who are interested in the customer, or are concerned with the customer's opinion of them.

You are human, of course, and you will make mistakes. Admit them before the customer calls your attention to them, and tell him you're sorry. When a customer complained to a printing salesman that the wrong color had been used on a circular, the salesman said, "I thought that was the color you wanted." He must have known that was a lie; the customer despised him for it; and he had to print the whole job over.

Another printing salesman brought a window streamer in to that same customer and said, "We ran the wrong color by mistake and will be glad to print the job over. We're sorry for the delay." The customer accepted it, and respected that salesman for his honesty.

Honesty does pay, particularly in selling. It is human to want people around us whom we can trust. There are not too many. See that your customers trust you in every respect, and they will want to do business with you. That is a basic principle of the *Human Side of Selling*.

Honesty pays, too, in a salesman's attitude toward his company. Many a man or woman who wouldn't think of taking one penny out of the boss's cash register will loaf during the day, and leave early whenever possible. They know it's wrong. It is stealing time, and that is dishonest.

Charles Fredrick pulled himself up from a driver-salesman on a delivery truck to vice-president and sales manager of his company by giving his employer more time, more hard work, than was demanded. His personal slogan was "Go that last undemanded mile!"

In sales meetings he would tell his men, "When it's four, or four-thirty in the afternoon, and you know there are a few more calls you should make, but you're tired—besides those stops are a mile out of town and it may be late when you get back to town, don't hesitate—go that last undemanded mile!"

The salesmen who followed that advice moved up rapidly. They became district sales managers. Some now own their own businesses. Charlie's slogan will work wonders for you. Try it.

Joseph H. Makler, president of Waterfill and Frazier Distillery Company, Bardstown, Ky., was an Army flier in World War I. Since that war he has been a highly successful salesman, noted for his integrity. He told me that he was thinking about this book one evening recently while he was lying awake in bed, and he remembered John McCrae's famous poem "In Flanders Fields." Do you remember this stanza:

> If ye break faith with us who die,
> We shall not sleep, though poppies grow
> In Flanders fields.

And Mr. Makler thought of the great importance of honesty and integrity to a salesman's success, to his self-respect, and to his happiness, and this wonderful message to salespeople ran through his mind:

> *If you break faith with us who live,*
> *You shall not rest, though grass will grow*
> *Beneath your feet.*

The greatest value to you as a salesman of complete honesty in your relations with your customers and your boss is this: You will *know* that you have their respect—and that knowledge will give you a feeling of confidence that will be a tremendous asset on the *Human* Side of Selling.

CHAPTER 21

He's So Darn Enthusiastic—It Must Be Good

FRED SCHNEIDER is membership director of the American Management Association. He knows thousands of the country's top executives. He told me, "As I meet more and more of the men who are leaders of American Industry I am impressed by the fact that there is one characteristic most successful people have in common. It is *enthusiasm*—contagious enthusiasm which makes you believe in them and their products."

Yes, Mr. Schneider, enthusiasm, contagious enthusiasm, is one of the qualities you invariably will find in successful people, and particularly in star salesmen. It is the jet propulsion that shoots a salesman rapidly to the top.

I walked into the office of a buyer of a large department store as an enthusiastic salesman was leaving. He was leaving with a big, confident smile and I heard him say, "Thanks again for that order. I do appreciate it, and I'm sure you will find that promotion I suggested a profitable one."

The buyer, an old friend of mine, turned to me and said, "There goes a real salesman, my kind of salesman. I have inventory problems and am in no buying mood. When he came in I automatically

Never Saw Such Enthusiasm—Sold Me the Tractor, Sold My Daughter ... Now I Wonder!

started to say 'No!' I didn't want to buy anything. But he didn't talk to me about buying at all. He told me he wanted to show me just two things—a new item he is introducing and the promotion other stores such as ours are using to move a surprisingly large volume. He aroused my curiosity. I didn't want to buy anything, especially any new, untried items, but I did want to know what other stores are doing and, of course, I do not want to miss any hot promotion opportunities. So I looked and listened.

"The merchandise looked all right. The price and discounts were satisfactory. Ordinarily I would have bought a few dozen and tried them in the department. You may believe it or not, though, that young chap was so darn enthusiastic about his product and about the success of other stores, I decided it must be good—and I bought five gross. I guess I caught some of his excitement. Anyway, I'm scheduling a series of ads and I think I can move at least as many as some of the other stores, and maybe more."

He caught some of the "excitement" of the salesman. That's what contagious enthusiasm does to your customer. It reaches beyond the power of reason. It arouses. It activates. It inspires confidence. It breaks down barriers. It gets results.

After a discussion of the selling power of enthusiasm at a sales meeting, one salesman complained, "Everyone can't be enthusiastic. It isn't something you can turn on and off like a faucet. Besides, I think it is corny! Today, buyers want the facts about your product and they want them quick. They are busy and they haven't time for a lot of conversation. You have to present your proposition in a hurry and you get an order or a turndown and get out. It's rough going, believe me!"

That man was right about a number of things. Enthusiasm certainly is not something you can "turn on and off like a faucet." Some sales counselors have advised salesmen to "act enthusiastic and soon you will begin to feel enthusiastic." I have tried it and it will not work for me. Perhaps I'm not a good actor. In any event, enthusiasm that is faked, or forced, is likely to be one-sided. *You* might begin to feel it. But your customer will remain as cold as ice.

You have to fire your enthusiasm with deep personal belief, you have to be thoroughly "sold" yourself, before you have the evangelical enthusiasm that is so contagious.

The complaining salesman said he thought enthusiasm is "corny." Well, these are sophisticated days, and so many alive, *human* qualities are now described by certain people as "corny." In some circles it is considered fashionable to be bored. Too many salesmen seem to have been bitten by the bugs of boredom and sophistication. Don't let them get you! They can ruin a good salesman.

The young man who called enthusiasm "corny" is no longer with the company at whose sales meeting he made the above statements. He has changed selling jobs three or four times in a year. He is smartly tailored, a handsome person about thirty. He has a college education. He "looks" like a salesman, but he hasn't the heart of a salesman.

When his sales manager called on some of the dealers in his area to learn why Bill wasn't making any sales, he found that Bill had made every call he reported. But he had made them too quickly. Evidently he would go into a store, introduce himself to the dealer, look around at the crowded store and say, "Guess you have enough of our line in stock. If you need any more, let me know. Here are some folders. You might put them on the counter where customers can pick them up." And away he would go. Occasionally a dealer would give him an order, but he was by far the low man in the entire sales organization.

Jack Bauer, the top salesman in that company, is quite a contrast to Bill. He is two hundred and eighty pounds of active, healthy enthusiasm. If he ever went to college, I'll bet he sold the school a new stadium. He is that kind of salesman. All selling heart and mind!

Bill couldn't earn three thousand dollars a year as a salesman. Jack earns more than thirty thousand a year selling the same products—washing and ironing machines.

At one sales meeting Jack was asked to show the boys how he sold such a large volume each year. He took off his coat, rolled up his sleeves, and said, "Gentlemen, I sell as much as I do because I believe in these products, and when I go into a store I take off my coat, roll up my sleeves, just as I have now, and I show that dealer why our washers and ironers are the best buys on the market today."

Then Jack walked over to an ironer—and sat on the open end of the ironer roll, all two hundred and eighty pounds of him. He said, "Sure I sit on the end of the ironer roll when I demonstrate the ironer. Believe me, when they see my weight on the end of that roll they accept my word that this is one ironer that is built to take punishment and give years of trouble-free service."

The superiority of those products is almost a religion to Jack Bauer. He knows every nut and bolt in them. He can and does demonstrate them everywhere he goes. He inspires so much confidence that dealers become enthusiastic. They buy and buy—and sell with confidence to their customers.

To Bill, that sort of enthusiasm was corny. He would never think of taking off his coat and bouncing up and down on an ironer roll to show his confidence in it. But that corny enthusiasm of Jack Bauer has bought him a new Cadillac every year and has made him independently wealthy. Who is right?

One of the most remarkable phenomena of present-day selling is the negative attitude of some salespeople. They call on a prospective customer believing that he is not going to buy. When customers come into their store, they half expect them to look around and walk out. It is amazing!

Walter Patrick McCarthy, one of the most enthusiastic salesmen I know, battles negative thinking wherever he finds it, and he finds it in too many places. When he was division sales manager for Oscar Mayer & Company, he sold Oscar Mayer Wieners. Who could become enthusiastic over a wiener? Few salesmen did. But Walter McCarthy was not an ordinary salesperson. He learned why his product was so good and went up and down the country like Billy Sunday preaching the gospel.

Woe to you if you were one of his brokers and thought you were selling just a plain yellow-banded frankfurter!

Walter told me he would call on a wholesaler, or a chain-store buying office, with one of his men, and he would be told on the way, "We're just wasting out time. They won't buy. They always turn me down." McCarthy would say, "We'll see why they won't buy. They can't know how good our products are, and how they can sell them in substantial volume, or they would buy. But we are not going to call on this man with the conviction that he will not buy. We are going in there with the belief that he will buy, if we can convey some of our knowledge and enthusiasm to him." And, more often than not, the prospective customer did buy.

Walter McCarthy soon increased the sales in his area to more than a million dollars a year and was always one of the top men in the entire sales organization.

He could make you believe that Oscar Mayer Wieners had personality, and I guess they did. He not only sold his customers, he sold his own family and friends. He wasn't fooling. He believed in those wieners. Don't laugh. I did, too. We served no other kind in our house. His enthusiasm was respected everywhere.

In fact, his brokers respect him so much they recommended him for a bigger position with another company. Today, Walter McCarthy is one of the principal sales representatives of Arcady Farms Milling Company. And he is just as evangelically enthusiastic about Arcady Farm products. Again he sells his friends as well as his customers. That is truly a characteristic of a star salesman—to be so enthusiastic that you sell everyone you can reach.

Joseph Kolodny, managing director of the National Association of Tobacco Distributors, Inc., is one of the most successful and best liked men in the entire tobacco industry. He is the head of his own distributing company and the dynamo of the national association. Everyone who comes in contact with Joe Kolodny gets a mental and spiritual lift. Why? His secretary, Gloria Piatek, who knows him as well as any one of his associates, said, "Of course he is a brilliant, hard-working, persevering individual who sets high standards for all of us to follow. But I think it is his overwhelming *Enthusiasm* (with a capital 'E') that makes the sale in everything he does. Mr. Kolodny has to be sold on something himself before he will attempt to influence those around him. When he is, he becomes enthusiastic about it, and it is that contagious, confident enthusiasm that wins everyone he meets."

One of Joe Kolodny's favorite expressions is: "People are people! Other people are just like you. Basically, they look like you; they act like you; they react like you! They are quick to sense your feelings . . . even if you hide behind a mask, the tone of your voice is pretty good evidence of your real feelings."

Enthusiasm, "contagious, confident enthusiasm," is one of the greatest selling forces a salesman can have. Why are there so few enthusiastic salespeople? What makes salesmen negative, or sophisticated, about their jobs? Possibly they take them too much for granted. Just as we take electricity and other conveniences for granted, perhaps. It might be a good idea to stand off at a distance and look at our jobs, at the product or service we sell, as though we were seeing it for the first time.

On one of the network radio programs I heard an interview of a guest who was a Mississippi farm woman. The announcer asked, "How are you feeling today?"

She said, "Oh, I'm very, very happy!"

And he asked, "What makes you especially happy, Mrs. Brown?"

Mrs. Brown told him. "You see, we've just got electricity on our farm, and it is the most wonderful thing in the world. Why, we bought all sorts of appliances, a vacuum cleaner, refrigerator, washer, and so on. And I could hardly wait to plug them all in and see them work in my own home. You should have seen us last night!"

The announcer asked, "What did you do last night?"

That Mississippi farmer's wife said, "Our electricity was turned on just after sundown. We ran from room to room and switched on all the lights. Then we plugged in all the electric appliances and ran them. What a thrill that was! Then we all went outside and stood there and just looked at our house. It was all lit up like a Christmas tree—oh, it was wonderful!"

Maybe we should go "outside" our jobs, ourselves, and look at all the lighted windows. Perhaps we would be almost as enthusiastic as that farmer's wife.

A confident, enthusiastic salesman who knows his products thoroughly and knows how they will benefit his customers will get a warm, interested reception everywhere. He will be respected by his associates and his customers. When his enthusiasm is based on a sincere conviction that he can help his customers, can be of genuine service to them, he will be close to the pinnacle of the *Human* Side of Selling. And that is the sure way to success in the selling profession.

CHAPTER 22

He Wears Red Neckties and Gets the Green Light

IF you know your products thoroughly, know how they benefit customers, if you are completely honest and are genuinely interested in serving the customer to the best of your ability, it would seem that your personal appearance and mannerisms should not affect your ability to sell successfully. But they do.

If you were a slot machine, merely offering some *thing* to a customer in exchange for his *money,* appearance and mannerisms would not have much effect on the sales you make. Yet, these days even mechanical salesmen are designed attractively in order to get the favorable attention of customers.

You are not a slot machine, however; you are *human.* And because you are *human,* your appearance and mannerisms affect your attitude toward yourself and toward your job.

Because your customers are *human,* your appearance and mannerisms affect their liking for you and therefore their willingness to buy from you.

Walk over to a mirror right now. How do you look? Not bad, eh? Suppose you were a prospective customer and the person you see

A Celebrity? Yes! He's a Star Salesman!

in the mirror were face to face with you and was trying to interest you in buying from him. How would you be impressed?

How you look when you stand in front of your mirror at the start of a day can determine your success all day long. Do you look gloomy or cheerful, downcast or confidently optimistic? Your appearance can sabotage your selling efforts or can make them a sparkling success. It is amazing, but true. And here is a remarkable true story which illustrates the change appearance can make in a salesman's success:

While flying from New York to Chicago I sat next to a man who was wearing a bright red tie and a light-gray suit. We introduced ourselves and I learned that he was the sales manager of a refrigerator company. When he found I had written *Man Alive* (the guidebook to successful salesmanship) he called my attention to his red tie. He said, "I have been wearing red neckties ever since I attended a convention in Toledo and heard Cy Burg, president of the Iron Fireman Manufacturing Co., tell the convention audience how red neckties have turned many salesmen from discouragement and failure to enthusiastic success. I decided right then to try wearing a red necktie—and, believe me, it works!"

Thousands of salesmen have been wearing red ties since they heard the power of a cheerful red necktie. The story Mr. C. T. Burg tells illustrates the effect appearance can have on your own attitude toward yourself and your job, and your customers' warmth or coldness toward you.

Mr. Burg said:

One gloomy gray morning a caller was announced at my office, and through the door came one of the sorriest looking salesmen I have ever seen. His approach was apologetic, and the most striking thing about him was his clothing—a somber dark suit, a dark hat that had seen better days, black shoes, and to top it all off, a *black* necktie.

Even before he had a chance to open his mouth I began to feel gloomy, and then he said, "I sell the Blank Super-8 automobile—would you be interested in buying a car, Mr. Burg?"

Of course I wasn't interested—I didn't want to buy a car or anything else from that fellow, even though at the time I had been wondering if it wasn't about time for me to invest in one of the new models being advertised and displayed.

I told him that my present car was giving good service. He acted as though that was exactly the answer he expected, and then can you imagine what he said? "How's business?"

"It's good," I replied. "We are having a fine gain in sales over last year."

His face took on an incredulous expression, and he said, "Really? You're the first man who has told me that in six months!" This ornament to the selling profession left shortly, and as I turned back to my work I started thinking to myself:

"Suppose that same salesman had come in radiating optimism and progress? Suppose, even though it *was* a dark morning, that instead of that sad getup, he had worn a good-looking gray suit and hat—and a cheerful red necktie.

"A red necktie," I mused, "why, isn't that the perfect symbol of cheer, optimism and enthusiasm, and why shouldn't we make it just that throughout our entire sales organization of several thousand men?"

We decided we had a real idea, and a few weeks later I "sprung" it at our national convention of dealers and their salesman. That was the start of the red-necktie tradition in our organization—just a symbol, I'll grant, but a powerful one when you get an entire organization recognizing it and using it—getting their chins up, and sticking their chests out behind that red tie.

In spite of all the charts, graphs, and statistics that economists use to explain the ups and downs of business, isn't it true that, basically, good business is founded on optimism and confidence?

If the buying public has confidence and is optimistic, won't this feeling cause them to buy, thus making factory wheels hum and cash registers jingle, and by their very attitude create the prosperity that everyone wants?

And isn't the professional salesman the proper man and the *ideal* man to spread, everywhere, the gospel of optimism and cheerfulness?

Not only will this attitude increase his own sales, and thus his own earnings, but it will create more work for the men and women who make the goods and create the services he sells—they in turn becoming themselves better customers for other salesmen.

That's why we tell our salesmen:

"Don't hang black crepe, or wear it, either! The last thing before you slip into your coat in the morning, tie a cheerful red necktie under your collar, get your chin off your shirt bosom, stick your chest out, and with a smile on your face go out and show your prospective customers how you can serve them."

As the refrigerator company sales manager who told me about Cy Burg's red necktie said, "It works!" Wearing red ties and light-gray suits has made a difference in his own selling success and it can in yours. Try it tomorrow, and see.

Your tie doesn't have to be all red, of course, but it should be bright and cheerful, preferably with red as the principal color. Your suit doesn't have to be light gray, but it should be a light shade—at least not dark, somber, gloomy.

You may be in a selling job where you are required to wear a uniform, as you do when you sell in a gasoline service station, when you're a dairy, bakery, or soft-drink driver-salesman. It isn't possible to wear red ties and light-gray suits in every selling job. But, keep the red-tie and light-gray suit idea in mind, and keep your appearance cheerful. Make yourself look like the confident, cheerful person you would be glad to see if you were the customer.

One successful salesman I know buys a new suit or a new hat when he is down in the dumps or when he plans to call on a particularly big and tough prospective customer. He claims the new suit or new hat gives his morale a boost, sends him into the prospect's office with a confidence and an assurance he otherwise might not have.

One salesman has his suit pressed and his shoes shined whenever he feels a gloomy spell coming on. Another buys a new tie, puts it on right in the store, and throws the old one away. He says the new tie gives him a fresh new outlook on life. These men are human, and so are you. Brighten your appearance in some way when you're feeling low and give yourself a confident lift.

A woman salesman buys a daring new hat when she feels low. She selects a bright, gay hat, and her spirits rise at once. She calls on her prospective customers with buoyant confidence in herself, and she gets the orders.

It doesn't seem necessary to discuss personal cleanliness. Many millions of dollars of soap advertising year after year has been selling the advantages of keeping clean. Nevertheless, the buyer of a large organization said, "When a salesman comes close to me to tell me about his products, or to demonstrate some feature—it is good to know that he has taken a bath recently. If he is neat and clean, I very likely will not notice, but if he is careless in his personal habits I will know that he may be careless in taking care of the business I might give him."

Of course, a breath that carries an odor of stale tobacco, of beer, garlic, or an upset stomach, will handicap even the best salesman. The salesman who understands the *Human* Side of Selling always thinks of his customer and consequently never takes chances on offending by unpleasant breath.

The tone of our voice can affect the impression we make on our customers. It is part of our "appearance," part of the *human* factors that affect the customer's regard for us. Ask your family and close friends to tell you frankly how your voice sounds to them. If it is shrill, high pitched, colorless, do something to improve it. Take voice lessons. Join a public-speaking class.

Breathing with your diaphragm will help you deepen your voice, make it richer, more vibrant. Try it. Put your hand on your diaphragm and practice inhaling and exhaling every morning and evening, and during the day whenever you can. You will soon notice the improvement in your voice.

What bad speech habits have you acquired?

Some salesmen talk so rapidly that customers find it difficult to understand them. Others slur over their words, run them together. I heard one prospective customer ask a salesman several times to repeat something he had said, but still he raced on, his enunciation so careless that he had little force or conviction in his words. He did not get the order.

E. F. Lukens, vice-president of *Farm Implement News,* said:

There are two things in personal selling that I believe deserve emphasis. One is proper enunciation and proper tone of voice so that the listener or one who is being sold does not have to strain to hear or understand at the expense of what is being said. I have noticed these faults in individuals in our organization—in individuals who otherwise, have the essentials of being successful salesmen.

Another thing that I believe deserves emphasis is expression by the use of one's head, hands and posture. A nod of the head or shake of the head and the use of hands to denote emphasis, disparagement or compliment adds to the effectiveness of what is being said and helps to maintain the attention and interest of the person we hope to sell.

In a class in public speaking an instructor gave a simple rhymed admonition which helped us a great deal. It was: "Speak clearly, or do not speak at all. Carve every word before you let it fall."

Say that aloud a number of times a day. Say it slowly. Enunciate every word as though you indeed were carving it, and you will begin to speak more clearly and distinctly. When you do, you will see your words impressing your customers more forcefully. You will receive more attention, and more respectful attention.

Unconsciously we develop speech habits which may become disturbing interruptions to the clear delivery of ideas from our minds (via the words we speak) to the minds of our customers. I have made a few notes of verbal idiosyncrasies of some of the salesmen I have seen in action. One interjected, "Do you see what I mean?" every few minutes in a way which indicated that it was a nervous speech habit, not at all a question, for he never stopped for an answer.

Another starts with "I don't mind telling you" and proceeds to tell you. But he injects an "I don't mind telling you" into his conversation at least once every two or three minutes, until you become aware of it and it detracts from the things he is telling you.

Another salesman uses "and one thing led to another" as a speech crutch. He doesn't realize it, but he is having one thing lead to another all through his sales presentation.

An exasperating habit of one salesman is the use of "and so forth" in the middle of a statement which he leaves hanging unfinished. The "and so forth" evidently is used to cover up disorderly thinking, much as some careless housekeepers are said to sweep dust under rugs when they don't want to bother with the vacuum cleaner.

A buyer told me, "Many salesmen make the mistake of saying 'Okay' instead of 'Thank you.' This comes from the general overuse of 'okay' which is an indication of carelessness." That buyer suggested that salesmen cultivate the habit of saying "Thank you!" sincerely when they leave a buyer's office.

Check your own speech habits. Ask your family and friends whether you unconsciously are using some expression over and over until it becomes a speech defect that identifies you just as would a wart on your nose. Once you find it, you can correct it easily.

What odd mannerisms have you acquired? Arthur H. ("Red") Motley, president of *Parade,* the Sunday picture magazine, learned that he had been talking out of the side of his mouth for a long time and didn't know it.

Red Motley said:

One night at a bar when another salesman and I got mellow enough to be frank and earnest with each other he said to me, "Motley, you went to college, didn't you? You've got a Phi Beta Kappa key, haven't you?" And I said, "Sure, why?" "Well," he said, "Why do you go to such great lengths to try and make people believe you're a tough guy with no education?" I said, "No such thing!" and he said, "You certainly do. Look at the way you talk out of the corner of your mouth!" I said, "You mean like this...?" and he said, "Yes, I mean like that!"

When I woke up next morning I remembered that conversation. I bumped into a good friend of mine that day and asked him, "Do I really talk out of the corner of my mouth?" He replied, "You certainly do and I've always wondered why! Have you ever thought how you look to the man on the other side of the desk?" Much to the amusement of my family, I started practicing my pitch before a mirror.

I thought I had discovered a great principle of sales training until I told that story to a friend of mine, a sales manager in Chicago. "Why, Red," he said, "that's old stuff. I have thirty-two men on the road and every year, for a six-week period, we have what we call the Mirror Contest. I ask each of my salesmen to practice his pitch in front of a mirror twice a week. It doesn't make any difference whether it's the worst salesman or the best, they all show increases during that period. Just remember this, if a man can keep on the track with his own funny-looking puss staring back at him out of a mirror, no stony-faced prospect in the world can put the chill on him."

Common sense. Since then I've never ceased to be amazed at the number of fascinating things salesmen do when they call on me. They put their eyebrows, their ears, and everything else into the sale to the point that I don't even hear what they're saying.

When Red Motley and other star salesmen unconsciously develop odd mannerisms, you know it can happen to you and to me. Let's keep practicing before our mirrors and catch those oddities before they become too much a habit with us.

A Hollywood movie star appeared on one of the major television programs for the first time. He had been before movie cameras for years. He should not have been nervous. Yet he kept pulling his nose all through the television show. On the movie set, those nose-pulling incidents could be eliminated from the film in the cutting room. Every pull of that proud nose before the television cameras, however, registered on the television screens in a million homes. Are you a nose puller?

A salesman who is tall, dark and handsome, well groomed, cultured, sat in a meeting where he was discussing a large order with several executives—and he kept scratching his head. His head could not have been dirty. He was too immaculately clean for that. It must have been nervousness. And I know he was not aware that he was scratching his head while he was trying to make some important sales points. It was a distraction, however, and may have been one of the reasons why he did not get the order.

Watch the salesmen you see in action. Some are chin holders. Some are pencil chewers. Some are tie straighteners. Some smoke too much. I heard the vice-president of a company, who does not smoke himself, tell a salesman who was chain smoking in his office, "Ed, you smoke quite a bit. Smoking doesn't bother me as a rule, but when I see you light one cigarette after another I must say it does take my mind off the business we are discussing."

Here is a good rule about smoking: "Don't smoke in the customer's office at all, or at least not until he smokes first. Then do not overdo it."

One salesman I know is slightly deaf and tries to hide it. If you can't hear clearly, don't be ashamed of that fact. Capitalize on it. I know another salesman who wears a hearing aid and he can hear as well as anyone. However, he tells his prospects and customers that he is slightly deaf, which is true, and they speak slowly, clearly, and a bit more loudly than usual in order that he may hear them. They like helping him, and he doesn't have to try to hear. The first man misses much of the words his customers speak and tries to guess what they said. They resent that fault of his, while the second man's customers love him.

How is your smile? Many a morning we get up "on the wrong side of bed," or we have a headache, or a quarrel with some other automobile driver on the way to work, and we definitely do not feel in a smiling mood. How can we smile?

Some people say we should just smile whether we feel like smiling or not, and soon we will begin to feel more cheerful and before long we will be smiling with no effort at all. That might work. Try it when you're not in a smiling mood.

But never, never call on a customer, or let a customer call on you, unless you smile when you meet him! A woman who stopped trading at a grocery store gave as the reason, "They never smile—they never seem glad to see me. I'm going to give my business to people who appreciate it and show they are glad to see me come in."

I once worked for the president of a company who had what I called an "automatic smile." When you opened the door of his office, that smile spread all over his face as though there was a photoelectric cell connection between the door and his smile muscles. I noticed that people who came in with a frown or a harried expression invariably smiled before they reached his desk.

That smile helped to relax the person who approached the president, and started discussions on a friendly basis. A smile tells your customer immediately "I am glad to see you." Give him a smile greeting and you will get a friendly reception.

The dog that meets you with a wagging tail gets a friendly pat, while the dog that growls or looks at you suspiciously usually is given a wide berth.

Many of the most successful salesmen take the mirror test frequently. They stand in front of a mirror and rehearse their sales presentations over and over. Try it today. It helps iron out rough spots, helps catch and correct odd mannerisms and queer speech habits. Because we're human we'll never be perfect, but we can reach the top only if we aim high.

Keep checking over your appearance, your voice, your enunciation, especially your attitude toward your customer.

Look cheerful. Keep smiling. Remember that many thousands of salesmen have put aside their dark gloomy clothes and have found that when they wear a light-gray suit and a red tie they get the green light of customer welcome.

Perhaps a cheerful red tie will turn on the green light for you. Try it. Keep on trying to improve your appearance and your mannerisms. When you look like a cheerful, confident salesman you are much more likely to feel and act like one who expects and deserves success—and then, lo and behold, you will find more and more success coming your way.

CHAPTER 23

He's a Showman—Corny, but Completely Convincing

YOU have heard the expression "They laughed when he sat down at the piano." You know the rest of it—they were amazed when he played that piano beautifully. When Martin Bazner left his office morning after morning carrying a heavy three-foot portfolio, other salesmen smiled and shook their heads. That big portfolio held an easel sales presentation—a "canned sales story," and most salesmen did not bother to carry it. They agreed it was "corny." They didn't need it. They could "tell" the story. They didn't have to "show" the customer the same story they were telling. Besides, customers didn't have time for a corny easel presentation.

But Martin Bazner carried that big portfolio all day long, through a steaming hot New York City summer. He set it up and used it on every call. Certainly some customers told him they were too busy to look at it. Everyone is busy. But Bazner knew that *no one is too busy to learn something that will benefit him*. So he firmly and

We Sure Are Convinced. Ship Us a Carload, but
No Elephants, Please!

politely opened that three-foot portfolio on every call. He set it on the prospective customer's desk, turned page after page—and read every word on every page!

Of course, he added his own comments and demonstration to the "canned" sales presentation. But, corny or not, he used the "props" his company gave him to put on a show for the customer—and he outsold every other salesman in his company by far. So far, in fact, that he was soon made branch sales manager. Today he is general sales manager of the Ammco Tool Company of North Chicago.

Showmanship in selling can be as simple as using the sales presentation, the display material, and other "props" your company gives you, or showmanship can be as elaborate as wrapping a two-story house in cellophane and having movie stars and the governor of your state attend the "grand opening," with Miss America there to cut the cellophane.

Showmanship is a powerful magnet. It attracts us and holds us.

When you watch people crowd along the curb, their eyes bright in anticipation as the calliope plays and the circus parade moves gaily down the street, you can see what magic power showmanship has.

It lifts us out of our narrow little routines. It stimulates our imagination. It electrifies us. It charms us with the color and warmth it brings to us. It awes us. It awakens the adventurer in us. We always respond.

Showmanship can be colossal, gigantic, stupendous. But it need not be. Millions crowd into the big tents to see the circus—"the greatest show on earth"—each year, but I dare say additional millions hurry to their windows to listen to the hurdy-gurdy and watch the red-capped monkey dance across the sidewalk holding his little tin cup.

Showmanship can be the ten-story high electric spectacular signs flashing high over Times Square in New York, or a ball player pointing to the left-field bleachers when he steps up to bat in a World Series game and then blasts a game-winning home run to that very spot.

HE'S A SHOWMAN

That showmanship of Babe Ruth in a critical World Series game electrified everyone in the ball park. It is a particularly good example of showmanship from a salesman's standpoint, because it was tied inseparably to the hitting of the home run.

Yes showmanship in selling, to be most effective, should be an inseparable part of the sales presentation.

When a Goodyear tire dealer, for instance, tells you that you ought to buy a new inner tube with your new tire, you probably wonder if you really need a new tube. You can see the wear on your tire, but you can't see it on the tube. However, when that Goodyear dealer simply lays your old tube alongside a new tube, you immediately see that the old one has stretched out of shape. The dealer then doesn't have to urge you to buy a new tube. His simple but effective showmanship convinced you quickly that the old tube had lost some of its life and might be dangerous, so you want a new one.

One of the basic principles of showmanship in selling is *demonstrate!* Never take for granted that the customer knows how it looks, feels, smells, tastes, sounds. *Demonstrate it*—show him!

Bob White, head of the Bob White Organization, is a nationally known food merchandiser. He is a master showman and has achieved sensational success in introducing new canned foods through his showmanship. He tells us:

If you question whether buyers, including the most difficult, respond to basic human appeals, try this program. Prepare any food product in attractive and readily presentable form that will appeal to these basic human senses:

> Sight
> Taste
> Smell
> Feel
> Hearing

Present your food product attractively, in ready-to-serve form to fifty buyers. Whether it be a quick-fix pie, canned crepe suzettes, frozen canapes, a specially-ground hominy, French fried sardines, processed beverages—just anything you wish—present it in the most appetizing, ready-to-serve form to wholesalers, chain-store and supermarket buyers.

Pick the tough ones. It is a safe bet that at least 49 will prove they are human. Not only will they look, but most likely all will taste, feel and smell your offering, and listen attentively to your worthwhile sales facts.

We urge that you try this simple ABC selling approach because our many and varied experiences consistently show that any salesman will increase his volume in proportion to his utilization of appeal to these basic human senses.

For example: In one instance, we quickly achieved national sales prominence for canned wieners. Prior to our appealing to buyers through their basic senses with a show-prepare-and-serve demonstration unit that had appeal for all five senses, canned wieners had been only a minor item with a questionable future. But giving the buyers a whiff, then showing that canned wieners are not too unlike their butchershop cousins, having them tasted either hot or cold, and at the same time telling buyers these wieners don't require refrigeration, etc., etc.—turned canned wiener sales into a volume product of national consequence.

Canned whole chicken had been on the market for years, but sales had always been pretty much to the epicurean trade. Within a few months we changed this product into a popular mass-market, big-volume item by showing grocers and chain-store buyers the bird as it comes from the can and then how it looks baked. We proved the flavor with cold and hot samples—and the aroma of the rich hot broth whetted so much interest that holding the necessary audience was never a problem.

This success was followed up a year later with the introduction of a canned half chicken cut up for frying. Here, again, the same basic approach was used and the buyers were fed fried chicken. If you ever question the effectiveness of appeals to the human basic senses, brother, I specifically suggest you let fried chicken convince you. You will find that you can't miss!

Showmanship will make any type of selling more successful. The salesman who understands the *Human* Side of Selling will dramatize his sales presentation—and he always will make the customer the hero of the sales drama.

According to Zenn Kaufman, merchandising director of Philip Morris & Co., Ltd., one of the biggest mistakes we salesmen could make is to assume that we are the heroes of the drama called selling. He said, "Your customer is the hero. The minute we take the spotlight off the customer our show is over. We might as well go home, believe me, our audience is gone."

Mr. Kaufman, who is coauthor with Kenneth Goode of the popular book *Showmanship in Business,* said, "Showmanship is the thing that packs a motion picture theater, a ball park, or a prize fight. The same thing that will pack people into your local movie will pack them into your store. People are the same in business as out of business. If you find the formula that builds 'box office,' that same formula will work in building sales for you."

Find the showmanship formula that builds "box office" in your own selling. If you are selling in a retail store, that showmanship might be dramatic window displays, attractive merchandise displays on the counters, all through the store. It might be a giant button on your lapel, an armband or a badge calling attention to a special sale. It might even be a special uniform or costume. For instance, why couldn't all the salespeople in a store wear cowboy outfits during a "roundup" sale!

Showmanship in a retail store certainly should include the "audience participation" principle so successful in radio and television shows. Let your customer take part in the act. Let her take part in the demonstration, push the buttons, turn the knobs, operate the machine, see for herself how easy it is to use, how it will save her time and work when she gets it home.

If you are promoting food, let your customer sample it, as Bob White suggested. Hills Brothers coffee became the leading brand in market after market when a pound sample was delivered to every home so that the whole family could taste the coffee while they listened to and read the advertising about it.

If you are selling men's shirts, for instance, hand one to your customer and ask him to feel it. While he is holding the shirt and looking at it, call his attention to the fabric, the double stitching, the pearl buttons, and the color, which will harmonize with his suit.

"Put it in his hands" is a good showmanship principle to follow in almost any type of selling. Milk-wagon salesmen found they substantially increased their sales of a new premium quality milk when they handed a bottle to the customer and told her the advantages of the higher priced milk while she held the bottle in her hands.

Some companies supply salesmen with sound slide films or movies, with flip-over charts and portfolios. Most organizations give salespeople proofs of advertising and advertising schedules. Show them everywhere! By all means use these modern showmanship "props" to dramatize your selling. The salesman who doesn't use them when they are available might be compared with a soldier who uses a bow and arrow instead of modern automatic firearms.

A "canned sales talk" is good showmanship. Have you ever stopped to think that every movie actor, every radio or television star, uses a "canned sales talk"? They all do. And they rehearse and rehearse those "canned sales talks" until they know them so well they actually seem spontaneous.

Take a tip from the world of show business—prepare a "canned sales talk" if you do not have one. Then you will know your lines, and you will not miss the cues you get from the customer. You will be able to improve the inflection of your voice and your gestures. If you would be a star, practice over and over until you're a skilled performer when you appear on the stage—before your customers.

We salesman can learn an important lesson in showmanship from great comedians such as Bob Hope, Jack Benny, Fibber McGee and Molly. The next time you see or hear them, notice how the jokes are always on them, how they give their audience a feeling of superiority. They laugh at themselves, make you laugh at them, and they make you feel important. Their humility is magnificent showmanship.

You will sell far more if you keep the spotlight on your customer and let him be important. For instance, you probably know much more about the products you sell than your prospective customer does. In most cases you will be rewarded if you are careful not to place him in a position where he displays his ignorance. You can preface your explanation of your products features with some such remark as "You probably know more about this than I do, but if I may I'd like to explain . . ."

Remember, the customer must be the hero of the show!

One of the most effective showmanship devices you can use is this simple statement: "I use it myself!" If you're selling something you and your family can use—buy it and use it. Recommend it to all your friends. You will find many ways of showing it to better advantage in selling it when you use it yourself and see it used in the homes of your friends.

Testimonials of users can be dramatized. Where possible, take the prospective customer to see your product being used by a satisfied customer. Robert Gust, who headed his sales organization for twenty years, used photostats of actual orders to dramatize the acceptance by big stores and chain buyers of the products he sold.

We have seen how an exceptionally successful farm equipment dealer carries a movie camera in his car and takes movies of his customers operating the equipment he sold them. He also uses modern showmanship to collect overdue bills as well as to sell farm equipment. When a farmer has neglected to pay an installment on a tractor, this dealer will drive out to see him. Instead of asking for the payment, however, he will take out his camera and tell the farmer he would like to photograph him operating the new tractor. Instead of humiliating the customer by reminding him that his payment is overdue, this dealer, who understands the *Human* Side of Selling, makes the customer feel important, builds up his ego, and the customer usually responds by voluntarily giving him a check for the unpaid balance before he leaves the farm.

Showmanship can help you become more successful, whatever you sell. And don't hesitate to be "corny." People everywhere are corny. At the suggestion of Radio Sales, the CBS radio and television representatives, a well-known bakery in Washington, D.C., bought station WTOP's Claude Mahoney program to sell more bread. Soon afterward the bakery announced, "Claude Mahoney is the perfect salesman for our bread in Washington. Some people call him corny. But he's made more friends for us than corn has kernels."

A popular song told us, "It's a Barnum and Bailey world—corny as it can be!" It is indeed a world that responds eagerly to colorful, exciting showmanship.

Remember that life can be a rather dull, humdrum routine at times for your customers. That is why they flock to parades, circuses, movies. That is why they will respond to your showmanship.

Use your imagination. Put yourself in your customer's place and ask yourself how you would like to see your product or service demonstrated, dramatized. Psychologists tell us that people learn nine times more quickly when you present your story to the eye as well as the ear. Don't just "talk" your sales presentation—act it—dramatize it! Have the customer take part in it. Keep the spotlight on your customer. He is the leading character in every sale.

Make your own selling performance the best showmanship possible and you will be gratified by your success on the *Human* Side of Selling.

CHAPTER 24

He Rides 'Em Hard—These Four Vicious Nags And One Mean Little Jackass

YOU have watched rodeos. You have seen cowboy after cowboy come galloping out of the chutes on a well-trained cow pony swinging his lariat around his head, and you've seen him rope and tie a scrambling calf almost before you could catch your breath. Exciting, wasn't it? And the bulldogging and the races and the trick horses—you probably were tingling.

Then came the big event. As the loudspeakers blared the announcement, there was an awed hush of expectancy over the entire arena. All eyes focused on the chutes.

Suddenly a cowhand swung open a gate and clambered up the fence in a hurry.

There Comes a Time in the Life of Every Man

Out of the chute, as though propelled by a powerful spring, came a snorting, angry, wild-eyed bronco, bucking and twisting madly, trying to throw the rider, who was digging in his spurs and waving his hat in arrogant defiance. What a moment!

Perhaps the leaping, jolting horse was a killer. Perhaps he had crippled dozens of cowboys who tried to ride him. It didn't matter. If the cowhands in the rodio drew his number, they rode him for all they were worth—let falls come and the bones break where they may.

There isn't a rodeo rider alive who hasn't been thrown. Many of the champion riders have had almost every bone in their bodies broken. They have them patched up, and as soon as possible they're back, waiting for a number to be drawn, ready to climb into that saddle again and pit their skill against the meanest horseflesh alive.

There are four vicious nags that every one of us salesmen draws sometime, and when we do draw one we either ride it or we take a painful fall. They are *Fear, Resentment, Regret,* and *Doubt,* and you couldn't find a meaner group in any corral!

No matter how good you are, one of these cayuses is going to throw you sometime, and probably many times.

What can you do about it? Learn all you can about their devilish tricks so that you know what to expect. Then dig in your spurs and ride them ragged!

Learn how to take the inevitable falls, too, so those painful falls will not cripple you. They can damage your mind severely if you're not prepared for them. Remember (Chapter 4), it is estimated that one American out of ten becomes mentally ill and may require psychiatric treatment. Mental invalids! They were thrown too hard.

Don't let yourself be hurt so badly that you have to carry your mind around in a sling! You don't have to ride these vicious nags blindfolded. Watch every move they make. Learn so much about them that you almost can tell what they're going to do next. Ride them hard, and here's hoping you stay in the saddle, and win!

The most vicious of all is *Fear.* And there isn't a man or woman alive who hasn't known the jolting, pounding, tearing experience of fear.

It was the late President Franklin D. Roosevelt who said the only thing to fear is fear itself. A young boy about to walk home late at night through a graveyard, or a salesman about to call on a tough prospect he knows wouldn't see the last five salesmen, might say, "I can't help being afraid. What can I do about it?"

Fear can take a lot out of a salesman, can weaken him before he realizes what is happening. One of the best salesmen I know was so tormented by the fear that his wife had cancer that his selling ability was almost paralyzed. She did have cancer. After an operation, she recovered and her health has been excellent ever since. He once more is one of the top salesmen in the country.

Fear threw him—badly. Fear of personal troubles or of family problems can throw you. Watch out for personal and family forms of fear.

Be on guard against the job type of fear. When you find yourself fearful of satisfying the boss, of your chances for advancement, of earning enough money, of losing your job, think it out—don't let fear throw you.

As a salesman there are times when fear will jolt you with worries about prospects and customers, about competition, about business conditions. Such fears can kick the daylights out of your ability to sell. Do something about them—quickly.

We salesmen cannot avoid fear. When our time comes we climb right up into the saddle of fear. What can we do to win our fight with this vicious nag? Learn everything we can about his mannerisms, and ride him hard!

I would not say, with Mr. Roosevelt, that the only thing to fear is fear itself. That is a passive statement. Fear is wicked action and requires a knowing hand on the reins and a courageous heart to dig in the spurs. However, I would say, and quite positively that

> *The only thing to fear is submitting to fear instead of fighting it.*

What do I mean? It happens that I have another friend whose wife thought she had cancer. He too loved his wife dearly. And he was afraid. Who wouldn't be! But he decided that fear could not help her in any way. It was a destructive emotion that could hurt her by making her more uncertain and unhappy. He decided to do everything possible to learn whether she did have cancer and what could be done. She did have it. Her operation, too, was successful. He dug the spurs into his fear, rode it hard, and won. Only his closest friends knew about his wife's illness. His selling (and he is one of the top salesmen) was not affected.

Fear can do a wide range of damage in your personal or family life. Whether the thing you fear is as dreadful as cancer or as minor as getting a ticket for a traffic violation, you don't have to submit to the fear. Study it. Know what it is doing to you. Then replace it with positive thought and action. Ride it—hard.

In your job, watch every movement fear makes, every form it takes. You can't avoid it, but once it comes you can control it by positive thought and action. What have you done that brought on the fear? Don't do it any more.

A salesclerk in a department store was almost obsessed with the fear that she was going to be discharged. She was sure the boss didn't like her. She reached the point where she dreaded to come downtown each day. Would this be the day she would be fired? During one lunch hour she became hysterical. While she was crying her heart out, she told another salesgirl her fear and the reason for it—her boss never said "Good morning" to her when he came in each day. The other girl said, "I can't understand why he does not say 'Good morning' to you. Do you say 'Good morning' to him?"

The crying girl thought for a moment and replied, "No, I thought a boss should speak first, I guess."

"That is nonsense," her friend assured her. "When you see him after lunch, you say 'Good afternoon, Mr. Jones,' and you say 'Good morning' to him every morning, and see what happens."

Of course, you know what happened. The boss responded to the friendly, if worried greeting. The salesgirl finally faced her fear, took positive action against it—and she won.

Don't laugh at that simple fear of hers. It may seem funny to you that she should place so much emphasis on a "Good morning" from her boss. It was tragic to her because her fear had distorted that into the possible disgrace of losing her job, a feeling of insecurity, of not being wanted, etc. etc. All because of something she herself was not doing!

What haven't you been doing?

Perhaps you haven't been getting to work on time. You haven't been working quite so hard as you could. You haven't been taking good care of customers. You haven't been making the calls you should, or writing the reports you should. You haven't been living up to your best in that job of yours. Do it. Give every facet of your job the best you have, and you'll ride those fears right out the gate!

The fears about customers or prospects which every salesman has sometime can be licked the same way. One of the top salesmen I know told me he had found the reasons he was fearful of a prospect were (1) he didn't know as much as he should about the products he was selling, the competition, and the market for products of that type, and (2) he didn't know as much as he should about the prospective customer and how the products could help him. The second was by far the principal cause of fear, he said.

Think that over. When you are about to come face to face with a prospect, do you really know what he wants, what you can do for him, the answers to all the questions he may ask about your proposition? Do you really want to help him, to be of service to him, instead of merely wanting to get on order from him? Answer those questions in the affirmative and you'll triumph over this type of fear.

Fear gives everyone a rough ride. It can shake a salesman so much that he is too weak to do anything more than just go through the motions of selling. Bob Zuppke, former football coach of the University of Illinois, told his team, "Boys, the best defense is a good offense." That applies particularly to winning the fight with fear. Study it as coolly as possible. When you find out what it is trying to do to you, pull up on the reins, dig in your spurs, and ride the hide off it. Most of the time you will win, if you try.

The next one of the vicious nags every salesman rides at times is *Resentment*. This is a sly one, looks harmless enough, but before you can turn around it kicks you in the teeth.

There are innumerable circumstances, real and imagined, that can cause you to tangle with resentment. Your wife never does put the top on the tooth-paste tube. And she didn't sew that button on the shirt you wanted to wear today. She didn't have to make such a fuss about your working late last night. You really did, and anyway can't a man have a night out once in a while! If she only would not listen to your mother-in-law so much—and so on. Isn't it amazing how one little thing can lead to another sometimes until resentment runs away with you and you get a real jolt!

Some other driver cuts in in front of you as you are driving to work. A traffic policeman makes you back up when you stop for a light. Someone behind you honks his horn impatiently the second the light changes. What you'd like to do to those guys!

At your place of business your boss tells you about a customer who complained about you. The nerve of that customer, when you had treated him all right—what did he expect? And the first few customers you see are abrupt. Maybe they're in a hurry, but they surely are not even polite. You feel slighted, ignored. You have an argument with one, and he tells you what you can do. You know you're wrong, and you're embarrassed. You begin to feel people are shoving you around, and how you resent it!

Watch out for this baby. You can win any struggle with him by looking for the reason underlying the resentment. Look for it fairly. People are selfish, and thoughtless. Recognize that. They're on the defensive, just as you are. Go back over the day. Deliberately make it a point to be nice to the people who brought on the resentment. You will be amazed what it does to you, and to them.

When a car blocked the street under an elevated structure one evening, I waited impatiently for several minutes. The driver could see me in his rear-view mirror, but he didn't move. Finally I honked my horn a number of times resentfully and he moved his car up enough to let me pass. I was burned up. After I drove a block, however, I began to think how foolish it was to make him resentful and to feel resentment myself over something so insignificant—who hasn't!—and I parked my car, walked back and apologized. He nearly fainted in surprise. Instead of scowling at each other as we

FOUR VICIOUS NAGS AND ONE JACKASS 217

had before, however, we parted smiling warmly and both easy winners in our battle with mean old resentment.

Another vicious nag that likes to toss salesmen for a loss is *Regret*. The sales you didn't make. The calls you passed up that your competitor sold. The things you didn't say in that last interview. The course of studies you didn't take that might have meant a bigger job. The kind word you didn't seem to have time to say—at home—or to a fellow worker—or to a customer. The investment you might have made. The money you could have saved and didn't.

Someone has said, the saddest words of all are "It might have been!" At times regret may get you down. Get back in the saddle, however, and ride that nag. Even Babe Ruth, Joe DiMaggio, Ted Williams couldn't hit safely every time at bat. In baseball a .300 average is exceptional—.400 is sensational. And that's only four hits out of ten tries.

Golf champs lose tournaments for which they've practiced for months. Champion football teams miss passes, miss kicks, lose games. But the mark of a champion is the ability to take the bad breaks, the bad judgment, and learn something each time, and try to do better next time—*and always keep trying!*

There isn't a salesman who hasn't been bounced around by *Doubt* at times, and possibly thrown badly by this brute. When you see customers come into your place of business, you doubt that they want to buy—they're "just looking around."

Or, if you call on a prospect, you decide he probably isn't going to buy, maybe he won't even see you. Besides if he does buy, your credit manager will tell you his credit isn't good. But you have to make so many calls each day, so you'll go in to see him anyway.

Doubt feeds on lack of confidence. Take away the feed and you weaken doubt so much that it is easy to tame. What causes lack of confidence? Principally thinking of what you want to get from the customer instead of what you want to *give* the customer.

You can win your fight with doubt by concentrating on the ways you can serve your customer, how the products you sell will benefit him, how you can help him do what he wants to do.

You can anticipate the questions he will ask, or have in his mind, about you, your company, and your products or service, and have the answers for him. You can be an authority on the merchandise or service you sell and their benefits to prospective customers. When you are you will remove the lack of confidence, and doubt will be a gentle horse you can ride without too much trouble whenever you draw his number.

Be sure to keep your doubts to yourself, unless you need help. Then get it. But don't get the reputation of being a chronic doubter unsure of yourself. Goethe said, "Give me the benefit of your convictions, if you have any, but keep your doubts to yourself, for I have enough of my own."

Almost as disastrous as the four vicious nags is the mean little jackass *Delay,* which every salesman finds himself riding at times. Why? Because salesmen are human, and putting off until tomorrow the things we should do right now can become a stubborn habit.

Those calls on prospects or old customers, the reports that should be made promptly, the letters that should have been sent yesterday, the orders that should have been followed up. Delay is a mean little jackass, indeed, because he backs up when he should go forward, holds a salesman back from success and advancement, in fact, often sits on a salesman so hard that he crushes his selling effectiveness.

Watch out for this mean little critter. Don't let him sit on you. That is easy to say, but it takes a darn good man to control this foxy one. When you see him coming, run—make those calls, take care of that customer, send in those reports, write those letters. How good you feel when you do them now, and know you're the master of delay!

Psychologists tell us that we have emotional cycles. What causes them no one knows. However, there are times when we feel we're sitting on top of the world and other times when we're scraping bottom.

It's a good idea to find out just what your emotional cycle is. Take a piece of ruled paper and write the days of the month across the top. Down the left side write "Extra good"—"Fine"—"Fair"—"Just so-so"—"Low"—"Very low." Each morning put an "X" on your chart at the point that expresses your feeling that day. At the end of the month draw a line from "X" to "X" and you will see how your feelings varied during the month. You will have a graph of your emotional cycle.

What good will that do? It will show you that you are going to have low days whether you like it or not, and you will make allowances for those days. Also you know you are going to have days when you can do anything with enthusiasm. You will plan to take full advantage of those good days.

Your emotional cycle does not vary much from month to month, so you will be able to tell broadly when your cycle is on a downswing and you will not let your lowering feelings disturb you too much. Knowledge is power, and certainly the most powerful knowledge you can have is knowledge about yourself as a human being.

Keep on studying yourself. The most profitable study you can make is the study of you. Particularly learn how you can control the four vicious nags—*Fear—Resentment—Regret—Doubt*—and the mean little jackass, *Delay*—which you will have to ride at times. Let them know you're their master and they will not throw you—at least not so often, nor so hard!

CHAPTER 25

He Is Proud to Be a Salesman— a Professional Salesman!

IF you met a friend you had not see for a number of years and he asked you, "What are you doing these days?" what would you say?

For Service to his Fellow Men (and Women) Far Beyond the Call of Duty

In reply to that question one man said, "I work in a hardware store." When his friend asked, "What do you do there?" he said, "Oh, I sell and make myself generally useful."

A girl replied to that question by saying, "I work at Macy's." Her friend had to ask, "What do you do?" Then she said, "I sell in the housewares department."

A gasoline station service-salesman replied to the question by saying, "I work in a service station. I'm a gas-pump jockey."

A laundry driver-salesman answered the question by saying, "I drive a laundry truck." Dairy, bakery, and beverage company driver-salesmen have given similar answers to that question.

Wholesaler's salesmen and salesmen who represent manufacturers sometimes answer that question by saying, "I'm a peddler." The sales representative of a large meat packer tells his friends, "I am a sausage peddler."

What are *you* doing these days?

It is certain that *you are doing exactly what you* think *you are doing*.

You are what you *think* you are. And your customers, your business associates, your family, and your friends will have just as much respect for you and your job as you have yourself.

Adolph Kroch chose bookselling as his career. He started to work as a salesclerk in a bookstore and pyramided his bookselling success into one of the greatest bookstore operations in the world. His love for his work and his pride in it have had much to do with his brilliant success. He said, "Such a wonderful profession, that of bookselling! In my position as a book salesclerk I began to feel terribly important. Here I was permitted to talk to strangers (who soon became friends) about books I loved. I sold them the books without any so-called sales effort and they came back for more books. And why? Because I offered them something I knew, something I loved, and because I transmitted to them my honest enthusiasm."

Don't you admire Mr. Kroch's pride in his work! You can't help admiring a man who loves to sell and is proud of his job.

The next time anyone asks you, "What are you doing these days?" answer promptly—and proudly—"I am a salesman!" And tell proudly what you sell. Notice how that gives your self-respect a boost—how your friends look at you with new appreciation. Everyone respects men and women who are proud of their work.

Why is it that some salespeople evidently are not proud to be salesmen?

First of all, many men and women just happen to have selling jobs. To them selling is simply a job, a way to make a living.

Secondly, there are some salespeople who have had little or no sales training, who have never even thought of taking a course in salesmanship in their spare time, who probably never have read a book on the subject. They have no interest in selling as a career.

Thirdly, there are salespeople who think of selling as a "game." Some even call it the "selling racket." In this group are the high-pressure boys who are responsible for the "caveat emptor" (let the buyer beware) attitude of prospective customers.

The natural law of selection will weed many of these misfits out of the selling ranks as salesmanship becomes recognized more and more as the most important profession in any free country.

When you are proud to be a salesman, when you understand and are guided by the *Human* Side of Selling—when you are enthusiastically interested in being of genuine service to your customers—then let a friend ask you, "What are you doing these days?"

Your answer will be "I am a salesman—a professional salesman!"

What is a *professional* salesman, in the finest sense of the word "professional"?

R. S. Wilson, vice-president in charge of sales of the Goodyear Tire & Rubber Company, defined the truly professional salesman as

a man who first of all has made Selling his chosen call—his lifework. In this he is unique, because most men who have the title of "Salesman" did not *choose* to be salesmen—they just *happen* to be salesmen. Selling is not a calling with them. It's just a job.

The Professional Salesman is the man to whom true service is of *paramount importance*. To quote Henry S. Dennison: "A Profession combines science and common sense into an art accompanied with a motive of *service* greater than that motive of *service to self* and also having a loyalty to a code of ethics."

The Professional Salesman is a man who is constantly studying to improve his proficiency. I am thinking of a surgeon whom I know well who personifies to me the Professional attitude. I met him at lunch one day not long ago and he told me he was leaving by plane that afternoon for Dallas. Why? He had read in one of the medical journals of a surgeon in Dallas who had performed a delicate cheek bone operation—in a manner that was new to him. He immediately called the Dallas surgeon on the telephone—found he was to perform such an operation the next day, so he dropped everything and left by plane to watch the operation and learn a new technique. This friend of mine was 56 years old when this incident occurred and to the end of his career he will go on studying and practising to improve his proficiency. He is a true Professional.

The Professional Salesman is a man who recognizes there is no substitute for hard work. Charles Kettering puts it this way: "I think this know-how we talk about is eternal *practice, practice, practice!*" Dr. Paul Ivey says, "If you want success in any profession you have to *pay the price* for it; that means *work!*"

The Professional Salesman is a man who above all else maintains his own self-respect, integrity, independence. In the final analysis, this matter of integrity is the sine qua non of the true Professional. I know of no man to whom I could give the title "professional" in any line who would sacrifice his own self-respect either through coercion or for the hope of gain.

In Chapter 12 we discussed a questionnaire Mr. Wilson had sent to 500 leading purchasing agents. When they were asked to describe the best salesmen who called on them, they used such adjectives as "dependable," "sincere," "honest," "friendly," "considerate," "intelligent," "loves-his-job." Notice that the purchasing agents respect the salesman who "loves-his-job." Everyone respects such a man regardless of the nature of his selling job.

A waiter in a restaurant is a salesman. He sells food to his customers. His interest in them, his attitude toward them, and the service he gives them can make them want to come back again and again and bring their friends. Lucien Caldora, a distinguished headwaiter at the Waldorf-Astoria, is one of the finest examples of men who are exceptional successes in serving their customers. His quiet enthusiasm shows that he is happy and proud of his work.

One day when I complimented him on his service he said, "It's a very real pleasure to serve. I love my work."

And then he made this significant statement: "If you love your work, Mr. Moore, nothing can bother you. A man's attitude toward his work is very much like a woman's love for a man. If she loves him, he can beat her and mistreat her and she will come back for more. If she doesn't love him, however, he can do everything for her and she won't appreciate it. Because I love my work customers can be grouchy or very pleasant and I like them just the same. It is a pleasure for me to serve them."

That is one of the distinguishing characteristics of a truly professional man, and particularly a professional salesman. He loves his work and is proud that he has so many opportunities to serve people.

Charles Ward, president of Brown & Bigelow, told me:

I have met thousands of salesmen, both Brown & Bigelow salesmen and others, and I have found there is no single "physical" quality that distinguishes a real salesman from the rest of humanity. They come in all sizes, shapes and appearance.

One of the best salesmen I have ever known is a Negro. Another is a Japanese. So even race has nothing to do with it.

Their personalities are as diverse as their appearance, too. Some are quiet, almost shy; others are blatant and overpowering. Some have Doctor's Degrees, and some can barely read and write.

If there is one quality that successful salesmen have in common, it is that of dogged determination to give the greatest possible service to every customer. A good salesman never quits until he serves the customer in every way he can—and customers seldom quit that type of salesman.

Whether you are a genius or couldn't graduate from grammar school is not nearly so important to your success as a professional salesman as is your attitude toward your job and your customers. Do you have a "dogged determination" to give the greatest possible service to every customer?

John W. Mock, sales and personnel training consultant and former professor of salesmanship at Northwestern University, has this five-step formula for professional salesmanship:

(1) *Be interested*
(2) *Be organized*
(3) *Be helpful*
(4) *Be human and*
(5) *Be yourself*

(1) *Be interested*—Ask questions. If you want the buyer to be interested in what you are offering, you must first be interested in the buyer, what she wants and why. And to show your interest is no problem at all; you simply ask "interested" questions—questions that show that you are interested in her wants and needs and that you genuinely are interested in helping her.

(2) *Be organized*—Talk about what it does! No one ever buys anything because of what it is—never! Purchases are made because the item will *do something* for the buyer.

Now, in explaining what an item *does,* don't worry about "buying impulses" or "motivating forces" or any other psychological terminology. You can study them—they are fascinating and good fun to know, but don't become confused by them. Just remember: There are only two things that any item can *do:* it can help you keep what you have, or help you get more than you now have, and, possibly, both.

In other words, an item can *save* (time, money, labor, material, energy, etc.) or it can *give* (pleasure, power, prestige, pride, satisfaction, success, etc.). Organize your thinking and your talking around these two good friends, *gives* and *saves,* and you will continue to increase in effective, happy sales ability because you are talking to your buyer in terms of what *she* (or *he,* as the case may be) wants and needs. Now you are ready for the next step.

(3) *Be helpful*—Help the buyer decide! Are you waiting for a discussion of the psychological moment—the crucial point where you "ask for the order"? Sorry! There's no place for such a tense and nerve-racking moment if you want to attract more and more business. Just summarize the discussion—point out the advantages and disadvantages—review the buyer's wants and needs as revealed by her answers to your questions (in Step 1)—make sure you've answered all *her* questions—and above all,

(4) *Be human*—Remember that your buyer is a human being, even as you are, with the same joys and sorrows, hopes and despairs, triumphs and defeats, ups and downs.

(5) Finally, *Be yourself*—You have been blessed with a personality that's all your own. Develop it. Don't try to be like someone else. Have faith in your own talents.

As John Mock suggests, be yourself—but be your best self!

A truly professional salesman never stops growing. His mind is always open—he is eager to learn new and better ways to serve his customers and his employer.

He seldom takes anything for granted. Even if he is told "We have always done it that way" he keeps on looking for a more effective way.

He joins sales clinics, takes salesmanship courses as often as possible. He reads books such as this over and over, discusses the subject matter with his fellow salesmen—and applies the know-how of other successful salespeople to his own work.

Selling is his lifework—his career—and he is mighty proud of it. He loves his job, and he knows specifically what his job requirements are.

If his company does not give him detailed specifications of his duties, he outlines his responsibilities as he understands them and reviews them with his boss. When the boss approves the job specifications, the professional salesman knows exactly what is expected of him and he therefore is better able to deliver fully.

He knows there is no substitute for hard work. He does not have to be urged to practice, practice, and practice his sales presentation. Most important, he knows that true service to the customer is the real measure of selling success. He is thoroughly honest and his customers respect him. He is enthusiastic, confidently cheerful. And he knows how to use showmanship to dramatize his selling. He is a credit to the selling profession—a star on the *Human* Side of Selling.

PART IV

Even The Boss Is Human!

CHAPTER 26

Who Is this Character—the Boss?

W<small>HY</small> are some salesmen and saleswomen afraid of the boss? Could it be that the mere fact that he is the "boss" (with the power to raise or lower salaries, to hire or fire) makes him an awe-inspiring figure?

Or could the fear of the boss, often a subconscious fear, be the result of a guilt complex? A guilt complex due to the salesman's knowledge that he is not selling as well as he could and should.

Let's put the cards on the table—how do you feel about your boss?

Do you wonder what he thinks of you, whether he likes you and is satisfied with your work?

Do you wonder whether he is going to increase your salary, or someday tell you that you're through?

Do you wonder whether there is a "future" for you in your company and whether the boss wants to see you move up into a better job?

Sure I'd Like to Help You with Suggestions, but I Don't Want to Stick my Neck Out

THE BOSS

Do you sometimes wonder what sort of person he really is and how you could know him better? Wouldn't you like to know where you stand with the boss?

Many salesmen do not know the answer to these questions because they have been so wrapped up in their own personal problems and desires that they have seldom taken the time to think about the boss—to ask themselves: Who is he, what is he trying to do, what does he want of them—how can they be of the greatest possible service to him personally and to the company?

A salesman in a downtown Chicago store telephoned his boss that he would like to come up to the office for a discussion. When he was in the boss's office he said, "I have been working here for some time now and I would like to know where I am going—what's ahead for me here?" He almost blurted that out as he stood beside his employer's desk.

George Williams, the boss (that is not his real name), suggested with a friendly smile, "Sit down and relax." Then he said, "You can go as far in this store as you want to go."

The salesman said, "I have had some ideas about improving the operations of my department from time to time, but I have hesitated to do anything about them because I didn't want to stick my neck out."

His boss told him, "We want people who are willing to stick their necks out. That's the way we can progress. You don't have to be afraid to stick your neck out, because there is nobody who will chop it off."

I happened to call on Mr. Williams shortly after this interview and he told me about it as an example of the difficulty he has in finding salesmen who are interested enough in the success of the store to do more than the specific selling job to which they are assigned. That particular salesman had been with the store for about a year. He has a pleasant personality and gets along well with the customers, but he has never done more than his routine selling job. Evidently he has been afraid "to stick his neck out."

His boss told me that he needs a manager for that store, and any one of the salespeople in the store could have that managerial job in sixty days—if he showed by his actions that he really had the interest of the store at heart and wanted to become the store's manager. All the salespeople, however, simply go on day after day behind their counters doing a fairly satisfactory selling job and exhibiting none of the initiative or active interest in the store's success that would single out some one of them as ready for advancement.

Mr. Williams said, "Why, if I walked into that store someday and saw that salesman with a broom in his hand sweeping the floor just because it needed sweeping and he wanted to see that our store was perfectly clean, I would say, 'There is a man I will keep my eye on, because he has the makings of a store manager.' But would he, or any of them, think of sweeping the floor? No! If you asked him to do it, he probably would, but he would think you were taking advantage of him because that is the janitor's job and not his." And he said to me, "Do you see what I mean?"

Let's take a good look at this boss and see what sort of person he is. He is an active member of his church in a small suburban community. He has a wife and several children and home interests that are similar to those of many of the salesmen. He plays a fair game of golf, likes to play cards occasionally, and works in his garden whenever he can. In other words, he is quite *human*.

As vice-president and a director of the company, he is responsible for purchases, for the operation of the company's stores, the finances, the public relations, stockholder relations, and sales. He reports periodically to the board of directors and must show them that the business is operating profitably and continuing its consistent growth. His chief interest is his salespeople because the success of his sales organization determines his own success and the success of the company.

It is difficult for many salesmen and saleswomen to believe, but this employer actually is more interested in the success of his salespeople than they are themselves!

That is true of your own boss, whether you are a salesman in a retail establishment, whether you sell for a wholesaler, a manufacturer, or any other organization.

THE BOSS

Harley V. McNamara, the dynamic president of National Tea Company, told me, "We are always looking for men in our organization who show that they want to—and are ready to—move up. It is difficult to move up one man until another is ready to take his place."

And Mr. McNamara continued, "The best way to move up in any organization is to help the man ahead of you move up, so you can step into his place—and be ready to!"

Harley McNamara knows. He has moved up steadily from grocery salesclerk to the presidency of one of the most successful merchandising establishments in the United States. Of course, he is a brilliant man, but his chief characteristic, I would say, is his humanness. In fact, in answer to the question "How do you account for your own success?" he said, "I learned early in my business experience that people are human. If you are human in your relations with your customers, your fellow workers and your boss, you will find that they will be human with you." And when you hear the National Tea Company truck drivers call, "Hi, Mac!" when they drive by him anywhere in town, you will know that Mr. McNamara must be human indeed.

Joseph Kolodny, managing director of the National Association of Tobacco Distributors, asked me, "What can we do to make more salesmen interested in becoming better salesmen, in getting themselves ready for advancement? There are many sales managing jobs among our distributors that salesmen could move into if they showed they were ready, willing and able to assume the sales manager's responsibility." Distributor executives are anxious to move salesmen up—as soon as possible!

The general manager of a nationally known metal-fabricating company told me that he needed a sales manager. I asked him why he didn't move up one of his salesmen into the manager's job. He said, "There is nothing I'd like to do better than that, but they don't seem to think beyond their own saleswork. They don't show that they are interested in the overall success of the company. They simply do the selling job assigned to them and seem to be satisfied to do that reasonably well."

The executive vice-presidents of two other companies have asked me to help them find sales executives. I know that each has moved men up from the selling ranks on other occasions but right now evidently there are no salesmen in their organizations who have been willing "to stick their necks out" and show that they are willing to sweep a floor, if necessary, or do anything else over and above their regular selling duties to aid the management in making the company's operation more successful.

Your boss is very much like the head coach of a football team or the manager of a baseball team. He has an investment in you—in money, in time, and his reputation as a successful leader of men. You are on his team for only one reason—he likes you and he believes you have the ability to succeed.

His interest in you is genuine, because his success depends on your success.

Your boss probably works far longer and harder than you or any other salesman. Very likely he works at home, holds meetings with other company executives in his home or in theirs. Time doesn't mean anything to him when he has a sales goal to reach. Edward Stiteler lost thirty-five pounds working ten or twelve hours a day when he became a partner and manager of the Matherson-Selig Company and was responsible for its over-all selling success.

Of course, the personality of sales executives and other company officials varies because no two individuals are alike. Some will be cool and aloof, others will be as friendly and easygoing as a fraternity brother. Some will be as eccentric as the brilliant Lewis Rosensteil, head of Schenley Distillers, who raised one man's salary from $6,000 to $50,000 a year and made him sales manager, and others will be as understanding and reliable as the noted leader Thomas J. Watson, head of the International Business Machines Corporation. Regardless of his personality, however, you can be sure of one thing—your boss is interested in you and will do everything he can to help you become more successful.

At an I.B.M. convention in the city of Endicott, N. Y., where the company's largest factory is located, Mr. Watson told the many successful salesmen gathered there:

I cannot tell you the feeling that I experienced last evening when I came into the tent to look at our present products and then looked at the products we had thirty-four years ago. These things mean more to me than they could ever mean to anyone else in this business.

I have had more pleasure out of the business and I owe a greater debt than any other person in I.B.M., because I never could have succeeded in this business without the support and cooperation which I have had from nearly everyone who has ever been associated with me.

I have tried to the best of my ability down through the years to impart upon all those who carry titles that they cannot hope to be helpful in the business and cannot hope to progress unless they can learn to forget their titles and deal with every man in accordance with the ideals on which I.B.M. was founded.

I.B.M. was founded on the ideal of the Golden Rule which is a very simple formula. I have never let an opportunity go by to call everyone's attention to what our duty is to the MAN, and that he wants to be treated just as we would want to be treated if our positions were reversed.

There you have the head of one of the greatest business organizations in the world expressing his gratitude to the members of his organization—and his concern for their welfare.

When the going is tough, your boss is more concerned about it than you are, and he constantly is looking for ways to give you a lift, to let you know that he is behind you and that he believes in you.

In 1946, when a postwar readjustment dipped Philip Morris business, Board Chairman A. E. Lyon (then president) turned the dip into a provocative challenge.

Calling his sales chiefs into his office, he asked them, "How much of the cigarette business are we getting now?" They told him the company was getting 8 per cent.

Walking over to an open window, and making a tossing motion, as though he were throwing something out the window, Mr. Lyon said, "Forget it—throw it out the window, and let's go out and get the other 92 per cent!"

Of course, every employer is not a Thomas Watson, an Al Lyon, or a Lew Rosensteil. Some sales managers and sales supervisors are strong, some are weak. Because your boss is an important factor in the *Human* Side of your selling, learn everything you can about him. If your immediate supervisor is weak, do your best for him because you may be able to help a weak boss become stronger and then you will become invaluable to him. He will need you and see that you move up with him.

If you find, however, that you cannot respect him you owe it to yourself, and to your boss as well, to find another job. If you should see that your boss is one of the few dishonest sales executives, don't allow yourself to be debased by having any part in a dishonest operation. Of course, you will want to be sure before you pass judgment. But you must respect your immediate superior, and the management of your company, in order to sell successfully.

Some salesmen, especially those with an inferiority complex, criticize their employers, if not to their customers at least to their own families and friends. Remember that your boss is human. Because he is human he will make some mistakes. He would not be in an executive capacity, however, if he did not have a good batting average. Never forget that you are on his team. He is relying on you. Play ball with him. You are working together for your mutual success.

Thousands of sales managers are members of the Sales Executives Clubs of this country. In national conferences, conventions, and in regular meetings in your community, sales executives compare experiences and are constantly trying to find ways to make *you* more successful.

Many sales executives are members of the American Management Association. Management representatives travel hundreds of miles to take part in clinics where your selling problems are discussed and methods for making you more successful are investigated.

In other words, the employers, and sales executives, have one primary interest—and are working toward one principal objective—to make their own salespeople as successful as it is humanly possible for them to be.

For your own success on the *Human* Side of Selling, remember that your boss definitely is on your side. He is a human being with much the same likes, dislikes and desires that you have. Make it your business to know him better. Try to understand his objectives for the entire organization. *Think* about the many additional ways you can help him. Stick your neck out with suggestions and additional effort—keep at it—and watch how he responds by moving you ahead as rapidly as you care to go.

CHAPTER 27

He's Working for You

IF you were going to plant a garden, what would you do? First you would decide what crop you wanted. Then you would select the best seed you could find. You would plant that seed under the most favorable circumstances. You would watch over it and care for it as it grew. You would pluck out the weeds around it, do your best to protect it from damage. You would be working constantly to give it every opportunity to develop to the fullest possible extent.

You would have quite an investment—in money and in work and time—in that garden. If you had selected weak seeds or the wrong seeds for your particular soil, or if perchance some of the seeds refused to produce, you would lose your investment in them.

Your boss is much like our gardener. If you want to make the greatest possible success of the *Human* Side of Selling, it will be well to remember that he has a substantial investment in you as a salesman. Actually he is working for you—investing his time, work, and money in your success.

Unfortunately, some salesmen and saleswomen are so myopic that they cannot see beyond the boundaries of their own self-interest.

It Would Be Tough Going Without Your Help, Boss!

HE'S WORKING FOR YOU

They are so busy thinking about themselves that they do not see that the best business friend they could have is their boss—the man who works for them.

Is your employer really working for you? When John Wilson worked in a department store in Kansas he thought many times that he would like to be in business for himself. He decided, however, to become a salesman of the National Cash Register Company. He said, "I found that I was able to go into business under the most unusual circumstances in that the man who was willing to put me into business would also be working for me." The man to whom Mr. Wilson referred was the late John H. Patterson, head of the National Cash Register Company.

At a sales conference in Dayton, Ohio, sometime later John Wilson told why he joined the sales force of the National Cash Register Company and why he knew that his boss actually worked for him:

If I were in the retail business for myself I would have to buy my merchandise and pay for it, whereas Mr. Patterson not only supplies me with the cash registers I sell, but he has an engineering department which is always anticipating the needs of the future for at least 15 or 20 years.

If I were in business for myself and my merchandise were sold on credit, I would be obliged to borrow money with which to finance the accounts. Mr. Patterson carries all the accounts for me.

If I were in business for myself I would not only be forced to plan my own advertising, but pay for it. However, Mr. Patterson has assumed this responsibility by providing me with the benefits of the finest advertising department of any company in the country.

The man in business for himself must reinvest most of the profits which he earns in merchandise and new fixtures, but my profit is in cash, it can be invested and pays interest to me.

Mr. Patterson agreed wholeheartedly:

This young man has just stated that I am working for him. All of us are working for somebody. You are working for your wives and children. I feel sorry for anyone who does not have some one dependent upon him.

Some of you may wonder why I work as hard as I do. My personal wants as well as the physical wants of my children have been amply provided for. Then why do I continue to work as hard as I do? As I have said, you have your family dependent upon you, but my family embraces all the members of the NCR family, which includes not only all the thousands of employees here in Dayton, but other thousands throughout the world.

Mr. Wilson said, I am working for him, which means that I am working for each and every one of you. When he made that statement he displayed a better understanding of my objective in life than anything anyone has ever said.

Mr. Wilson knew the importance of understanding that his employer was definitely working for his success. When he made the above statements in a speech, he was one of many NCR salesmen. His understanding of his employer, plus his great faith in the valuable service he could give his customers with NCR equipment, helped move him up steadily in his company until today he is vice-president in charge of sales and director of the world-wide National Cash Register Company.

Look at your own selling job as John Wilson looked at his. In effect, you are in business for yourself. Your boss is working for you. Take advantage of the help he gives you. Follow his suggestions. Use the selling tool that he provides for you. If you are really interested in your success, he will help you become as successful as you care to be!

If you represent a wholesaler or manufacturer and have a territory assigned to you, think of that territory as your own private domain. You are in business for yourself in that territory, with your employer working for you to give you everything you need to make your own business successful.

Zenn Kaufman, merchandising director of Philip Morris & Company, Ltd., Inc., and one of the greatest showmen of our time, dramatized the backing given every salesman by his own company with the following dialogue at a company sales meeting.

The dialogue was presented by Zenn Kaufman, with sales promotion manager Robert Larkin assuming the role of a Philip Morris salesman:

Mr. Kaufman: "Mr. Larkin, here is your New England territory, known for the moment as 'Larkinland.' As you can see Larkinland represents almost nine million people, with some 5 million smokers, and our share of that market is 8 to 9 per cent. That is your territory, all yours! Of course, it would be nice if you owned it yourself!"

Mr. Larkin: "Sure would, Mr. Kaufman!"

Mr. Kaufman: "That idea appeals to you, Bob. Did you ever figure out what it might be like to own your own cigarette company? Probably you would call your cigarette a 'Larkin,' right?"

Mr. Larkin: "Yes."

Mr. Kaufman: "I have a Larkin Cigarette right here (exhibiting cigarette package labeled 'Larkin')! Does that look nice to you?"

Mr. Larkin: "Sure does!"

Mr. Kaufman: "Fine! I can see your advertising: 'Stop your Barkin, Smoke a Larkin!' There is just one catch, Bob. To make Larkin Cigarettes you would need a plant."

Mr. Larkin: "Right."

Mr. Kaufman: "You know these big machines down in Richmond that go buzzz-z-z?"

Mr. Larkin: "Sure!"

Mr. Kaufman: "Well, you have to have one of those machines even for New England, and they cost $90,000! Have you got $90,000?"

Mr. Larkin: "Not right handy! Not on my expense account."

Mr. Kaufman: "Well, let's make believe you could go around to Household Finance and borrow that $90,000. Then you would be in business."

Mr. Larkin: "Right!"

Mr. Kaufman: "No, not yet! Because you would have to have an advertising expense and a payroll. For a company to do the volume you want to do you need around $17,000 a month, so just for a few months you would need $50,000. Do you think the finance company would give you $50,000?"

Mr. Larkin: "I guess I'd be over my head!"

Mr. Kaufman: "Well, let's suppose you have a rich old aunt who dies and leaves you $50,000. Now you really are in business for yourself."

Mr. Larkin: "Right!"

Mr. Kaufman: "No, no! You are still in trouble. I'll tell you why. In order to make cigarettes, you would have to have a stockpile of aging tobacco, wouldn't you?"

Mr. Larkin: "Oh, yes, I forgot about that!"

Mr. Kaufman: "That's right. And for the volume you expect to do in New England alone you would need about 3 million dollars' worth of aging tobacco. Do you think you could count on a rich old uncle for that 3 million?"

Mr. Larkin: "They're all too young!"

Mr. Kaufman: "Well, then, you really are out of business."

Mr. Larkin: "Yes."

Mr. Kaufman: "Well, I don't know whether you are or not. The fact is that I think that being with us you are really in the cigarette business for yourself. I will show you what I mean.

Here is New England (and he pointed to a large map). You see that it represents some 9 million people, some 5 million smokers. And it really belongs to you, because you are in charge of New England. What you do with it is entirely in your hands. You have some 110,000 retailers to do business with and it is up to you whether or not they do business with you. They can be with you or against you.

Here is New England (handing a New England-shaped piece of the map to Mr. Larkin). I want you to hold it in your hands and realize that actually it is *yours*. It belongs to *you*, and the success or failure of the Larkin Company in New England depends on you."

As Zenn Kaufman explained so clearly and dramatically, your employer has invested a great deal in you and has set you up in business as a salesman. How successful do you want to be? Your boss, when he selects you as one of his salesmen, gives you what amounts to a blank check on the Success Bank; you can write in any amount you want, and he will help you cash it.

So your boss is working for you—what does that mean to you? It means that you need never be afraid of him. You need never wonder whether he is interested in you. You need never think the cards are stacked against you in your organization. You are on your employer's selling team because he believes in you and is willing to invest in you and work for you to make you as successful as you want to be.

It has been said that the salesman who moves up rapidly in earnings and in position spends 60 per cent of his time selling his customers and 40 per cent of his time selling his boss. You don't have to "sell" your boss, except in the sense that you let him know by your work, by your interest in the success of your company, that you definitely are anxious to work with him straight down the line, without regard for time or tide, so to speak.

When you are in *en rapport*—in complete harmony—with your boss, when you work as an understanding, smoothly functioning team, then you are reaching for the heights on the *Human* Side of Selling. You are bound to be more successful because together you will go all out in serving your customers, and you will move to the top in the selling profession.

CHAPTER 28

If You Were the Boss

YOU have heard salesmen say, "If I were running this outfit, I'd . . ." and they usually imply that they could do a better job than the boss does. They often say it belligerently—as though their thinking hit the front of their own heads and then bounced right back inside. Very likely they were thinking only about their own ideas and were not trying to understand the boss and his sales objectives at all.

Spoken belligerently, critically, egotistically, "If I were running this outfit . . ." is bad medicine. It breeds disloyalty. It short-circuits constructive thinking. It undermines enthusiasm, makes selling hard work.

The same words, however, can lead you to a warm, appreciative understanding of your boss which can help make you one of the happiest, most successful salesmen. It just depends on your attitude, your point of view. If you know the *Human* Side of Selling you will never put on mental boxing gloves with your boss. You will keep your thinking in his corner of the ring.

You do not have to be a yes man. No intelligent employer respects a salesman who agrees with him in everything. I sat in a

So You Want a Raise? Well Let Me Tell You, Young Fellow . . .

IF YOU WERE THE BOSS

sales meeting where the sales manager deliberately proposed a change in selling practice that would not have been good for the company. He asked the men whether they had any comments to make about the proposal. Twenty men were there. Only two hands were raised. Both men stood up and told the boss why they disagreed with his suggested change. The change was not made.

Later he told me, "I made that suggestion to see whether we have any men who are more than yes men. I was looking for men who will think about company policy and sales objectives. I don't want to make all the decisions around here. I can make mistakes, and I want men near me who will correct me when I do. Thank goodness there are at least two men in our outfit I can keep my eye on as management prospects."

In your relationship with your boss, try to put yourself in his place and understand his objectives. Remember, he actually is working for you, for your success. When you try harder to help him you are helping yourself.

Bill learned the truth of that last statement. He is an ex-GI. Bill received one of those "invitations" to join the Army shortly after he left high school. When the war was over and he was back home, he married Sarah and got a job selling in a grocery store.

There were four other salespeople in that store, all older than Bill. Not one of them worked harder than Bill. No one was liked better by customers. Bill is a friendly, sincere guy who really likes people, and consequently people like Bill. Yet, despite his interest in the customers and his conscientious hard work, a year went by and Bill received only a small increase in salary.

After dinner one evening he told Sarah he was beginning to be a bit discouraged. He wanted to earn more money so they could buy a house someday, and he wondered whether he ever could earn enough in that grocery store. The four other salespeople were older and had been there longer. What chance did he have?

Fortunately for Bill, Sarah was not the kind of wife who would say, "Why don't you tell the old boy to give you more money, or else . . ." Nor did she say, "You're right, they don't appreciate you. Go on out and find another job." Sarah listened to Bill while he told her the reason he was becoming discouraged. Then she asked, "What sort of man is your boss, Bill?"

That stopped Bill. He couldn't answer for a minute. Then he said, "Well, Mr. Johnson has worked hard all his life, I guess. He's in the store every morning before any of us gets there and he is still there when we leave. From remarks he's made at different times, I'd say he takes bills and other things home and he and his wife work on them together. He's pretty decent to us, but he gets sarcastic sometimes with one or two of the boys who come in late or when they drop everything and leave at quitting time. I don't blame him, though, I'd feel the same way."

Sarah said, "Bill, I think you've got something there!"

Bill asked, "What do you mean, honey?"

"Why, you just said that you'd feel the same way. Now, if I were the boss, I'd be looking for an assistant, maybe a partner in my business, who'd feel the same way about things as I did. Does that make sense, Bill?"

Bill thought about that for a few minutes, and then exclaimed, "Holy cow, Sarah, I think you have the answer. I'm going to do everything I would do in that store if I were the boss. And I know where I will start.

"Mr. Johnson is a bearcat about having everyone in the store promptly at starting time in the morning. You know I'm always there on the dot. And next to Mr. Johnson I'm often the first one in. But beginning tomorrow I'm going to get down to the store a half hour ahead of time. Just a hunch. We'll see what happens. And say, I'll be home twenty or thirty minutes later, too."

Bill told me that he walked into the store the next morning while Johnson was going over the vegetables, sorting out those which had spoiled and freshening the vegetable display for the day's business. The boss looked up at Bill with a surprised smile. "Why, Bill, you're early this morning!"

And Bill said, "Yes, I thought those vegetables looked a little sad last night, so I decided to come in early and look them over. I'll take off my coat and be with you in a minute."

Several weeks later Bill arrived at the store before Mr. Johnson.

He was waiting when the boss arrived. Johnson actually apologized for being late. He had slept a bit longer than usual. He said, "Bill, I think you should have a key to the store. You seem to be taking a real interest in it. I've been telling my wife about you, and she would like to have you and Sarah over for dinner. When can you make it?"

Before another year went by, Mrs. Johnson had confided to Sarah that she did not want her husband to work as hard as he had been working all his life and she thought he ought to have a partner, someone who was as much interested in the business as he.

Today, less than two years after Bill was beginning to be so discouraged that he thought he might be in the wrong selling job, he is a partner in a large and profitable grocery business. He and Sarah now can afford to look for that house they wanted.

What made the difference in Bill's success? Did he change? Did he suddenly develop "selling personality"? Did he marry the boss's daughter?

No. Bill, thanks to Sarah's thoughtful suggestion, began to think about his boss, began to try to understand him and his ambitions for the business.

Then Bill started to take as much interest in the business as he would if he were the boss himself. When he did that, he was in!

That is the *Human* Side of Selling your boss. It is a sure formula for advancement in selling, provided you are absolutely sincere in your interest in your boss and his objectives for his business.

When I drove into a large corner gas station one morning, after an all-night snowstorm, the snow was piled about two feet high everywhere except just in front of the gas pumps. Three servicemen were standing around a desk in the little office. After one had filled my car's gas tank, I asked, "Why don't you shovel off this snow so more customers can drive in? Now only one car can drive in at a time."

Here's the reply I got to that question: "If we shoveled off the snow today, they'd expect us to do it every time it snows, and that is not our job!"

I happened to know that the owners of that station, one of whom manages it himself, are looking for a manager. Any one of those servicemen could have the job if he followed Bill's example and put himself in the boss's place and did the things for that business he would do if he were the boss. Isn't it amazingly easy to move ahead in any form of selling—if you just think about the *Human* Side of your selling job!

Ask yourself today, "What would I do, how would I work at my selling job, if I were the boss?" Let your answer guide you to greater success in selling, whether you work in a retail establishment or sell for a wholesaler or manufacturer. Many of the great men who achieved fame and fortune in business owe their rapid rise to the fact that they refused to do only as little as others around them did. They went all out to help build their employer's business, doing everything they could no matter how menial or how big, and they moved up to the top.

Mr. J. C. Penney is one of the great men of our time and a tremendously successful business leader. At the age of twenty-three, however, he had lost his last dollar in a small store he had bought in Longmont, Colorado. He heard that a clerk in a dry goods store in that town was ill and he got a temporary job there for the holidays. When the clerk came back young Penney was sent to Evanston, another small town where the firm had a store.

Would you like to know the "secret" of J. C. Penney's early and rapid success? You can use it. And you can be certain that it will work for you too. It never misses.

Mr. Penney worked in that Evanston store as he would if he had been the owner! And within three years the owners did make him a partner in their whole group of stores.

Here is an incident in Mr. Penney's experience in the Evanston store which illustrates so well the difference between selling in the usual routine way, doing as little or as much as you think you're being paid for, and doing everything possible (even if it's sweeping the floor) to contribute to your firm's success. Mr. Penney relates:

> Once settled in Evanston, I worked as I had never worked before. Here was a business with which I was familiar, and I determined to make the most of my opportunity. On my first day in the store I went

out to lunch with the head clerk. As soon as we had finished, I got up.

"Where are you going?" asked the head clerk.

"Back to the store," I said.

"You've got an hour for lunch. Don't be a fool!"

None the less, I hurried back. And the next day the incident was repeated. In the store I worked early and late, never leaving until the last suit had been brushed and piled, the floors swept, and everything dusted. Each night the head clerk, with a sardonic smile, fired the same question at me: "Don't you know when to quit?"

Apparently I didn't. But in eight weeks he was discharged, after twenty years' experience. I was given his job.

Put yourself in the place of Mr. Penney's employer. What would you have done? You would have been just as interested, as every boss is, in finding someone who really takes an interest in your business and goes all out to further the business, even as you do. Probably you would want Mr. Penney as a partner to be sure he continued in your business.

Three years after he had lost his last dollar, Mr. Penney became a partner in the business which he has expanded to one of the leading mercantile organizations in the world.

It can happen to you. Now you know Mr. Penney's secret. Use it and grow!

In your particular selling job, do the things you would do if you were the boss. Keep putting yourself in his place and keep on trying to know him better, to understand how you can help him attain all his objectives.

Follow that practice even in matters that may seem unimportant in your selling success. If you travel, for instance, look at your expense account as you would if you were the boss. That doesn't mean that you have to save every possible penny. It does mean, however, that you will exercise good judgment in spending the company's money to the best advantage, as though it were your own.

A young salesman of *Parents' Magazine* told George Hadlock, his boss in the Midwest, that he was proud of the fact that he had not had to spend a cent on entertainment; he had not even taken one customer to lunch. George Hadlock gave him a lesson on the *Human* Side of Selling. He said, "Hank, to be successful in selling you must like people. And if you like your customers you will want to take some of them to lunch—not because they may give you business, but because you enjoy doing business with them and appreciate the opportunity they give you to serve them. It isn't particularly smart to be penny wise and pound foolish."

Mr. Hadlock is right. Learn your boss's policy in regard to expenses for travel and entertainment and follow it as carefully as you would if you were the boss yourself.

George Davis, a star food salesman, became sales manager of Phillips Packing Company. He has a policy which all of us salesmen can adopt profitably. George told me that he decided every boss dislikes to hear alibis, excuses, stories about complaining customers, or any other unpleasant information. He said, "The boss hired me to take care of customers in my territory, to settle complaints if necessary, to keep the sales volume coming in. So I make it my business to see to it that he never hears anything unpleasant from me. If I have any news for him, it is good news. That's why he is always glad to see me." No wonder he was moved up rapidly until he became sales manager.

Think that over! If you were boss would you like to hear excuses, alibis, complaints, unpleasant reports? Or would you prefer to know you had a salesman who never griped or brought you bad news, who could take care of any unpleasantness that might come up in his selling job, settle complaints, and bring you only pleasant constructive reports?

Of course, if competition or other market conditions should be brought to the boss's attention, don't hesitate simply because they might be unpleasant. But keep your personal contacts with the boss on the pleasant, constructive level you would appreciate if you were the boss.

If it is true that a salesman to be most successful should spend 60 per cent of his time selling the customers and 40 per cent selling the boss, you can spend your 40 per cent to the best advantage if you will put yourself in his place and then do the things in your own selling job that you know you would if you were the boss.

Remember, the boss is human, too. Whether he is your department manager, district manager, region director, or sales manager, he is human. And his own success depends on your success. Think about his objectives, go all out in helping him by doing far more than he expects of you, and you're sure to be a greater success on the *Human* Side of Selling.

CHAPTER 29

How to Sell Yourself into the Job You Want

IF you understand the *Human* Side of Selling, it is entirely possible that you will be so happy in your present job that you may never be interested in getting another, unless it is a better one with your present employer.

There may come a time, however, when circumstances beyond your control can make it necessary to look for a job. When that time comes, what will you do?

Suppose we put that question another way: what do most salespeople do? First they usually tell their families and then their friends, "I am looking for a job. If you hear of anything, let me know." They answer classified ads for salesmen. They get a few leads and call on the prospective employers. They fill out applications and wait.

Eventually they are hired by someone. Too often the selling job is not exactly what they wanted. They can't become particularly excited about it. But it is a job. It will do until something better comes along.

Now Do I Get that District Manager Job?

The haphazard practice of finding a job is one of the principal reasons for the costly turnover in selling organizations. Job changes are costly—to the salesman in lost time and opportunity, to the employer in the loss of his investment in the salesman and the loss of sales volume.

What can be done about it? Many employers are endeavoring to match the right man to each selling job by careful selection, aptitude tests, preemployment analysis. In some cases this scientific employee selection method is too highly "mechanized," especially in the analysis of salesmen. John M. Wilson, vice-president of the National Cash Register Company, has one of the most *human* and one of the most successful methods of selecting salesmen that I know. This is the way Mr. Wilson describes it:

"When interviewing an applicant, I have always been able to put him at ease by telling him that I was going to dismiss from my mind the interests of our company and decide whether it would be a good thing for him to come into our business. If it is a good thing for him to come into our business it automatically will be a good thing for our company to have him."*

That might well be called "the *Human* Side of selecting a salesman." To anyone it can be a guide to the choice of the right selling job. Before agreeing to work for any employer, ask yourself, "Will it be a good thing for me to go into this business?"

Of course you have to know what you want before you can answer that question fully.

Many job seekers come to Walter Lowen, noted New York employment counselor, and ask, "What do I do about getting a job in selling or advertising?" Walter Lowen says, "We answer with two highly significant questions of our own: (1) What can you do now—what do you have to offer an employer at the present time? (2) What is your ambition—what do you want to be doing ten years from now?"

Mr. Lowen explains, "In the combined answer to those two questions is the key to the kind of job you should seek." It is difficult to find the best job for you unless you know what you want.

* *Man Alive.*

An employment manager of a large company said, "Many of the applicants I interview give me the feeling they are not sure what they want. They expect to sell their services, yet they don't even know what it is they're trying to sell, or whom they really want to sell."

Finding the right job for yourself is much like selling a product. First, you must know what it is you are selling. You must know your product thoroughly. How well do you know yourself? In *Man Alive*, I suggested that you draw up a personal "Balance Sheet" at the end of each month.

That Balance Sheet would be just a plain sheet of paper with a line drawn down the middle. On the left you would write "Liabilities." "Assets" on the right. Your assets, if you were looking for a job, would be your education, experience, enthusiasm, initiative, and all the other good qualities you would want in a salesman if you were hiring him. Your liabilities would be the weaknesses, lack of training, indifference, and other negative qualities you would not want in a salesman if you were the boss.

Look over your own analysis of yourself. Ask yourself, "What am I fitted for?" And then, "What sort of job do I really want? What would interest me so much I would be enthusiastic about it and would do my best to become a star?"

When you decide the answers to those questions you know "your product"—yourself.

And you have a general idea of your potential market—the type of selling job you should have.

When you know the general type of selling job you would like, make a list of the businesses that might have such a job. Then go over your list and rate the organizations in the order in which you would prefer to work for them.

Remember that you want a selling job where you can reach your maximum success. You want to work for a firm of which you can be proud and sell products or services you can sell with enthusiasm. You want to be with an outfit that is growing, so there will be room for you to move up as you produce and show you are ready to assume additional responsibility. Most important, you want to work for sales managers and department heads you can respect, so you can build up that old team spirit that can make the difference between championship performance and mediocrity.

Now you have your "prospect" list of businesses for which you might like to sell. And you have rated the list in the order of their possible importance to you. What do you do now?

You are ready for your own selling campaign. How will you conduct it? Before you do anything else, you will prepare a presentation of your qualifications. And that presentation should be a *human* document, not merely a dry historical table of the dates of your birth, graduation, marriage, and job experience. More than nine out of ten of the applications we receive are mere statistical outlines. Employers are interested in the statistics of your background, of course, but they are not interested in hiring just statistics; they want to hire a *human* being.

When you have an interesting general presentation of your background (written the way you would tell it to a friend) you are ready for the next step in your job campaign—approaching the prospective employer.

You can call on him, write him, or telephone for an appointment. You can contact him first through a mutual friend. Or you can consult a recognized employment counselor, who often can save you a great deal of time and expense by finding the job you want and arranging an interview with the prospective employer.

When you have a definite job prospect, learn all you can about it and slant your presentation to fit the specific job requirements.

When I analyzed my selling experience, education, and other qualifications and decided I wanted to work for an advertising agency I was in my early twenties. I had had some advertising experience, but no agency experience. Before I applied for a job I looked in an agency register and learned what clients the agency served and who the executives were. I learned all I could about it. Then I asked myself, "If I were in the place of the head of that outfit, what qualifications would I want in the man I hire?" I made a list of those qualifications and wrote a letter of application in which I said, "If I were on your side of the desk, Mr. Johnson, it seems to me that I would want a young man who . . ." and I described each quality I would want and then showed how my background matched those qualifications.

The manager of that advertising agency told me he had received more than a hundred applications, and had called in only the few who showed what might be called some application initiative. He evidently liked the idea of a prospective employee trying to put himself in the boss's place and look at the job from the employer's standpoint because he hired me.

You will never make a mistake by putting yourself in the place of your prospective employer and doing the things that would impress you if you were hiring a salesman like yourself.

A young salesman asked my help in securing a job with an electric appliance manufacturer. He had been invited to come in for an interview with the sales manager. I suggested that he call on as many of the company's dealers as he could, learn what appliances made by his prospective employer were selling best, how they compared in quality and price with competition, and so on. He asked, "Do you really think I should go to all that trouble? Would it make an impression on the sales manager?"

My reply was a question: "If you were that sales manager, wouldn't you be impressed by a prospective salesman who had enough initiative and interest in your company to learn something about your products, your dealers, and your competition before he called on you?"

He said, "Yes, I guess I would."

Remember, your prospective employer is *human*. Put yourself in his place and apply for a job with him in the way that would sell you if you were choosing a salesman.

If I had had the time I might have told that young man how I learned the lesson I passed on to him the hard way—by an unsuccessful search for a job in New York City for two long months. Yes, I had come to the big city from Rockford, a community of about a hundred thousand sprawled along the banks of the Rock River in northern Illinois. I was his age, almost thirty, and I was convinced I was ready to move into the big league.

For two very long months I kept pumping up my enthusiasm as I applied for job after job in the Manhattan skyscrapers. Very courteously, I was told time after time that my background was excellent but I had had no New York experience. It seemed that to every New Yorker Illinois was still Indian country.

One day I managed to solve the mysteries of the New York subway long enough to reach 120 Broadway for an appointment with John Cole, then advertising director of National Distillers Products Corporation. Mr. Cole wanted an assistant to take charge of sales promotion operations. While I had had no sales promotion department experience, I had a selling and advertising background and I thought I should be able to do a good sales promotion job.

Mr. Cole kindly said he liked what I told him about my experience and would consider me for the position. He did not ask me to come back, however, and I suspected his answer was 99 per cent "No!"

When I went back to my hotel room I thought over my experience of the past two months and my interview with John Cole. All at once I realized the principal mistake I had been making. In each interview I had been talking about the most interesting thing in the world to me—the job I wanted and my qualifications for it. And I had been neglecting the most interesting thing in the world to my prospective employers—what specifically could I do for them, how could they be sure I was the man who would do the job best for them?

I liked John Cole. There, I decided, is a man with whom I would enjoy working. Of course his primary interest was the advertising and promotion of his company's brands. What did I know about them? Nothing. So I hurried out and made retail calls all over New York. Several days later Mr. Cole had on his desk a memorandum report of my calls and a number of recommendations for specific promotions. Within a week I was invited to come back to 120 Broadway.

Mr. Cole told me he had hired another man to fill the position for which he had interviewed me. Nevertheless, he had decided he needed a second promotion man and he wanted me. I was placed in charge of promotion of two divisions, and a year later when all divisions were merged I was made sales promotion manager of the entire company.

What helped me get a job for which I had had no previous experience in one week when I had been unsuccessful for two months in my efforts to get other jobs for which I was well qualified? For the first time I remembered to forget the job, the salary, and the other "things" I wanted and to think of the *prospective employer*—and what he might want. When I got over onto the *Human* Side of Selling I made my sale.

When applying for a job, do not ignore the prospective employer's assistants or his secretary. I know one man who lost his chance for a good selling job when the sales manager's secretary said he was busy and asked the applicant to tell her what he wanted. He said, "I'll wait and tell Mr. Andrews," and right then he was through. He might as well have said, "You're not important enough for me to bother with. I'll talk only to your boss."

The salesman-applicant waited. When the sales manager's caller left, the secretary went in to announce him. The boss asked her, "What's he like?" And, being human, she said, "I don't like him. He isn't very courteous." Two strikes against him. He didn't get the job.

If you have been honest with your customers, have tried sincerely to serve them well, you may get a boost from them when you apply for a new job. On the other hand, if you have misrepresented or have been careless in your treatment of customers, you may pay heavily when you are applying for a new job or when you are being considered for advancement in your own company.

I happened to be visiting the vice-president of a big drug wholesaler when a manufacturer telephoned him to ask what he thought of a man who was being considered for a selling job. The v.-p. said, "We can't believe what he tells us. He's a nice fellow, but we've lost confidence in him." Needless to say, that man was not hired.

Another manufacturer called, evidently a friend of the v.-p., and said, "We're thinking of promoting Charlie. Do you believe he'd make a good sales manager for us?" The v.-p. replied, "Charlie is an all-right contact man for you, but he's more a good-will builder than a salesman. He has never made a promotion or merchandising suggestion to us. You ought to have someone who can help your wholesalers sell your products. We'll buy all we can sell, you know." Good old Charlie probably will never know why he is not sales manager of his company today.

It is amazing how few applicants for selling, or any other positions, ever follow up their first call with a "thank you" letter. How in the name of common sense can you expect anyone to believe you would be a successful salesman if you do not demonstrate the principles of successful selling in applying for a job? The minute you get back from an interview, get out that pen and paper. Put yourself in the prospective employer's place and write him what you would want to hear if your places were reversed.

When you are successful in getting a selling job that makes it necessary for you to move to another city, don't go right out and buy a home. One salesman I know did that and his sales manager resented it, because he thought it obligated him to keep the man whether he produced or not. The salesman did produce, but his hurry to buy a permanent residence strained the relationship with the boss unnecessarily for a time. A good rule to follow might be the admonition scrawled on dressing-room walls in old vaudeville theaters: "Don't send out your laundry until the manager has seen your act!"

Selling yourself into the job you want is not difficult when you understand and are guided by the *Human* Side of Selling. Once you have found the right selling job for you, however, keep yourself the right man or woman for that job by making good use of your leisure to study and improve yourself. On the very first day, begin to prepare yourself for the job ahead.

The president of one of the largest transcontinental airlines told a meeting of the Sales Executives Club in Chicago, "When we select salespeople, we are more interested in men and women who enjoy going out of their way to help others than in people who have been behind the counter for five years."

That, my friend, is the *Human* Side of a modern employer's

measure of prospective salesmen. If you knew the *Human* Side of Selling you would be sure to get along with that executive, and could move up in his selling organization or virtually any other as rapidly as you care to go.

CHAPTER 30

Loyalty is the Badge of a Noble Man!

FOUR salesmen were having an after-dinner smoke in a hotel lobby in a northern California city one evening.

After discussing the weather and current politics one of them said, "Business is certainly lousy these days. I haven't had an order all week. I got a lot of chances to quote but I guess our prices aren't competitive, or maybe our terms are wrong. The stuck-up sales manager of our outfit doesn't know what is going on in the field."

The second salesmen said, "Yeah, I know what you mean. I have made a few sales this week, but not as many as I should have made. I have got a sales manager who cracks the whip when we don't send in reports promptly and he gets pretty nasty about expenses. Why, I was late for an appointment this morning and I had to tell the customer that I had been busy making out my expense report. That customer was sore because I was late for my date with him and said he would have to see me on my next trip; he didn't have any business for me today."

The third salesman cut in: "You ought to work for my outfit. Our washing machines are supposed to be inspected before they leave the plant. Sometimes they are shipped without casters—why, I even

I Know it's the Boss, but I Can't Let Him Drown!

had a customer who received a shipment without motors. How the hell can anyone operate a washing machine without a motor? We have a plant manager who doesn't know enough to come in out of the rain."

The fourth salesman stood up and said, "Well, fellows, I'll see you later," and started to walk away. One of them said, "Hey, what's your hurry, don't you like our company?"

The salesman who was about to leave said, "To tell you the truth, fellows, I couldn't take part in this conversation because, first of all, I haven't a single thing to complain about. I believe that my company and my management are tops. Sure, such people as our credit manager, the boys in the factory, and even my own boss are human; they might make mistakes occasionally. They wouldn't be human if they didn't. I am sure, however, that they are doing their darnedest to back me up in every way they can, and I don't mind telling you, fellows, that I am proud to be associated with my outfit.

"As a matter of fact, boys," he went on, "I am the sort of guy who wouldn't work for a boss if I didn't believe in him, and I wouldn't work for a company if I could not be proud to represent it. How in the world could I sell with confidence otherwise—and how could I have any self-respect?"

What do you think of each of those four salesmen? Which one would you want as a personal friend? Which one could you respect? If you were a prospective customer, from which one would you prefer to buy?

Loyalty is far more than a matter of ethics to a salesman. It has a definite dollars and cents value. It can have an important influence on a salesman's success and on the speed with which he moves ahead in his company.

Above and beyond the dollars and cents value, however, loyalty can influence the salesman's happiness in his job and in his home. Yes, a salesman's family and his friends might sympathize with his gripes, his complaints about the company and his employer, but the family and friends of a salesman who is proud of his company and his boss will have a great deal more respect and admiration for him.

THE BADGE OF A NOBLE MAN

Does loyalty have a definite dollars and cents value to a salesman? Let's examine a few cases and see.

A driver-salesman for a laundry lost so much business on his route that he lost his job. Why did he lose the business? Why did he lose his customers? When they complained about the loss of a button or about the quality of the work he would say, "I can't understand it. I guess they are just plain careless. They don't seem to care about my customers at all." The customers lost their confidence in the laundry and the driver-salesman lost his job.

Another laundry driver-salesman seldom loses a customer although his laundry tears off just as many buttons and makes just as many mistakes. When the customers complain he sympathizes with them, but he says, "Our people do their best but they are human, you know, and any of us can make a mistake. However, we want our customers to be completely satisfied and if any work we do is not satisfactory we will do it over."

Do you see the difference? With which driver-salesman would you prefer to do business?

One salesman of automobile insurance has a difficult time making a bare living. He is a "good fellow" and when his customers complain to him about his company's claim adjusters he agrees with the customer that the claim adjusters are cold, indifferent, soulless people who don't care about the policyholders at all. He wonders why his customers do not renew the policies. They have lost confidence in his company.

Another salesman who has been selling automobile insurance for only a few years makes $15,000 to $20,000 a year. When a customer complains about his claim adjusters he says, "Our people want to take care of your claim promptly and completely. I will write them or, if necessary, telephone them long-distance and I will see that you get prompt action. Our office, of course, processes a lot of claims; sometimes an adjustment takes longer than a customer likes or we like. However, we have the best claim department in the country and you can be sure that you will get better service than you can anywhere else!"

With which insurance man would you prefer to do business?

The purchasing agent of a large company told me that he was about to gives a salesman an order for a carload of paper when the man started to tell him about the bad deal he thought he was getting from his company. He said they were short-changing him on expenses. They were unfair in cutting his territory, and so on. The buyer told me that he decided if the company was not treating its own salesmen fairly how could he expect any better treatment?

Who lost through that salesman's disloyalty to his firm? His company lost a carload order, certainly, but he lost the commissions on that carload. He also lost the respect of that purchasing agent and he lost much more, because disloyalty can undermine the salesman's own character.

Frederick Raiter, sales representative of the Heinn Company, manufacturer of loose-leaf binders, called on a large television manufacturer. He knew this television manufacturer was printing thousands of catalogues and needed loose-leaf binders. He asked to see the advertising manager, who told him that the company was indeed in the market for loose-leaf binders; in fact, he thought that the purchasing department had already bought them. Many salesmen in Mr. Raiter's place would have said, "I am sorry I didn't get here earlier; perhaps I can get your order next time," and would leave.

Fritz Raiter, however, was so enthusiastic about the management of his company and the craftsmanship of the men and women in the factory who make the Heinn binders that he said, "Gee, I hope that the order hasn't been placed because I believe you would prefer to do business with our company if you knew what intense pride everyone from the president down takes in producing the finest quality binders that can be made."

And then he went on to tell the advertising manager a glowing story about the president of the company, the sales manager, and the men and women in the factory. Before long the advertising manager picked up his telephone, called the purchasing department and said to the purchasing agent in charge of advertising material procurement, "There's a young man up here in my office who represents the Heinn Company and I think you might want to hear his story about Heinn loose-leaf binders."

When Fritz Raiter walked into that buyer's office, the buyer told him, "I will be glad to talk with you but I want you to know that I have already made out the order to another company. I haven't sent it to them yet, but I am afraid it's too late to change it."

Again Fritz Raiter enthusiastically told the same story—not about his product alone, but about the character of his company's management and the craftsmanship of the people in the plant. Before long the buyer said, "Well, Mr. Raiter, I promise you that I will not mail this order today. Let me think this over overnight."

When I saw Fritz Raiter that evening he said, "You know, that purchasing agent and the advertising manager were so much interested in what I told them about Mr. Wood, our president, and Pat Finch, our sales manager, and about the people in our plant that I think they actually *wanted* to give me the order."

Mr. Raiter was right. When he called the purchasing agent of that large television manufacturer the next day he was told that he would be permitted to submit a quotation. The other order would be held up until his price was received. You will be interested to know that his quotation was higher than the price that had been quoted by his competitor—yet he got the very big order and made well over a thousand dollars in commissions on that sale.

You see what I mean when I say that loyalty has a definite dollars and cents value!

Customers prefer to do business with a salesman who is enthusiastically loyal to his boss and to his company. Put yourself in the customer's place. Wouldn't you? Of course, you would, because you would have far more confidence in an organization represented by a man or a woman loyal to it.

When I walked into the office of a sales manager friend one day he asked me, "Did you see the man who just walked out when you came in?" and I told him that I had noticed the man. He was a rather handsome, well-dressed young man. The sales manager told me, "Yes, he looked good to me too. He applied for a job as salesman and I would like to hire him. In fact, I would have hired him in a minute if it were not for one thing: he criticized his present employer and the policies of his company so much that, frankly, I am afraid to hire him. I can't help feeling that he might talk about me the same way he talks about his present employer, if he were on our sales force."

That sales manager, who came up through the ranks himself and ten or twelve years ago had been a route salesman himself, said, "One of the many lessons I have learned in observing hundreds of salesmen is this: *The salesman who belittles his boss belittles himself!*"

Loyalty not only influences your customer, it also influences your relationship with your employer, or your prospective employer if you are looking for a job. Every sales executive wants to have men on his selling team who are completely loyal to him and to the company.

I know of one case where a salesman had been moved up rapidly to the position of sales manager in a large company, principally because of his intense loyalty for his immediate superior. As his boss moved ahead in the company he brought this salesman up with him. Other men had more ability, but no other man was more loyal.

The next time you hear some salesman criticize his boss or complain about the management of his firm, hand him this book and tell him to read this chapter. Perhaps you will save his job. Your help may make him realize the actual monetary value of loyalty to him and straighten out his thinking so he, at least, will have an opportunity to advance in his organization without the handicap of questionable loyalty.

A salesman's loyalty can affect the happiness of his family. When a salesman goes home and complains about his boss and about his firm, his family probably will sympathize with him, but they will begin to worry about his job. They will have a feeling of insecurity. They probably won't tell him but they will wonder from week to week when he is going to be fired or when he will decide to give up his job and leave.

The family of a salesman who is intensely loyal to his employer and to his firm, however, will be proud of him. The family's feeling of pride will be a great bulwark of confidence that will strengthen the salesman and help him become far more successful.

The attitude of the salesman's friends is affected by his loyalty to his firm. He may not realize it but friends, even though they are sympathetic and may agree with the salesman that his outfit is lousy, can't help thinking that there may be two sides to the story. There usually are. The salesman who is enthusiastically loyal to his boss and to his company, on the other hand, is respected by his friends, who will admire him and his organization.

Yes, loyalty does have a dollars and cents value (even though that may seem to be a cold way of putting it) in a man's success in selling his customer and in his relationship with his boss. And loyalty definitely can affect the salesman's happiness at home and the respect that his friends have for him.

Of the greatest importance, however, is the effect that loyalty has on the salesman himself. To reach your maximum development as a human being, you must be proud of your work, the management of your company, and the men and women with whom you associate in your company. You must have the feeling that you are a vital part of a team. You must realize that the other members of the team are human, just as you are. Certainly, they will make mistakes, too. They wouldn't be human if they didn't. However, they are working for the success of the whole enterprise, just as you are, and therefore you should learn to know them and to understand them—so that you can have complete confidence in them.

Loyalty to your boss and to your organization will give you a feeling of security—and a faith in your future—that nothing else can give you. Loyalty is the difference between a mental and spiritual Lilliputian and a real man. Truly it is the mark of a noble man, and a characteristic of the great salesmen who understand the *Human* Side of Selling.

Conclusion

CHAPTER 31

America Needs a Great Army of Salesmen

WHEN our nation is threatened by some foreign power, our government recruits millions of men and women for the armed services. Every red-blooded American is glad to fight to keep our country free, to protect the liberties that we cherish, to fight for our rights to our own American way of life.

When war is declared, we are a united people. We will fight for each other and for the land that we love.

When we are not at war, however, most of us Americans are easygoing people. We tolerate propaganda attacks on our country and on the way we like to own our own property and our own businesses, because we believe in freedom of speech and are willing to let the other fellow shout his head off, if he behaves himself and just lets us alone. There comes a time, however, when some of the propaganda becomes vicious, when it might even endanger our freedom to work and live as we choose. The American Eagle is a mild-mannered bird—it can be pushed around quite a bit, before it goes into action. Then, watch out!

The American people have been attacked by two major propaganda campaigns in recent years: first, advocating various forms of

Isn't our Kind of Music . . . Wonder if We Could Teach Him to Play "Yankee Doodle"

socialism and, second, communism. What is propaganda? As a salesman you know what propaganda is. It is a form of salesmanship. Some smart boys on the other side of the ocean have decided that they want to sell their way of life, their system of government, to the American people. And they have come over here with a crew of their own salesman—and have enlisted some gullible Americans—to sell their ideas to us. Are we going to let them?

The socialists and communists are pitting their salesmanship against American salesmanship. Are we going to admit that they are better salesmen than we are? If a socialist or communist country declared war, we would send our armed forces into battle with them and whale the daylights out of them until they cried "uncle"—Uncle Sam. We are in a propaganda war right now, and it's a war of salesman against salesman—of certain foreign salesmen against American salesmen. And America needs a powerful army of patriotic salesmen—to sell and resell the American way of life to our own people.

Why should it be necessary to sell the American way of life to our own people? Because some of us may take it for granted and listen to the slick anti-American salesman who tries to convince us that the socialist or communist grass in the field across the ocean is greener.

Certainly we believe in the United Nations. As Arthur Hood puts it so well, "We believe in the Fatherhood of God and the Brotherhood of Free Men everywhere." We have watched the people of many nationalities and tongues live together in peace and mutual respect in the great little nation of Switzerland. We know that it isn't necessary to talk alike and live alike and believe alike to get along. We don't want anything any other country has. We want only to work with other people, cooperate with them for our mutual good, and live on this little spinning planet of ours in peace with our neighbors everywhere. Unfortunately, some of our neighbors are bullies, some are tough mugs who like to shake their fists in our direction, some are smooth, envious hombres who like to dip their hands in our national piggy bank. So we must keep our country strong. And we must keep our eye on our own government officials

A GREAT ARMY OF SALESMEN 269

to see that they aren't sold a bill of goods by the city slickers from across the seas. We pay the bill—and we elect them—and we can vote back in only those whose actions show they love the Mississippi, the Ohio, the Hudson, and the Columbia rivers at least as much as the Thames, the Seine, the Danube, and the Volga. No, we salesmen are not "isolationists" but our selling experience brings us into contact with all sorts of people and we do become "realists."

As salesmen we have two great opportunities to serve our country. First, we can sell the American way of life everywhere we go, particularly when we see that our "competition" has made an impression on someone we know. Secondly, we can keep our American free enterprise system strong and healthy by constantly improving our own selling effectiveness, by living up to our own best as a professional salesman.

Dr. George S. Benson, president of Harding College, and recognized throughout the land as a militantly patriotic American, believes that selling America is a challenge to every patriotic salesman. He said:

Selling America ought to be second nature with all good salesmen.

Surely nothing could have a more stimulating effect on a salesman's enthusiasm than a clear understanding of the history and achievements of this great country of ours. Once he has such an understanding—and likewise appreciates the fact that our American system is being challenged—a good salesman will consciously and unconsciously be a crusader for the American way of life.

By the same token, no one can sell America—however great its merits —who doesn't know the product, the market and the competition. That has been an important factor in our drift toward socialism in the past 20 years. Our people have not been adequately informed and thus few have done anything to effectively counteract the propaganda for socialism.

Freedom, America's greatest asset, is jeopardized today because no group of our population has taken the trouble to equip itself with the facts and then do a selling job. Only 30 per cent of all our colleges require students to study American history or to have studied the subject in High School. And a great many of our educational institutions in recent years have considered our free enterprise system—which is the motive power of our progress—to be controversial. They do not endorse it. To do so, they say, would not be "academic."

It has been only recently that business and industry have done anything at all to sell America to Americans. Many companies now are doing a creditable job, especially among their own employees. Some labor unions, civic and trade groups, have begun lately to join in conducting educational programs on free enterprise and Americanism.

But the one great need is for missionaries—American zealots to go out and reach the people at the grass roots, the cross roads, and in person-to-person or over-the-counter contacts.

Salesmen thus have an opportunity to make a vitally needed contribution to the future security of freedom in America. In times of war or peace, America sorely needs this force of crusaders going about the country constantly calling attention to the positive greatness of our nation and defending it against the halftruths and the outright falsehoods of socialist propagandists.

There is really only one basic issue in America today, and that is the issue of big government. The socialists, and an amazing number of our citizens who do not consider themselves socialistically inclined, think that big government can improve the lot of the citizens. But this is contrary to every fact of history. Once it begins to have dominant control over the economy, big government swiftly expands itself until it has full control over not only the economy but the lives of the people. In its ultimate form it destroys utterly the individual freedom of the people. It becomes then the harsh Master and all the people become slaves.

Government can only be big in our free, democratic America when we permit it to levy big taxes. We, the citizens, can control its size precisely by controlling the amount of taxes and refusing to permit it to practice deficit financing, or operate on borrowed money. That means, in the final analysis, curtailing its services in the field of subsidies, aids, grants, etc., and certainly its powers (in peace time) in the fields of finance, production and distribution.

The one simple truth we must get across to the people of America is that freedom goes along with self-reliance, that no people can be both dependent and independent at the same time.

If we do not rely on government for services that we can render better ourselves in the field of private enterprise, then we can hold down taxes, hold down the size of our government . . . and remain free! It is a challenging mission—the spreading of these truths to everyone in our land! The challenge is ringing in the ears of the salesmen of America.

No one is better able to sell America to our own people than the American salesman.

As Dr. Benson has suggested, a good salesman knows the product that he sells. When you sell America, your "product" is the American way of life. James J. Nance, president of Hotpoint, Inc., is a fervent believer in our country and the unlimited opportunities our American system offers all of us, particularly the men and women who have what it takes to sell.

Mr. Nance, who is himself a great salesman and a recognized leader of salesmen, said:

It is literally true that the American citizen today is the only citizen of the world who directs and has control over his own destiny. That is why I believe our future will be what we make it. We have it completely within our power to reverse the trends that could break down our private enterprise economic system and deny us the progress that is within our grasp. And I have enough faith in the good sense of the American people to believe that the trend toward socialism will be stopped in time.

The American Yankee is a sharp trader. Why should America abandon the free enterprise system? With all the experimentation throughout the world, no system half so good has been developed. Why should we give up a good thing?

The test of an economic system is the standard of living it produces, measured by goods received for labor put forth. Under the American system, in which individuals make the decisions and control their own labor and their own capital, we have made more material progress in the last 50 years than mankind made in all the earlier centuries combined.

Fifty years ago, at the start of this century, the standard American work week was 59 hours; the average weekly wage was $12.75. Today the standard work week is 40 hours, and the average weekly wage is $56.50. In terms of purchasing power the average American can buy twice as much goods with his earnings from 40 hours of work as his father or grandfather could buy in 1900 with his earnings from 59 hours of work.

Some of us know from our own experience what at least a part of the last 50 years of progress has meant. Where a comparative handful of families had horses and buggies, which passed for personal transportation less than 50 years ago, there are some 44 million passenger automobiles in operation today.

Telephones, which now are in the great majority of American homes, were a curiosity in 1900. Central heating, which is almost universal today, was a luxury reserved for the very well-to-do. A smaller percentage of our people attended high school in those days than now attend college.

Foods that now are standard items of diet in the average American home were unknown in 1900. Modern refrigeration has made the greatest contribution to this. The state of medical knowledge and the physical stresses of living were such that the life expectancy of a baby born in 1900 was 48 years, compared with the life expectancy of today of 66 years.

The electrical industry was in its infancy in 1900. Today 93 per cent of all American people live in electrified homes. More than 50 per cent of the nation's wired homes have not one but several of the many time and labor saving electrical appliances that have done so much to take the drudgery out of the homemaker's life. For example, almost 90 per cent have electric irons; 80 per cent have electric refrigerators; 53 per cent have vacuum cleaners; 70 per cent have washing machines. In the realm of home entertainment, some 94 per cent have radios, and already many millions have television.

The economy of America is a selling economy. Concurrent with the efforts and the genius of the men who created the products that make today's high standard of living was a powerful selling effort that convinced the most adamant prospect that these things were good for him. There never were more highly skilled salesmen than those who pioneered the sale of automobiles, refrigerators and the other wonders of America which have become universal in the last 25 years.

For more people to have more things requires creative selling. So I say to you, *"Now is the hour for all of us in business to prove that we have what it takes—what it takes to sell."* And *sell* we must, for not only is our prosperity at stake, but literally, our American way of life, our system of free enterprise. The responsibility is ours to see that the American economy of plenty is kept moving forward in high gear.

Occasionally you find a salesman who tells you "Selling is getting tougher every year. We are reaching the saturation point. When people have all they want, what chance will a salesman have?" Whenever you hear a salesman talk like that, take a few minutes to teach him the facts of life, as they are today.

In the first place, human wants will never be satisfied. In the second place, our American economy is a rapidly expanding economy. For instance, more than 4,300 marriages are performed every day—and that means more than 4,300 new buying units are formed every single day.

More than eighteen million new families have come into being in the past ten years alone. Think what that means in new selling opportunities of all kinds—not only food and clothing, automobiles, electrical appliances, real estate and building materials, but all the raw materials, the parts, and the machinery to make the products needed by these eighteen million new families and their millions of children.

As an American salesman you are one of the most important men or women in the whole world. If you do your selling job successfully you will help keep our American system strong and healthy, you will help keep our American standard of living rising higher and higher, and one by one other nations will see that our free way of life is truly the most desirable of all. Then they will stop trying to sell us their ways of life, and they will begin to buy the American way!

When an American salesman was traveling in England some time ago, he was introduced to a stranger who had a cockney accent. He asked, "Are you an Englishman?" The stranger answered, "Yes, I am a subject of the crown."

When the salesman said he was an American, the Englishman remarked, "Oh, then you are a subject of the United States."

The American salesman said, "Subject, hell, brother, I own a piece of it!"

Yes, you own a piece of this country of ours. As a salesman you are one of your country's most important citizens. Your success as a salesman provides jobs for countless people, keeps our standard of living rising, keeps our free enterprise system strong and healthy.

As A. E. Barit, president of the Hudson Motor Car Company, expressed it, *"The American salesman is the man of the hour!"*

Mr. Barit explained:

Every guide post along our way points directly to the fact that we have unprecedented ability to purchase on the part of the American people. And coupled with this, we have unprecedented ability to produce on our farms, in our mines, forests and factories all the necessary, useful, glamorous and entertaining goods and services our people want!

What we need now, to accomplish the American dream of even higher standards of living for more and more people, is more and more effective salesmanship.

The American salesman is the man of the hour!

Yes, the American salesman has within himself the power to help brighten and improve the lives of millions of consumers—and to help make the great American story come true to every producer who is willing to live and work as an American.

I salute the American salesman. Wherever he is and whatever he sells, he has a great and thrilling mission that is his heritage in this hour of shining opportunity for us all.

As an American salesman you are indeed the "man of the hour!" America needs an army of patriotic salesmen to sell America across the counter, down the aisles, from door to door, office to office, factory to factory, and farm to farm, from city to village, up and down the highways and byways of this great land of ours. There are no salesmen in any country in the world who can outsell American salesmen, and that's why the "patent medicine" boys who are trying to sell this country their communist or socialist snake oils and other cures for our economic ills will not get to first base if the salesmen of America are really determined to sell our own Land of the Free to our own people.

While America remains the Land of the Free, it will be a land of tremendous opportunity for salesmen. Remember, as a salesman you are one of your country's most important citizens. She is relying on you to keep the products of her farms, forests, mines, industry, moving on to the consumer so that employment may remain at a high level and peace and prosperity, and peace of mind, may prevail throughout the land. As Mr. Barit put it, you have a great and thrilling mission that is your heritage in this hour of shining opportunity for us all.

CHAPTER 32

You Can Make Your Community Proud of You

IT has been said that only a doctor or a minister of the gospel meets and influences as many people as does a salesman. Whether people come into your place of business to buy from you or whether you call on them in their homes, factories, offices or on their farms, you are sure to have some influence on everyone you meet.

If you show by your attitude and your actions that you are interested only in the sales that you can make, and have no interest in your customers as human beings, then your influence will have a shriveling effect on their natures.

On the other hand, if you have an alive interest in every customer and prospective customer and show that you appreciate the opportunity you have to serve them, then, to some extent at least, you will make the world a better place for everyone with whom you come in contact.

To reach your fullest personal development and your greatest success as a salesman, take part in the life of your community outside your own business. Use your salesmanship ability to benefit your community in many places where the additional work you do can't possibly bring you any immediate benefit. There is no better way to strengthen your understanding of people and intensify your interest in them as human beings than to use your ability as a salesman to serve your community without hope of any material reward.

Many salesmen help organize and operate boys' clubs, off-the-street clubs, help to raise funds for playgrounds and recreation centers. Other salespeople assist in community chest drives and help

Wait Till I Get the Guy Who Talked Me Into Being a Scout Leader!

various charitable organizations raise the funds they need. Usually there are many ways in which you as an individual salesman can engage in some public-spirited activity that will benefit your community.

By all means, join some religious, fraternal and community organizations. Your church undoubtedly has social clubs for men and women, societies and other groups who sponsor recreational activities, engage in charitable work, in campaigns to reduce juvenile delinquency, and other public-spirited activities. Salespeople make excellent Sunday-school teachers, organizers, and leaders of church groups.

N. C. Volkay of Pittsburgh is past president of the local furniture club and president of the National Wholesale Furniture Salesmen's Association. He has been active in many community projects, such as raising money for a new American Legion home, managing and coaching a Legion baseball team, and serving as commander of the Legion during the critical war period.

He is interested in the Civic League of Mt. Lebanon and the Youth Committee to promote playgrounds, dances, and other activities for the youth of the community. In addition, he finds time to be vice-president of the University of Pennsylvania Alumni.

Other members of the Furniture Club of Pittsburgh take part in the raising of funds for the Salvation Army, Cancer Fund, and other worthy causes. They contact veterans' hospitals and donate movie machines and other wanted things to make the boys happy.

Mr. Volkay said, "I believe these activities are excellent not only for the community but for the salesmen as well, for they build poise, confidence, and they give a real meaning to life."

Every salesman should belong to a public-spirited fraternal organization such as the Elks, Lions, Moose, a civic club such as the Kiwanis and Rotary. Why should you join? To be a "joiner"? No, indeed! To make valuable contacts, meet prospective customers? No, again. If you become a member of any club or group just because you want to get something out of your fellow members you will not be popular. In fact, the self-centered club member is like a miser sitting in the corner counting his pennies of good fellowship while unbounded richness is all around him. As a salesman who understands the *Human* Side of Selling, you will become a member of the fraternal and community organizations of your choice because *you have something to give your fellow members,* and because membership in those organizations will bring you more and greater opportunities to *serve your community.*

"Why should I do anything for my community?" one salesman asked. "What has this town ever done for me?" Don't criticize that man. He is suffering from a common malady which we might call "ingrown thinking." Ingrown thinking is like an ingrown toenail in many ways. It turns in instead of growing out healthily. It can hurt, too.

People suffering from ingrown thinking always ask this question before they make any decision or take any action: "What's in it for me?" If they can't see an immediate reward, they are not interested.

The salesman who understands the *Human* Side of Selling knows the answer to that question and therefore doesn't have to think about it at all. His experience in serving his customers has shown him that "the greater your service the greater will be your reward."*
And that law of action and reaction applies particularly to the service you render your community.

Your village, town, suburb, or city is not an inanimate object; it is a community of people. And the rewards you receive for service to your neighbors and fellow townspeople will be many indeed. First, and most important, you will have the rich satisfaction of *giving* without expectation of reward. That is an ennobling feeling which can make you a bigger, finer person. Secondly, you win the friendship and appreciation of many people. Thirdly, you find that your own family and business associates have more respect for you. Finally, there comes a time when your whole community is proud of you.

In addition to joining religious, fraternal, and community organizations where you will have greater opportunities for service, begin now to take more interest in your local government. A salesman in

---

* *Man Alive.*

a suburban community outside a large metropolitan city was discussing a proposed change in zoning laws with two of his neighbors one evening. All the men owned their own little mortgage-covered homes and none of them liked the changes the town council wanted to make in the zoning laws. One said, "I guess we can't do anything about it, though. The local politicians probably have already made up their minds."

Another said, "They're holding an open meeting tomorrow in the council chambers. Why don't we go down and see what happens." They agreed to go to the meeting in the town hall the next evening.

During the meeting, when the council was ready to vote on the proposed changes in the law, the salesman stood up and asked to be heard. He said later that he became so convinced that the vote would be unanimous for the changes and the new law would be so unfair to the homeowners of the community that he just had to get up and tell the councilmen why they should not change the law. He presented his reasons logically and coherently, just as he would make a sales presentation. The president of the council thanked him and took a vote. The bill to change the zoning law was defeated. That salesman had made a sale which benefited his whole community.

The town hall was crowded. Many homeowners were there, but the salesman was the only one who stood up and asked to be heard. After the meeting, people he didn't know crowded around him and thanked him. Ever since, his neighbors have had a new respect for him and wherever he goes in his town people smile and wave a friendly greeting. He rendered a service to his community and the respect and friendliness of his fellow townspeople are a great and continuing reward.

Many salesmen have become interested in the Junior Achievement movement. If you do not have a Junior Achievement organization in your area, you could start one yourself. Junior Achievement helps teen-agers organize what might be called miniature companies. Businessmen sponsor these companies and act as counselors. The teen-agers themselves determine what their companies will manufacture or sell. Then they appoint a president, vice-president, treasurer, elect a board of directors, and determine who will do the various jobs in their company. They sell stock in the company for 50 cents a share. They go into business, and learn the operation of a business organization by running one themselves. They prepare profit and loss statements and declare dividends when the business is profitable.

As a salesman you, of course, would be an invaluable counselor to a Junior Achievement group in the important selling operations of their company. And you would be helping to prevent juvenile delinquency by giving teen-agers constructive, interesting spare-time activities—and you would help teach them the American way of life.

A 17-year-old president of a Junior Achievement company which embosses and sells book matches said, "We read a lot in the papers about strikes, high prices, conflicting economic theories, and so on. There seems to be a lot of discouragement about our future. Yet on the basis of what I've learned in Junior Achievement it doesn't seem to me that there is anything wrong with our system, but simply that too few people understand it enough to want to work together."

In Chicago there are more than a hundred separate Junior Achievement companies which make and sell metal, wood, textile, leather, plastic, and many other types of products. Over $25,000 has been invested in these companies by people who bought 50-cent shares, and no one person is permitted to buy more than five shares. When you read the remarkable insight of that 17-year-old Junior Achievement president, don't you think the salesmen and other businessmen who are sponsoring and counseling the Junior Achievement companies are making a worth-while contribution to their community? You can take part in this great national Junior Achievement movement in your locality.

Many high schools have Career Days once or twice a year. On these days representatives of different businesses and professions are called in to tell the students about their individual work so that the boys and girls will be better able to decide on a career. As a salesman who understands the *Human* Side of Selling, why don't you arrange to take part in the career days of your local schools? You know the advantages of selling as a career. From any standpoint the selling profession should attract the best men and women in the country.

Listen to Lawrence A. Appley, president of the American Management Association, on the necessity of showing young people the advantages of a career in selling:

Take the matter of financial rewards. How many of our school and college students know that it is not impossible to find salesmen who earn more than the presidents of their companies? How many realize the number of those presently in the top echelons of management who came up through the sales route? How many have any idea of the number of salesmen in the $20,000 to $30,000 brackets?

Or, to look at the matter from a different angle, how many know that there are a good many sales jobs which require considerable technical knowledge—some, even, that require a degree in engineering? How many know that, far from hiring "just anybody" as a salesman, companies consider sales selection so important that they are devoting large sums of money to research in the procedures? How many know about the company training schools for salesmen?

Even considered from the viewpoint of "security" the sales field stacks up well against others. In the first place, in a competitive era there is bound to be a large and continuing demand for good salesmen. In the second place, the salesman has a type of security not possessed by any other type of businessman, security which stems directly from the nature of the work itself. Because results are more measurable than in any other field, the salesman may be confident that he will be judged largely on actual performance.

And there are other satisfactions. The salesman is much more on his own, much more independent than the ordinary jobholder. Salesmanship is a thrilling, dynamic activity. It's interesting, fascinating, and gratifying.

You will render a great service to your community and to the selling profession by speaking at Career Days in schools and at church gatherings or wherever you can talk to young men and women and show them the advantages of selling as a career.

As a salesman you can't help meeting and influencing many people. If you understand the *Human* Side of Selling, you will find that people look up to you, ask your opinion. You must be careful about giving your opinion on such subjects as religion and politics because they so often mean different things to different people. As one of the most important people in your community, however, you should know your city officials, your county and state representatives, and the congressmen and senators who represent you in Washington.

It is amazing how many people do not even remember the names of their government officials, their state and federal representatives. You elect those men and women. They work for you, but they cannot represent you intelligently if they do not know what you are thinking about the problems of the day. Write them. Write them again and again. Attend meetings at which they are present and talk with them. Know who they are, and let them know you and how you want them to represent you in Washington or in your state capital.

Life can be full and vigorous for you as a salesman if you will reach outside yourself and seize every opportunity to serve your fellow men. As a salesman you will have countless opportunities to be of service to your customers. As a salesman you can find many, many opportunities to be of service to your whole community.

Step up and give yourself, your experience, your selling ability, to your neighbors, your fellow townspeople. Make your community proud of you, and you will have the rich, warm surge of quiet, confident self-respect that will make you one of the most popular and happiest citizens of your own little spot in the universe.

CHAPTER 33

Follow the Way of Champions to Success

FIELDING YOST, one of the greatest of all collegiate football coaches, achieved national fame because he produced so many magnificent winning teams at the University of Michigan. Year after year

You Know What It Takes to Be a Champion—Go on out There and Show the World!

they won the Big Ten Championship. When they went to the Rose Bowl, they defeated their opponents by a top-heavy score. They were true champions—they fought hard and clean, and they *won*. Almost everyone is familiar with the record of the great Michigan football teams, but few know how Fielding Yost instilled the poise, the confidence, the tremendous power into his squads at the start of each season.

Mr. Yost always gathered around him in the dressing room at the start of the football season all the players who hoped to make the team. While they waited expectantly he would pick up a piece of chalk and write one word on the blackboard. Then he would turn to the players and tell them that no one could play on the Michigan team unless he fully understood the meaning of that word. He would talk for two or three hours about that one word, amplifying its meaning and showing the football squad how it could make them think, and feel, and act like champions—how it could help them give Michigan another winning team.

The word Fielding Yost wrote on that blackboard in the University of Michigan football team's dressing room at the start of each season, the word he discussed for hours, was "love." Yes, l - o - v - e . . . LOVE!

Mr. Yost would point out to the players that if they were to be successful they must have love for the game they were playing, they must have love and respect for their fellow players, and for their opponents too, and they must have a deep love for successful accomplishment. They must love to learn how to play football like champions, and love to work hard to win.

There you have the way of great football champions to success. All through this book you have read about the way champion salesmen outsell run-of-the-mill salespeople by an amazingly wide margin. What makes the difference between the plodders and the selling champions? Invariably the champions understand the meaning and the power of *love,* particularly for their own selling jobs and the opportunities they have to serve their customers. That word "love" is a he-man word, in football or in selling. It takes a healthy, virile, clear-thinking man to understand it. That word, with everything it implies, can make you a winner year after year—a winner of all the good things you want in life.

Follow the way of champions to success in your own selling. It is so much easier, and so sure!

Try this today—write three words *"love that customer"* on a little card and paste it on your mirror where you will see it each morning, or carry it with you all day. You are sure to sell more, earn more money, have more fun, and make more friends if you do. Better still, write those words in your heart.

In Chapter 4 we discussed the customer as the "man behind the dollar," and we know he can spend his dollars wherever he chooses. We know it is the customer who really pays our salaries, commissions, bonuses, and makes a profit for our employers. And we also know that a satisfied, happy customer can become a "center of influence" who will direct many other customers to us.

We know above all that the customer is a flesh-and-blood *human* being, with feelings and emotions, with frustrations and problems, with pride and prejudices similar to our own.

He definitely prefers to give his business to the salesman who appreciates him, who shows that he appreciates the opportunity to serve him, who recognizes him, respects him, serves him well, and expresses his appreciation.

It was William James, the great psychologist, who said: "The deepest need in human nature is the craving to be appreciated." You know how you love the friends who do not simply take you for granted, who really respect and appreciate you. Well, your customers are *human,* too!

Become sincerely interested in every customer, in every prospective customer, as a *human* being. Look for the many good qualities you will find in everyone, and show that you appreciate them. Particularly look for ways to be of service to your customers and show that you are grateful for every opportunity to serve them.

A salesgirl asked, "How can I look for the good qualities in my customers, or think of each one as a human being, when I see so many all day long? When you stand behind a counter and have to wait on people one after another, you don't have much time to be interested in anyone."

Try it, I suggested. You said you "see so many all day long," but do you really "see" them? Beginning tomorrow, look into the eyes of every customer who comes to your counter and greet her with a smile—a warm, friendly smile. If the customer is a girl, ask yourself whether she goes to school, works, or is married. If the customer is an older woman, does she have a large family, is she a widow or a spinster? Look for something to admire in each one—her hair, her eyes, her clothes, her voice, or her manner.

If the customer gives you her name when she asks you to have the purchase delivered or charged, thank her and be sure to use her name. Don't just say, "I'll have it delivered." Say, "Thank you, *Miss Peterson,* I will have it delivered." And when she leaves say, "Good bye, *Miss Peterson.*"

Thinking about each customer, looking for something to admire, using the customer's name will make you more interested in each one as a *human* being. You will not spend a second more with anyone, but your attitude will be one of real interest and appreciation which the customers will feel. Try it for a while, I suggested, and tell me what happens.

She agreed to try that simple way to become interested in her customers *as people.*

A few months went by before I saw her again. Unless you understand the *Human* Side of Selling, the change that had taken place in her would be difficult to believe. She had more poise, more confidence, was a happy, charming person. What had happened to her?

She told me, "That suggestion you made that I become interested in my customers as human beings has changed my whole outlook on life. I didn't like this selling job. I was tired out every evening, glad to get away from the store. Customers irritated me. Now, however, I like them. And, would you believe it, several of them have invited me to come to their homes. Many come back to me again and again. And they have asked my name—and, oh! I've made so many friends!"

Her eyes were sparkling as she said, "And do you know the

biggest thrill I get? It's when some woman comes up to my counter looking tired and unhappy and I can make her smile just a little bit and go away with some of the tiredness gone and a feeling that some one appreciates her and likes her. That is a very wonderful feeling indeed!"

That young lady had learned the tremendously uplifting power of the *Human* Side of Selling.

Another salesman asked, "How can you be nice to customers when they return merchandise and complain about it, especially when you know their complaints are unfair? When they know they are wrong they're especially tough; they come in ready for a fight. I sometimes feel like giving some of them a good swift kick in the pants."

If you ever feel like giving a complaining customer a "good swift kick," or if you ever argue with him, you are thinking only about yourself and not about the customer. Under the same circumstances you probably would return the merchandise and complain just as he did. If you have the customer's interest at heart you will remember that someone has said, "There are only about eighteen inches between a pat on the back and a kick in the pants."—and you will choose to give the customer a pat on the back.

When a customer returned some wallpaper to Art Witzleben, when he was manager of the Wallpaper Department in Gimbels, New York, and started to tell what was wrong with it, Art would say, "You need not explain why you do not want it. We will be glad to take it back. And you can have a full refund of the purchase price or select any other wallpaper you want. We value your good will and appreciate your business."

The customers invariably would relax and smile. Instead of a "kick in the pants," they received a "pat on the back." And usually they selected another pattern, often buying a better grade.

What probably happened, Art philosophized, was that their families did not like the pattern they chose and sheepishly they had to bring it back. So he showed by his friendly and prompt action that he understood their predicament, appreciated them, and wanted to help them in any way he could. You know the result of that "pat on the back" treatment—the complainers became well-satisfied customers who recommended that department and store to their friends.

No one likes to be wrong. Being told we're wrong accentuates our subconscious feeling of littleness, of unimportance.

When you think your customers are wrong, don't tell them. First try to understand their point of view. Put yourself in their place. Then go out of your way to *help them to be right!* They will love you for that.

Many of the most successful businessmen know the great importance of helping your customer to be right. Marshall Field, with his slogan "The customer is always right," probably is the best known. Another is Ellsworth Statler, founder of the Statler Hotels, who established this stern rule which even today Statler men must follow: "No employee of this hotel is allowed the privilege of arguing any point with a guest."

You do not have to be a Pollyanna or a yes man, of course. A customer who refuses to buy your products or one who demands special concessions may be very wrong. By putting yourself in the customer's place and trying to understand his point of view, you may often be able to show him that you can see why he takes the stand he does, but you wish to show him why the course you propose would be more profitable to him.

When you are genuinely interested in your customers and prospective customers as *human* beings you will get along with them much better. Why? Because they see that you appreciate them, and as William James pointed out, "the deepest need in human nature is the craving to be appreciated."

Your interest in your customers must be genuine. You can't fake that interest. It must come from the heart.

Pascal, the great French writer, said, "All bodies [all material things] are not equal to the lowest mind; for mind knows all these things and itself, and the bodies are nothing. All bodies together and all minds together and all their products are not equal to the least feeling of charity. This is an order infinitely more exalted."

The dictionary gives several definitions of "charity." One is "kindness in judging other people's faults." Another is "Christian love of one's fellow men." Without question, love of one's fellow men is "an order infinitely more exalted" and greater indeed than all the material things and all the minds in the world.

When you as a salesman carry the three words "Love that customer!" in your heart, you are carrying the greatest selling power in the world, far greater than all the minds and all the material considerations combined. Remember that. There is tremendous power in love. You had to understand it to play on the championship Michigan football teams. When you understand it, you can reach your highest championship form as a salesman. It is the very essence of the *Human* Side of Selling.

The Reverend Clarence H. Cobb, minister of the First Church of Deliverance in Chicago, recommended an investment to his congregation which he guaranteed would never depreciate in value and would pay dividends as long as each person lived. He said: "Some of you invest in General Motors stock, and some of you invest in Chrysler or the stock of other large corporations. Sometimes that stock goes up, sometimes it goes down. When things get bad, the stock you buy in the big companies can go down so far it is worth less than its par value and maybe the company can't pay dividends any more. There is one investment, however, which never goes down, which always pays dividends. Brothers and sisters, I am going to recommend that you *invest in the love of your fellow man*. The more you invest in the love of your fellow man the richer will be your dividends. And if you keep on investing, the value of your investment will keep right on growing and your dividends will increase year after year."

And the Reverend Mr. Cobb said, "Remember, as you sow, so also shall you reap. Brothers and sisters, sow courtesy and consideration, honesty and fair play, sow love of your fellow man, and you will be making an investment that will pay you the biggest dividends so long as you live."

If you are suffering from the sophistication that is almost an occupational disease with some salesmen, you may be interested only in the fact that the *Human* Side of Selling will bring you more profit, more sales, more earnings than you ever expected. I hope you are thinking and feeling far above and below the superficialities of sophistication, however, because then you will make the investment the Reverend Mr. Cobb suggested in all your selling contacts—you will know the full meaning of the *Human* Side of Selling, and it will bring you countless friends, more fun, more happiness, more of the deep satisfaction of serving your fellow man, and of course all the material rewards you ever hoped to receive.

CHAPTER 34

The Radar of Human Relations

YOU have heard the expression "He puts his heart into his work." Usually that means he likes his occupation, approaches it with enthusiasm, and works hard at it. When you understand the *Human* Side of Selling you certainly do put your whole heart into your work, because you are proud to be a salesman, you are enthusiastic about your employer and the products you sell, and you work harder than ordinary salesmen because you want to stand out from the crowd as a top performer.

As a salesman who understands the *Human* Side of Selling, however, putting your heart into your work means even more. It means that you are eager to be of service to your customers, you like people—you sell with your heart, as well as your mind and body.

THE RADAR OF HUMAN RELATIONS

The great religious teachers, world-renowned psychologists and philosophers, the learned men and women of all time knew the great power of the heart in human relations. Pascal spoke of three orders of existence. There is the order of the material: bodies, the universe, those things which are incapable of thought. Then there is the order of the mind, the order of reason. Above all, there is the order of the heart, or the order of charity. And Pascal said, *"The heart has its reasons which reason does not know."*

We are all familiar with the five senses—sight, hearing, taste, smell, touch—through which we receive the routine impressions of our surroundings, of people and things, of the world in which we live. We have a receiving apparatus, however, that is more powerful, more sensitive, and more far reaching than all our senses. That receiving apparatus—that "radar" of human relations—is the heart.

Whenever you meet a customer or prospective customer, his heart tunes you in. It picks up your wave length, and he listens intently. He listens for the answer to the biggest question in human relations: *"Is he with me or agin me?"*

He "feels" the answer. And if he feels that you are going to give him a "quick brush-off" or if he feels that your interest is only in making a sale and selling him as much as you can, if he feels that you have no real desire to be of service to him, no interest in him personally, then he knows that you are "agin" him—and whatever you do or say will make little impression on him.

The New Testament put it this way: "Enough I speak with the tongues of men and of angels, and have not charity [love of your fellow man], I am become as sounding brass, or a tinkling cymbal."

The heart knows. Invariably the heart knows!

Emerson said, "Who hears me, who understands me, becomes mine—a possession for all time."

When your customer feels in his heart that you are genuinely interested in him, that you understand him, that you want to help him, then you become "his salesman," the one with whom he prefers to do business. Sooner or later you also become his friend, and he enjoys doing business with you.

Charles Ravetta, dean of students at the School of Business of The University of Chicago, told me of a building supply salesman who called on him when he directed the purchases of many thousand dollars worth of material for International House. That salesman "took a personal interest" in Mr. Ravetta's plans for redecorating the house. He went out of his way to find just the right type of material even though much of it was not sold by his own firm. When he made a recommendation, Mr. Ravetta said, "It came from inside him. He was so sincere you could see it was his heart speaking!"

And Charles Ravetta added, "We developed a kindred feeling and eventually became good friends."

If you understand the *Human* Side of Selling you will look at customers and prospective customers not merely as potential sales, but as potential friends. When your attitude is one of sincere friendliness, of appreciation for the opportunity to be of service, customers will "feel" it and *they will want to do business with you.*

In *The Science of Salesmanship,* Sheldon said, "Make the man right and the sale will be right and all that follows will be right."

If you are right in your heart you can become a great salesman, a very successful salesman, and as wealthy as you care to be.

"The heart has nothing to do with successful selling," one salesman told me. He said, "The mind is the important thing. You have to outthink the customer. You have to dominate the interview. You have to go into the man's office determined that you are not going to let him turn you down."

That salesman is not a sales scarecrow, nor a mere order taker. He is one of the hardest working salesmen I know. Yet there is something that keeps him from being a great salesman. Customers admire his hard work, his knowledge of his products, his enthusiasm, but they are on the defensive with him, careful that they don't buy more than they need. His attitude might be expressed as, "You dumb so-and-so, you're going to buy this stuff and I'm the guy who is going to sell you", and his customers feel that. He never gets particularly close to any customer.

In his relationship with his employers he has been as egocentric as he has with customers. In the three selling jobs he has had during the past few years he has thought that he knew a great deal more than his employers. They were a bit on the stupid side, he thought. That attitude crept into his reports, into an occasional sarcastic remark he would make in sales meetings, into his condescending reference to the management in discussions with customers.

Evidently he didn't know that his employers would "feel" that he was "agin" them. They did. He should have been a brilliant success, based on his experience, his knowledge of his products, and his hard work, but he hasn't learned that he can't reach his peak of success unless his customers and his boss get a positive answer when they ask the all-important questions: *"Is he with me or agin me?"*

The salesman who understands the *Human* Side of Selling has a deep respect for his boss and complete confidence in him—or he would not continue to work for him. He appreciates the help he gets from the boss. He is a "team man" and will carry out instructions with all the enthusiasm and determination that makes a football player fight his way down the field to win for his coach.

His boss has a job to do, and the salesman will help him succeed in that job and break all records if possible. In his relationship with his boss, he remembers Lord Chesterfield's advice: "Make other people like themselves a little better, and I promise you that they will like you very well."

When your boss likes you very well, and your customers like you very well, and you know in your heart that you are doing everything you can to be of service to them in business and personally, you are sure to be a happy, confident, successful salesman with many, many friends.

Remember that all of us are little people in relation to the vast universe, and we know it. However, although we are all little people, in each one of us there is a potential greatness, *a magnificent divinity*. You and I know it is there, and we love those who recognize it in us and respect it. They become our friends.

In Emerson's Essay on Friendship, he wrote:

> In spite of all the selfishness that chills like east winds the world, the whole human family is bathed with an element of love like fine ether. How many persons we meet whom we scarcely speak to, whom yet we honor, and who honor us! How many we see in the street, or sit with in church, whom though silently, we warmly rejoice to be with! The heart knoweth . . .
>
> My friends have come to me unsought. The great God gave them to me. By the oldest right, by the devine affinity of virtue with itself. I find them, or rather not I, but the Deity in me and in them . . .

There you have the "secret" of the tremendous power of the *Human* Side of Selling.

As Emerson expressed it, "In spite of all the selfishness that chills like east winds the world, the whole human family is bathed with an element of love." You know the source of that love. It is the Deity in you and in everyone with whom you come in contact. Don't let the callouses of cynicism and sophistication short circuit the radar of your human relations. When your customers, your boss or your fellow workers "tune you in" and listen for the answer to that vital question, "Is he with me or agin me?" see that you are answering sincerely, *"I am with you, friend—all the way!"*

Keep that thought in your heart, and you can be a star salesman—and a happy one, with innumerable friends. You will be a Very Important Person to your customers and to your employer—and your family will be proud of your success and your stature as a truly professional salesman, a *Man Alive*—in the Greatest Profession in the World!

Index

Index

A. B. Blankenship & Associates, 38
Action, 3
Adams, K. S., 141
Advertising, 111 f.
Advertising buyers, 126–33
Ahrens Publishing Company, 57, 103 f., 107
A.I.D.A., 3
American Machine and Foundry Company, 111
American Management Association, 78, 186, 234, 281
American Restaurant Magazine, 55
Ammco Tool Company, 204
Analysis, of customer, 114–15
 of distribution methods, 75
 of territory, 74, 76, 115 f.
Appearance, personal, 139–40, 193–96
Appley, Lawrence A., 281
Application for job, 253
Appreciation, 28 f., 153–58
Arcady Farms Milling Company, 190
Attention, 3, 28
Attitude, 83–84, 86 ff.
 critical, 259 ff.
 negative, 189
 positive, 214
 toward boss, 242
 toward selling, 220–26
Audience participation, 207
Augsbach, C. Edward, 113
Automotive News, 54

Badger; *see* E. B. Badger & Sons Company
"Balance sheet," personal, 252
Barit, A. E., 273 f.
Bauer & Black, 76

Bauer, Jack, 188–89
Baum, Harold, 12, 66, 164
Bayuk Cigars, Inc., 28
Bazner, Martin, 202
Bell, George, 36 f., 138
Benson, Dr. George S., 269, 271
Birth of a Salesman, The, 171
Bishop, Arthur, 67
Blankenship, Dr. A. B., 38
Bloomington [Illinois] *Pantagraph, The*, 126
Bob White Organization, 205
Bond Clothing Store, 43, 153
Boss, characteristics of, 228–35
 interest of, in employees, 236–41
 point of view of, 242–49
 salesman's relationship with, 243
Bradley, Fred, 98
Bristol-Myers Company, *preface*
Brown & Bigelow, 224
Brown, Ed, 76
Buick automobiles, 11
Burg, C. T., 194
Burgess Vibrocrafters, Inc., 36, 138
Business Week, 111 f.
"Buymanship," 27

Caldora, Lucien, 223
Campbell Holton Company, 76, 161
Career Days, 280–81
Carnegie, Dale, 159
CBS radio and television, 209
Celotex Corporation, 67
Chesterfield, Lord, 293
Chicago, University of, 292
Chrysler Corporation, 177, 289
Cleanliness, 196–97
Clothes, 139–40, 193–96

INDEX

Clubs, 103, 106
Cobb, Rev. Clarence H., 289 f.
Cole, John, 255
Colgate, Palmolive Peet, 132
Colleges; see Universities and colleges
Communism, 268
Community, the, 275–82
"Comparison Chart," 51
Competitive bidding, 99
Confidence, lack of, 217
Consumer benefits, 45
Contract departments, 106
Courtesy, 28
Covert, Bessie, 102
Criticism, 259 ff.
Curiosity, 177
Customers, dealer, 60–72
   importance of, 151–58
   industrial, 108–17
   institutional, 97–107
   management, 134–42
   need of, for salesmen, 159–66
   problems of, 25 ff.
   prospective, 143–50
   retail, 31–42
   salesman's interest in, 19 ff.
   satisfied, 157
   wholesaler, 73–81
   women, 32–35
Customer analysis, 114–15
"Customer benefits," 51
Customer relationships, 28–29
C. Wendel Muench & Company, 132

Dave Robertson Electric Company, 116
Davis Appliance Company, 40
Davis, George, 248
Davis, William V., 40
Dealers, 60–72, 106–107
Deeley Company, 92
Deeley, Hack, 92 f.
Delay, 218
Demonstration, 205 ff.
Dennison, Henry S., 222
Dental profession, 89–96
Desire, 3
Distribution methods, 75

Distributors; see Wholesalers
Dodge automobiles, 50 f.
"Don'ts" for salesmen, 47–48, 90–92, 134–41
Dotts, H. W., 58
Doubt, 212, 217–18
Drug Topics, 156
Duffy, Edward V., 65, **71**

E. B. Badger & Sons Company, 111
E. B. Malone & Company, 65
Edison Electric Institute, 17
Education, definition of, *preface*
Edwards Dental Supply Company, 95
Einson Freeman Company, Inc., 174
Electrical South, 40, 116
Emerson, 291, 293
Emotional cycles, 218–19
Enthusiasm, 186–92
Essay on Friendship, 293

Fabian, Victor, 132
Factory Management and Maintenance, 111
Farm Equipment Retailing, 48
Farm Implement News, 197
Fear, 212–15
Ferguson, W. P., 58
Field, Marshall, 24 f., 28, 288
First Church of Deliverance, Chicago, 289
Fitz-Gibbon, Bernice, 41
Fortune, 13, 32
Fox, John, 18 f.
Francis, Clarence, 180–81
Fraternal organizations, 277–78
Frederick, Charles, 184
Free enterprise system, 174, 269, 272
Freeman; see Einson Freeman Company, Inc.
Friendship, 71, 96, 159 ff., 293–94
Furniture Club of Pittsburgh, 277

General Electric Company, 27, 171
General Foods Corporation, 181
General Motors, 289
George Spies Industries, 12

INDEX

Gimbel Brothers, 41, 149 f., 287
Goethe, 218
Goode, Kenneth, 207
Goodrich, B. F., 14
Goodyear Tire and Rubber Company, 124, 205, 222
Greenberg, Al, 39
Guide to Automobile Selling, A, 54
Gust, Robert, 209

Hadlock, George, 247–48
Hansen, Harry, 10, 32, 45
Hardie, Joseph, *preface*
Hardin College, 269
Hart, Laurence C., 78 ff.
Heinn Company, 123, 262
Helpfulness, 19 ff., 27 f., 225
Hills Brothers, 207
Hitz, Ralph, 58
Holton, Campbell, 76, 163
Honesty, 96, 179–85
Hood, Arthur A., 45, 47, 268
Hospitals, 100–103, 106
Hotel Management, 57, 104
Hotels, 103–107
Hotpoint, Inc., 271
How to Win Friends and Influence People, 159
Hudson Motor Car Company, 273
Hughes, A. M., 142
Human relationships, 290–94

Illinois, University of, 215
Imagination, 210
Indianapolis *Star-News*, 6
Industrial Budgets, Inc., 113
Industrial customers, 108–117
Industrial Distribution, 114
Institutional customers, 97–107
Insurance, selling, 82–88
Integrity, 223
Interest, 3, 19 ff., 28, 225
International Business Machines Corporation, 232 f.
Interview for job, 251
Iron Fireman Manufacturing Co., 194
Ivey, Dr. Paul, 223

Jack Lacy Sales Clinics, 18
Jacob Miller, Inc., 63
James, William, 285, 288
Jerman, Reginald, 114 f.
Jewel Tea Company, Inc., 58
Job hunting, 250–58
Johns-Manville Sales Corporation, 45, 78 f.
Johnson, J. Sidney, 62
Jokes, telling stories and, 141
Journal of the American Dental Association, 92
Journal of the American Medical Association, 92
Junior Achievement, 279–80

Kaufman, Zenn, 206 f., 238–40
Kellogg Switchboard Company, 108
Kettering, Charles, 223
Kolodny, Joseph, 190–91, 231
Kriesberg, Dr. Ralph, 88 f.
Kroch, Adolph, 221

LaBounty, Perry, 126
LaCrosse Breweries, Inc., 157
Lacy, Jack, 17, 19, 83, 84 86, 155
Lacy Sales Institute, 17, 155
Ladies' Home Journal, 32
Lampman, Howard, 127
Larkin, Robert, 238–40
"Lazy" salesmen, 128–29
Leigh, N. J., 174 f.
Lido Market, 35
Loeffel, Charles, 57, 107
Look, 26
Love, 164, 283–90
Lowen, Walter, 251
Loyalty, 259–65
Lukens, E. F., 197
Lyon, A. E., 233

McCarthy, Walter Patrick, 76, 189–90
McCrae, John, 184
McGraw-Hill, 111
McIntyre, Simpson & Woods, 147
McKesson-Robbins, 76
McNamara, Harley V., 231

INDEX

Mahoney, Claude, 209
Makler, Joseph H., 184
Malone; see E. B. Malone & Company
Man Alive, 160, 194, 251 n., 252, 278 n.
Management customers, 134–42
Mannerisms, 193, 199–200
Marcus, Stanley, 42
Marketing Conference, 78
Markham, Donald, 83, 87–88, 147, 155 f.
Massol, Merwin B., 76, 92
Materials & Methods, 111
Matherson-Selig Company, 232
Mayer; see Oscar Mayer & Company
Mecherle, George J., 83, 86–87
Medical profession, 89–96
Megelin, Carl, 108
Merchandising counselor, 67, 71, 78, 157–58
Miles Laboratories, Inc., 69, 129
Miller; see Jacob Miller, Inc.
Minchin, H. W., 5 f.
Mitchell, Charles, 156
Mock, John W., 152, 224 f.
Modern Hospital, 100, 102
Montgomery, Mrs. Charlotte, 33
Moore, M. K., 29
Moore, Dr. Rolland B., 93
Morrison, Gordon, 67
Motley, Arthur H., *preface*, 199
Mowry, Don, 65
Muench; see C. Wendel Muench & Company
Mulliken, Paul, 47 f.
Munn, John O., 54

N.A.D.A., 54
Nance, James J., 271
National Association of Tobacco Distributors, Inc., 191, 231
National Biscuit Company, 62
National Cash Register Company, 237 f., 251
National Distillers Products Corporation, 255
National Retail Farm Equipment Association, 47
National Retail Furniture Association, 39

National Soap Company, 180
National Tea Company, 231
National Wholesale Druggist Association, 62
National Wholesale Furniture Salesman's Association, 65, 277
Nation's Schools, 98
Neal; see R. C. Neal Company
Negative attitude, 189
Neiman-Marcus, 42
New Testament, 291
New York *World-Telegram and Sun*, 10
Nolan, Thomas, 43–45, 153–54, 156

Oral Hygiene, 76, 92
Osborne, David R., 51
Oscar Mayer & Company, 156, 189 f.

Packard automobiles, 11
Palmolive Company, 132
Parade, preface, 18 f., 199
Parents' Magazine, 247
Pascal, 288, 291
Patterson, John H., 237
Patton, Carl W., 63 f.
Penney, J. C., 4, 246–47
Personal appearance, 139–40, 193–96
Personal "balance sheet," 252
Personal relationships, 290–94
Philip Morris & Company, Ltd., Inc., 206, 233, 238
Phillips Packing Company, 248
Phillips Petroleum Company, 141 f.
Piatek, Gloria, 190
Positive attitude, 214
Presentation, 76, 79–80, 129–30, 205 ff., 225
Price, 115–16, 122
Production Equipment, 110
Professional salesman, 222–26
Progressive Grocer, 35
Promotion, 67, 71, 76
Promptness, 77, 138
Proofs, 92 f.
Propaganda, 268
Prospect list, 147
Psychology of selling, 17

INDEX

Purchasing agents, 118–25

Quigley, John A., 28

Radio Sales, 209
Raiter, Frederick, 262–63
Rapides Bank & Trust Company of Louisiana, 55
Ravetta, Charles, 292
R. C. Neal Co., 114
Recognition, 28
Regret, 212, 217–18
Relationships, customer, 28–29
  personal, 290–94
Resentment, 212, 215–17
Respect, 28, 177
Restaurant Management, 57, 104
Restaurants, 103–107
Retail customers, 31–42
Richard, Dick, 35
Robertson, Dave, 116
Roosevelt, Franklin D., 212 f.
Rosensteil, Lewis, 232
Ross Roy, Inc., 51, 177
Roy, Ross, 51
Rubins, Ben, 154
Ruth, Babe, 205

Sales Executive Clubs, 18, 234, 257
Salesmen, and the community, 275–82
  need for, in America, 267–74
  professional, 222–26
  selection of, 251
  traits essential to, 168–72
  types of, lazy, 128–29
    scarecrow, 9 ff., 32, 38, 45, 176
    wondering, 129–30
  wholesaler's, 75 ff.
Saturday Evening Post, 132
"Scarecrow" salesmen, 9 ff., 32, 38, 45, 176
Schaeffer, Nate, 12, 66, 179
Schenley Distillers, 232
Schneider, Fred, 186
Schools, 98–100, 106
Schultz, Maxwell, 3
Schwab, Charles M., 3

Science of Salesmanship, The, 292
Secretaries, 136–37; *see also* Subordinates
Self-respect, 223
Selling, attitude toward, 220–26
  "in depth," 65, 71
  psychology of, 17
  satisfactions of, 281
Selling to Restaurants and Hotels, 103
Service, 96, 222, 224
  to America, 269
  to the community, 275–82
Showmanship, 76, 203–10
Showmanship in Business, 207
Shupert, Perry, 69, 129 f.
Sincerity, 141
Smiling, value of, 201
Smoking, 94, 200
So You're Going to the Hospital, 100
Socialism, 268
Specialty Salesman Magazine, 5
Speech habits, 197–99
Speech-making, 76–77
Spies; *see* George Spies Industries
Star-News (Indianapolis), 6
State Farm Insurance Companies, 86
State Farm Mutual Automobile Insurance Company, 86
Statler, Ellsworth, 288
Statler Hotels, 288
Steltz, William George, 74
Stitler, Edward, 232
Stone, Dickman, 6
Stone, Richard, 176
Strobel, Harold, 157
Studebaker automobiles, 51
Subordinates, 136–37, 140–41, 256
Super Market Institute, 33
Superior Sleeprite Company, 12, 66, 164
Supplee-Biddle-Steltz, 73 ff.
Supply houses, 106–107
Sutherland, Fred, 12
Sweeney, A. M., 27

Tanis Company, Management Counselors, 139
Tanis, Tom, 139

Territory analysis, 74, 76, 115 f.
Testimonials, 209
Thornton-Fuller Company, 51
Thornton, George H., 52, 54
Tide, 33
Today's Health, 26
Trage Brothers Appliance Store, 39
Trage, Fred and Ed, 39
Trust, 95

United Airlines, 58
Universities and colleges, Chicago, 292
   Hardin, 269
   Illinois, 215
Unselfishness, 96

Valentine, Dan, 55 ff.
Vance Publishing Company, 45
Voice, tone of, 197
Volkay, N. C., 277

Waldorf Astoria, 223
Walsh, John, 156–57
Ward, Charles, 224
Waterfill and Frazier Distillery Company, 184
Watson, Thomas J., 232
Webster, Helen MacDonald, 95
Wentz, John, 139
Wheat Flour Institute, 127
White, Bob, 205, 207
Wholesaler customer, 73–81
Wholesalers, 106–107, 163–64
Willmark Research Corporation, 3
Willmark Service System, Inc., 32
Wilson, John K., 110
Wilson, John M., 237 f., 251
Wilson, R. S., 124, 222 f.
Witzleben, Arthur, 149–50, 287
Women customers, 32–35
"Wondering" salesmen, 129–30
Wood, William, 123
Woods, Leonard, 147–49
World-Telegram and Sun (New York), 10

Yost, Fielding, 283–84
Young, Gunnar, 155–56

Zuppke, Bob, 215